EIGHTY *PLUS*

Eena Job retired from her position in the Department of Sociology at the University of Queensland in 1982. Since then, she has lectured widely on the subject of ageing and has developed a course, "Fending Off Forgetfulness", which she teaches for the Continuing Education Unit at the University of Queensland. The book based on the course will soon be available as a UQP paperback. She is a council member of the Australian Association of Gerontology (Queensland Division), and serves on the Research and Education Committee for the Queensland Council on the Ageing.

Dr Job has written radio documentaries and plays, a television play, and a novel entitled *I Camp Here*. She has published many short stories under the pen name Esther Roland.

EENA JOB

EIGHTY *PLUS*
OUTGROWING THE MYTHS OF OLD AGE

University of Queensland Press

ST LUCIA • LONDON • NEW YORK

First published 1984 by University of Queensland Press
Box 42, St Lucia, Queensland, Australia
Reprinted in paperback 1985

Printed in Australia by Dominion Press — Hedges & Bell

Distributed in the UK and Europe by University of Queensland Press,
Stockley Road, West Drayton, Middlesex UB7 9BE, England

Distributed in the USA and Canada by the University of Queensland Press,
5 South Union Street, Lawrence, Mass. 01843 USA

Cataloguing in Publication Data

National Library of Australia

Job, Eena M., 1918–
  Eighty *plus:* outgrowing the myths of old age.

  Bibliography.
  Includes index.
  1. Age discrimination — Queensland — Brisbane.
  2. Aged — Queensland — Brisbane — Social conditions.
  1. Title.

305.2′6′099431

Library of Congress

Job, Eena M. (Eena Marie), 1918–
  Eighty *plus:* outgrowing the myths of old age.

  Bibliography: p.
  Includes index.
  1. Aged — Australia — Brisbane — Case studies.
  2. Stereotype (Pyschology) — Case studies. I. Title.
  II. Title: Eighty *plus:* outgrowing the myths of old age.
  HQ1064.A88J63   1984   305.2′6′099431   83-21708

ISBN 0 7022 1895 2

People who live to be 80 are likely to have been assaulted by tragedy at some time during those years. They carry the loss of loved ones around with them, the pain of remembering equalled only by the horror of forgetting. It is part of them, as are all their experiences.

This book is dedicated to the memory of Jonathan Job, who did not live to be old. Through him, I salute with reverence all those who people our past, acknowledging their continuing presence in our lives, and according them due recognition for their fashioning of the future.

Contents

Illustrations   ix
Acknowledgments   xi

Part I   Setting the Scene

1. The Nature of Ageism   3
2. The Toowong Survey   10
3. The Place, the Period, and the People   23

Part 2   The Drama of Living

4. Childhood   43
5. Education   56
6. Work   71
7. Leisure   87
8. Sexuality   100
9. Marriage   113
10. Parenthood   126
11. Politics   139
12. Religion   155
13. Health   168

Part 3   Finale

14. On Being Very Old   189

15. Towards an Age-integrated Future   208

Bibliography   219
Index   229

Illustrations

1 Now 97, she still lives alone   4
2 In modern Toowong   11
3 Toowong railway station in the 1893 flood   26
4 A boy was granted freedom to take risks   51
5 School days   65
6 Paid work for females   76
7 "Kids had more fun"   89
8 Sexuality, an historically relative concept   111
9 The first girlfriend   116
10 Parenthood, the central experience   127
11 The 1912 Tramway's strike   146
12 Most wives gave their lives to network-maintenance   167
13 "Life is wonderful"   196

Acknowledgments

My family, my respondents, and members of my university department all helped to make this book. Some — especially among survey respondents — prefer that I do not mention them by name. But I am happy to record my lasting gratitude to Gillian Lupton, to whom I owe many ideas, and to Jake Najman, whose patient re-reading of preceding drafts made eventual publication possible. They are members of the Department of Anthropology and Sociology at the University of Queensland, whose staff, both clerical and academic, proved a resource of incalculable value; as did the professional services of the John Oxley Library in Brisbane.

Special thanks are also due to Mrs Alice Andrews and Mrs Olive Fogarty, who are still living independently in Toowong. They are among those respondents who very kindly supplied me with treasured family photographs to illustrate the book.

Part 1 Setting the Scene

Chapter 1: The Nature of Ageism

It used to be said that blacks were inferior to whites, and women inferior to men, and those who supported these assertions claimed that the inferiority of blacks and women was biologically based. These ideas have been successfully challenged, and their remaining proponents identified as racists or sexists. But the notion that the old are inferior to the young, and that their inferiority is biologically determined, is still very widely accepted.

Ageism, like racism and sexism, creates its own self-fulfilling prophecies and promotes lifestyles that damage individual potential. It is a cumulative process: the older people get, the more inferior they are assumed to become, and the more difficult it is for them to swim against the social tide that can so easily swamp them. Those who get to be 80 or more have had to marshall their own resources to resist the impact of what Raphael (1979) calls the "decades of loss", and have had to actively challenge social pressures that would reduce them to vegetable status.

People aged 80 and over are the most rapidly increasing segment of modern industrialized populations. This well-known demographic fact of late-twentieth-century life is usually taken as a prediction of gloom and doom, made personal because most of us, especially if we are female, are more likely than not to live to be 80 plus. We are warned of an

At 97, this lady still lives alone in a house she keeps as immaculate as ever.

"epidemic" of senile dementia, of a future characterized, as Bernard Isaacs (1972) puts it, by "the survival of the unfittest". Some are touting the possibilities of an Hitlerian final solution, disguised under the term euthanasia.

Yet most people who are aged 80 and over right now refute these ageist horror stories in their daily lives. They live independently, either with other family members or alone. They deny that they are lonely or neglected. They enjoy good health, both mental and physical. They do face increasing problems, but they cope with them creatively and courageously. These people are not "marvellous for their age" — they are *normal* for their age. They are the majority — the *large* majority. This is the inescapable conclusion reached from all existing international research.

Until recently, there was very little systematic knowledge about people aged 80 and over. Information about them tends to be tucked away as addenda to data about the aged in general. Often it consists of little more than documentation of the assumption that disabilities — physical, mental, and social — "naturally" increase with increasing age. In a famous three-nation study, Shanas (1968:440) admits to surprise that the increase with age is less marked than expected; and in the earlier work on which Cumming and Henry based disengagement theory, the evident well-being of panel members who were 80 and over is put down to biological elitism (Parlagreco, 1961). The ready resort to a biological argument in explaining deficits of ageing is reminiscent of nineteenth-century preoccupation with the weight of the female brain, a biological given which was taken as proving inferiority to the male.

Gerontologists are not immune to ageism. Indeed, gerontology began as the cataloguing of deficits taken for granted as due solely to biological ageing. The fact that some of these deficits are observable from infancy did not deter researchers from adopting the premise that development peaks in young adulthood, then promptly reverses into decay. In this view the youthful body-and-mind is recognized as a living system with a capacity for growth, but with the attainment of maturity it is conceptualized as a machine which, like all machines, wears out with usage over time. The fact that the human body-and-mind remains a living system until the moment of death, and that living systems require use of all their faculties if those faculties are not to atrophy, does not fit easily into theories of ageing that do little more than elaborate lay presuppositions. Evidence for dialectical relationships between development and decay, with the one dependent on the other, has only slowly been accepted.

Ageing is a lifelong process, beginning at conception, and development and decay are two sides of the same coin. Physiological growth depends on the orderly decay of cellular structures. We lose our tail and our gills to become more human; similarly, we shed old skills such as crawling to develop new ones such as walking. According to one theory, we discard brain cells, without constantly replacing them, as the price of the consolidation of memory (Kimmel, 1974:346). Youth is a period when development is more evident than decay; middle age is a period when more or less of a balance is achieved; and although decay becomes more obvious in old age, there is a plethora of evidence that possibilities for continuing development are still present. Yet many gerontologists, along with the general public, continue to take it for granted that after some variously specified chronological age biological decay takes over and becomes the definitive characteristic of the ageing person. "Deteriorating", rather than the more accurate "maturing", has become a synonym for "growing old".

In 1969 a North American psychiatrist, Robert Butler, coined the term "ageism", and described it as another form of bigotry — comparable to racism and social class discrimination (he does not mention sexism). Defining ageism as "prejudice by one age group toward other age-groups", Butler does not confine its use to prejudice by younger groups against the aged, but this is the kind he emphasizes. His example is a campaign by middle-aged householders against plans to purchase a high-rise apartment building as a public housing project for the aged. As Butler points out, the prospective tenants were not only old, they were poor, and many of them were black. So, as an example of ageism *per se*, it is confounded by other prejudices, and Butler himself admits that, "colour and class were surely most significant" (1969:244). He states, but fails to establish, that these two issues were insufficient on their own to account for the degree of opposition that arose, and his argument skips disjointedly from the protest movement to a psychoanalytic discussion of ageism and back again without providing his reader with any firm structure as guide. Yet, although his evidence is faulty and his presentation muddled, his main point comes through loud and clear: age-based prejudices pervade our society; and particularly prevalent, particularly damaging, is prejudice against the old.

Ten years later Richard Kalish elaborated and refined the concept by pointing to a type of ageism additional to the open antagonisms usually associated with the term. This he calls the "new ageism", found most often amongst advocates of the elderly — including Robert Butler himself. Inexplicably, in his castigation of Butler's "distressingly excellent" book *Why survive?*, Kalish fails to make ironic acknowledgment of Butler as originator of the term ageism. But in the course of an article that meanders from one point to another in much the same way as Butler's earlier one, Kalish succeeds in making a compelling point. Advocates of the aged, in their anxiety to do their best for their clients, portray those clients as failures, by stereotyping the majority in terms of the few who are "least capable, least healthy, and least alert . . ." (1979:398).

The degree to which ageist attitudes are embedded in what Berger and Luckmann (1966) call "the social stock of knowledge" has been explored in some depth. Erdman Palmore's Facts on Ageing Quiz (1977) is a simplified version of earlier attempts to tap factual knowledge and ageist stereotypes in the general population. Despite the controversy that still surrounds the scale, it remains a useful index of the extent of misconceptions about the aged. Most surveys in which it has been used reveal that the proportion of old people in long-stay institutions, and the proportion of old people in the population in general, are greatly overestimated. Moreover, old people are incorrectly assessed as being bored, lonely, set in their ways, and unable to change. Fictions such as these have such a considerable currency that they are difficult to dislodge; and in the meantime, some of the best-established "facts" about the ageing process are themselves under challenge.

Indeed "facts", even about biological aspects of ageing, very often turn out to be little more than myth or conjecture. Nathan Shock points out that there is no evidence that the rate of change in physiological characteristics can be related to any specific chronological age, and some physiological systems are maintained with minimal alteration almost to the point of death (1973:57). Even slower reaction times, classically regarded as one of the very few verifiable facts about ageing, are minimized by physical fitness and higher motivation. Moreover, individual differences are so great that many old people react faster than the young (Botwinick, 1978:203). Memory lapses occur throughout life and are associated more with depression than with age (Gault and Reeve, 1982:12). Further, the work of Labouvie-Vief and Blanchard-Fields questions the whole taken-for-granted principle of "assessing the competencies of ageing adults as deviation from a youthful standard"; rather, these competencies may reflect "a mature mode", hitherto under-valued, of "socially integrated thought" (1982:206).

In Australia, the first signs of this radical re-structuring of theories about ageing surfaced in an article by Bennett and Ahammer advocating a social deficit model (1977a). Attacking the biological decline model for its methodological and theoretical deficiencies, they put forward an impressive body of evidence for the view that "Regressive changes in the latter part of the life-span appear to reflect environmental or experiential deficits rather than intrinsic ageing phenomena" (1977a:3). Later in the same year Bennett expanded on this theme by postulating that the outcome of the ageing process for any one individual might be found in the degree of congruity or otherwise between the self-image and the social image of the ageing person — a symbolic interactionist approach (1977b). That this is a fruitful basis for the study of ageing is illustrated, both in Australia and abroad, by such works as Myerhoff and Simic's *Life's career — aging*, Hazan's *The limbo people*, and Russell's *The ageing experience*. All these works provide sensitive portraits of old people coping, or failing to cope, with the social effects of ageing, including stigmatization, although one or two of the authors might be said to verge on Kalish's "new ageism".

More promising is the wider and more forthrightly sociological view taken by Levin and Levin (1980). Their *Ageism: prejudice and discrimination against the elderly* may prove to be only the first of many works to use the concept of ageism as a central focus in gerontological theory and research.

None of the works so far cited deals specifically with the "old-old" group, a term coined by Neugarten (1974). In fact, even today there is an almost total lack of specific research concerning them. There are a few studies of very old cohorts: centenarians in North America (Beard, 1967) and in Japan (Shigiya, 1978); North American nonagenarians (Gallup and Hill, 1959); and an unpublished account of Spanish-American war veterans (Richardson and Freeman, 1964). Despite the concern so frequently expressed about the economic and social significance of the increase in numbers of those who are aged 80 and over, the only research directly concerned with them as a group in their own right, to this author's knowledge, remains the survey conducted by the author herself in 1978–79.

Findings from that survey are reported in the pages that follow. And the major finding, overwhelmingly supported by gleanings from the general literature on ageing, is that the old-old, despite the problems that face them, do not conform to the stereotypes thrust upon them by the ageism of our society.

Chapter 2: The Toowong Survey

Being old simply means having lived a long time; and far from being a problem, long life is a universal human goal. But derogatory connotations — such as frailty, sickness, loneliness, mental vacuity, physical helplessness, unproductiveness, rigidity of outlook, financial dependence, powerlessness — have become encrusted around its chronological meaning. All of these decremental attributes can be found in human beings of any age, and most of them are especially characteristic of infancy. To a lesser extent, they are also more frequent in extreme old age than during the middle years of life. It is not old age itself that is the problem, but the difficulties that commonly attend it.

Such difficulties are likely to be most acutely felt by those who have lived beyond early old age into the final decade, or two decades, of human life; and it is they who are most likely to be considered a "problem" by the society of which they are a part. As has already been pointed out, people of advanced age are rapidly increasing in numbers and in proportion to the rest of the aged (Myers, 1979:25), but they have been the subject of very little research. In 1978 I set out to try and redress this situation somewhat, although the resources at my disposal ensured that the attempt remain a modest one.

Planning the research

The first task was to find a sample, and this proved a stumbling-block. If I had gone only to institutions for the aged, I would have been sampling only 18 per cent of those aged 80 and over; senior citizen centres would have yielded fewer than 10 per cent; Meals-on-Wheels, home nursing, and other community services, even in combination, would have led me to 21 per cent at most. The great majority of people aged 80 and over are indistinguishable from younger people in the way they live, and seeking them in any specialized setting introduces unacceptable biases. It is true that since 1973 all Australians aged 70 and over are eligible for a government pension, but the Social Security Department could not supply the names and addresses I required because it would have involved a breach of confidentiality.

In the end I decided to attempt a door-to-door census of one fairly typical Brisbane suburb — Toowong — and to try to locate every resident of the required age, including those living permanently in the four institutions (two nursing homes, a hostel for old men, and a general hospital). Detailed maps of the area were obtained from the General Post Office. The Bureau

A view of modern Toowong.

of Statistics informed me that the 1976 census had found 366 persons aged 80 and over living in Toowong, representing 3.1 per cent of the total population of the district (11 713). For the Brisbane City Council Local Authority as a whole, the percentage of this age-group was 2.3 per cent, so in this respect Toowong was higher than the mean, but much less so than some more densely settled suburbs.

Socio-economically, Toowong is much like the rest of suburban Australia in being largely middle class, but it has pockets of upper-middle near the Brisbane River, and others of blue-collar workers closer to the inner city. Perhaps the most typical attribute of Toowong, however, is that like many other suburbs in Australian cities, it is in a process of rapid change. What was true of Toowong in the 1971 census was less true in 1976, and in the early eighties some of the run-down areas closest to the city heart are showing signs of becoming fashionable.

With the population to be investigated decided upon, guidelines for intensive interviews about the life-history and present circumstances of the participants were prepared as advised by Lofland (1971). These had pre-coded cover-sheets showing age, sex, marital status, residential situation, use of community services, and whether or not an interview was agreed upon (with reasons for refusal where this occurred). On the back there was space for interviewer's impressions about the respondent's appearance, personality, residential situation, and health status variables.

I then arranged some advance publicity in the local press. On hindsight, there should have been more, as this serves to familiarize people with the aims of the research and circumvent possible misunderstandings.

Interviewing

In July 1978 I began knocking on doors along the south-western boundary of Toowong. Not every dwelling was visited; reports by neighbours who seemed knowledgeable were accepted as sufficient evidence that it would not be worth calling at a particular house. In many cases there was nobody at home, usually because, according to neighbours, both husband and wife were at work. Those people who came to the door were very cooperative, and by the time the first respondent was finally located, several people in the vicinity had indicated where to find her. The lady herself, aged 89, was interested and helpful; when the interview continued longer than expected, her daughter supplied lunch and invited me to come back next day.

A few interviews were completed in August and September, but other commitments made it impossible for me to devote as much time to this part of the work as originally planned, and in October I decided to engage a team of interviewers. The map of Toowong was divided into eight sections, and each interviewer was allotted one section to cover, street by street. Training took the form of group discussions, explaining the project, the interviewer's duties, typical difficulties encountered up to that date, and a revision of interview techniques. Some tapes of completed interviews were distributed, although there were none that could really be considered exemplary. Interviewers (some of whom were experienced, some not) soon discovered the importance of learning from their own and others' mistakes.

A major ingredient of the research design was that the interview should, as far as possible, prove an enjoyable experience for the old people concerned, who were encouraged to set their own pace and, to a large extent, to choose their own topics. They were not pressed to answer a question they preferred to avoid, nor to clear up inconsistencies or mis-statements. Apart from considerations of the courtesy due to participants, I believe that this strategy was justified by the amount and quality of the information many respondents volunteered. However, the open-ended nature of the interviews and the type of data that emerged from them do not, in my view, justify a rigorous mathematical analysis. I make no claim for statistical representativeness. The numbers responding to different questions varied widely; this should be kept in mind where percentages are reported, and readers seeking more precise information should consult my thesis, "The Social Construction of Old Age".

The first eight interviewers engaged were all women, whose

age varied from the early twenties to late fifties. Later, two young men were employed to interview some of the male respondents. For a variety of reasons some interviewers were unable to continue, and were replaced as they dropped out. Five women and one man stayed with the project to completion, at the end of May 1979. By then cover-sheets with at least a minimum of information had been obtained concerning 94 men and 246 women — 340 in all — but of these only 205 agreed to a tape-recorded interview. Of the 119 people contacted who were not interviewed, 41 were classified as being judged "too sick" or "confused" — more often by relatives or the matron of a nursing home than by the subjects themselves.

This raises the possibility of a bias favouring good health and mental alertness among those who were interviewed compared with those who were not. On the other hand, in 10 cases direct intervention by relatives rescinded approval already granted for an interview, and the majority of refusals were because the old person was "not interested" or "too busy", or because they saw the interview situation as an invasion of privacy. Sometimes these judgments, too, were made without consulting the person involved, but they tended on the whole to represent more autonomous decisions, and suggest that most people who preferred not to be interviewed were as healthy and alert as those who consented. The most usual condition for refusal seemed to be a lack of privacy for the interview.

Some of the difficulties encountered were of a kind to be expected in any door-to-door enterprise — one interviewer felt that she learnt even more about dogs than she did about people. Others were undoubtedly because of the age of the people sought. Old people may take longer to attend to early morning chores, and sometimes prove less tolerant of interruption; lunch is often early, and a considerable number are accustomed to taking a daytime sleep. Evening calls were ruled out because many old people retire early, and because of the higher risk of alarming the 28 per cent of the sample who lived alone. This was something to be guarded against even in the daytime, but in fact the best response rate (74 per cent) was obtained from those living alone, and the worst (48 per cent) from those in institutions.

Definition of the interview situation

An interview, as very old people see it, is something that happens on television, usually to celebrities. Incongruities arise the moment a stranger appears on the doorstep, carrying a brief-case and an unfamiliar electronic device and professing, more or less ingratiatingly, an unlikely interest in one's personal affairs. Respondents' definitions of the situation could not be expected to coincide with the interviewer's. For the interviewer, academic and in particular, sociological concepts were salient, but for those respondents who accepted that the study's aims were academic, the preferred disciplinary frame of reference was historical, never sociological. This is not surprising; history, after all, is an ancient and understandable endeavour, whereas sociology is a johnny-come-lately without much claim to general comprehensibility or respectability. For these respondents it was the history of Toowong itself, not of the people living there, that was seen as the subject of inquiry. Attempts to draw them out about their own experiences were initially resisted; they kept returning to accounts of the locality. Eventually, however, their sense of history prompted full cooperation, and they gladly delved into a well-remembered past. This type of response was not restricted to those with higher educational achievements; it seemed mostly to be associated with an alert and inquiring mind.

Others appeared to define the situation as the first step in an official process designed eventually to achieve some form of improved social welfare for the aged. Sometimes they were fully accepting ("It's time something was done for old people"), sometimes suspicious ("If they want to know how they can help old people, what's all this got to do with it?"), and sometimes they alternated between the two. Whether suspicious or accepting, they tended to be guarded in their statements and uneasy about the tape-recorder; if they forgot that it was running, as most did after awhile, they remembered it again with real alarm:

"That thing hasn't been going all the time, has it? Oh dear, I shouldn't have said. . . ."

The tape-recorder certainly introduced a major awkwardness into the situation, but the guided conversations on which the survey was based would not have been possible without it. Only one respondent, however, insisted that the interview be recorded by other means. For some, the end of tape-recording signalled a redefinition of the situation from the incongruous to the understandable. With "all that business" over, the interviewer became a guest to be offered tea and cakes, shown photographs and bits of fancywork, and regaled with stories about the past and reflections on the present and the future, which had been disclosed much more reluctantly while the situation was still being defined as an interview.

It was not always possible to ensure a one-to-one interviewer/respondent situation, though the desirability of doing so became more and more apparent. The presence of a spouse or other family member imposed obvious constraints on the respondent's freedom to report, on the interviewer's freedom to question, and on the type of understanding that might develop between them. Occasionally a loving daughter could be helpful ("Tell her about your experiences when you went nursing, Mother"), and in the one joint interview by husband and wife, the pair proved mutually encouraging. However, in those instances where married couples were seen separately, differences in points of view (including estimates of the happiness of the marriage) added to the richness of the data. A spouse off-stage, as it were, was sometimes a disruptive element; one old lady who was sick in bed made it plain that she was annoyed by her husband's eager reminiscences to an invisible stranger; and men as a rule seemed to find it necessary to make some sort of jocular reference to a wife who, though unseen, was probably within earshot. One interviewer was quite unnerved by a respondent's son, who lounged in the doorway throughout the interview with an inscrutable smile on his face.

Whether or not other people were somewhere in the background, the chief interactional focus, of course, was between interviewer and respondent, each of whom contributed something particular to the resulting interview. Interpersonal dynamics of this kind are not limited to open-ended as opposed to structured interviews, although a rigid interview schedule may serve to obscure them.

For many respondents — perhaps the majority — the situation was always simply a matter of personal interaction with an obliging stranger. As previously noted, the response rate was higher for those living alone than in other residential situations; apparently any fear of strangers tends, for most old people, to be outweighed by the pleasures of engaging in friendly conversation. Different styles of interaction ranged from the monosyllabic to the garrulous; it was possible to spend three hours with the latter and learn a great deal about the people next door, without getting essential information about the respondents themselves.

Social desirability was a paramount consideration for many; one old lady made this quite explicit by explaining, "I don't want to say anything you disagree with." Degrees of candour varied; some were at pains to present themselves and their families in the best possible light, while others seemed quite disconcertingly frank in their criticism. Inconsistencies abounded. This, of course, is to be expected. Human beings normally hold "conflicting opinions, values, attitudes, or tendencies to act" (Dean and Whyte, 1969:106), and the selective processes at work in reporting recollections are seldom efficient enough to eliminate even blatant contradictions. The fact that inconsistencies were not screened out by a prestructured interview schedule brought the transcripts a step closer to reality, and encouraged an appreciation of the dialectical complexities always at work in the thought processes of real-life human beings.

The interviewing situation was appreciably more difficult in all of the four institutions included in the survey. Although some excellent interviews were obtained at the hostel, and a few from the other institutions, on the whole most interviews were not of the same quality as those from respondents still living independently in the community. There are several reasons for this. The first and most obvious is that the institutionalized are, by definition, the "frail old" (except the men at the hostel, where nursing services are not provided), and it is to be expected that people in poor health would be less inclined to devote their failing energies to the demands of the interview situation. In addition, the fact of institutionalization posed its own constraints. Respondents were far less in command of the situation than those in their own homes: meal-times and other routine events could not be delayed; third parties were either continually present or kept coming and going; and rostering ensured that there were always some members of staff who had not been informed about the project or were not entirely in sympathy with it.

One-visit interviews place the investigator in an observer-as-participant role (Gold, 1969:30), with effects on the recorded product contributed by all the people present. Important among those effects were those emanating from the interviewers themselves.

Interviewer effects

In an exhaustive report on interviewing in the social sciences, H.H. Hyman concludes that the most competent interviewers are usually female, married, and between 35 and 44 years of age (1954:289). Several of the 12 interviewers employed in the Toowong study fitted this prescription, but the youngest was 20 and unmarried, and the oldest in her sixties. Initially, it was assumed that it would be important to establish rapport, and that this would be more easily accomplished with older interviewers. The first assumption was borne out by experience, but the age gap between an octogenarian and even the oldest interviewer amounted to a whole generation, and in practice the youngest achieved excellent rapport through her genuine interest in and liking for the old folk. These transcended the misunderstandings that sometimes arose when they spoke from a perspective outside her knowledge and experience. The old men tended to flirt with her; the old women tended to mother her; in either case, they were usually willing to tell her a lot about themselves.

The greatest difficulty posed by the age difference applied to all the interviewers, though to some more than others; this was the slower reaction time which — though it is amenable to training and highly variable among individuals — is a well-documented accompaniment of old age (Botwinick, 1978). The slowness may be because old people have so many experiences to sort through before deciding on a response. Whatever the cause, it tends to put them out of phase in conversational interplay with most younger persons, who will often, finding a pause too long for their personal comfort, consider a question or remark unanswered when in fact a reply was about to be made. The old person sees this as an interruption; valuable material may be lost, and rapport suffers.

Interviewer/respondent matching is an issue which, in the opinion of at least one authority, rests on assumptions about person-to-person interaction for which it is difficult, if not impossible, to establish adequate evidence (Moser, 1967:267). In other words, the constituents of rapport are largely unpredictable. The possibility of achieving greater rapport (and therefore validity) through matching at least for sex seemed worth attempting, and two male interviewers, both young married men with previous interviewing experience, were employed early in 1979. Both were responsible for some excellent interviews, but it should not be assumed that same-sex interviews are invariably superior. One old gentleman who rang me personally, and in the course of quite a long conversation expressed interest in being interviewed, was disappointingly reserved when confronted with a male interviewer. Like many men in our society, he apparently related better to women in a situation involving confidences of a personal nature. It was felt that women could only be interviewed by women, because of such questions as the age of menarche, but most men responded freely when asked by female interviewers about birth control, or their wife's experiences in childbirth and menopause.

As it happened, an opportunity occurred to compare an opposite-sex with a same-sex interview situation. One old gentleman was first interviewed in the men's hostel by a lady interviewer; he must have enjoyed the experience, because later, when he had transferred to a nursing home because of a deterioration in his physical condition, he readily agreed to another interview, without mentioning that he had already been included in the survey. This time the interviewer was male. The two interviews were factually similar, but there were slight differences in choice of language (including occasional mild profanities in the male-conducted interview) and in the type of material reported.

Interviewers were successful to the extent that they felt comfortable with the aims of the research and interested in the old people themselves. All had their own sensitivities that made certain sections of the inquiry awkward for them. Financial items were the most sketchily reported. Not only did interviewers dislike asking them, but many respondents seemed to find these questions offensive, and it seemed preferable not to press the point if this seemed likely to damage rapport for the rest of the interview.

Other difficulties arose in the area of religion. Most interviewers were practising Christians, for whom the meaning of life was clearly defined by their beliefs. Seeing this as unproblematic, they were inclined to skirt around related questions or apologize in advance for their inclusion. Subtle nuances of tone in the interviewer's voice may have engendered a similarly apologetic stance on the part of some respondents, who may have felt that the interviewer would not approve of non-attendance at church or disbelief in life after death. One of the less experienced interviewers could never quite conquer a tendency to murmur a congratulatory "Good!" whenever a respondent revealed values consonant with her own.

Awkwardness was anticipated in questions related to sex, but this proved in large measure unfounded. An attempt was made to place all such questions within a general health framework, but it soon became obvious that most of the interviewers were more nervous about introducing these questions than respondents were about answering them.

Despite all the difficulties, however, a wealth of detailed and often uninhibited information was obtained, its unevenness and contradictions reflecting real-life experience rather than a rationality imposed upon it by a less accommodating process of research. As one of the interviewers summed it up, "Research

... is like a newspaper photograph — in spite of the real epistemological difficulties, each little blurred blot contributes something to a discernible pattern ..." (Jones, in Job, Jones, Johansen and Spenceley, 1980).

Transcribing, coding, computer, and analysing

My own part in all this, in addition to the general organization, consisted chiefly of receiving and listening to the tapes (sometimes over and over again), and transcribing them onto stencils as Lofland (1971) advises. Transcribing began on completion of the first interview, and continued throughout the survey period. One minor tragedy was the accidental erasure of one of the interviews, leaving 204 complete interviews available for transcription. Again following Lofland's advice, multiple copies were made of each transcript; one copy was attached to the cover-sheet, and the rest colour-coded for a particular subject matter. When interviewing had ended and all transcripts were completed, a code book was constructed for 135 variables, with up to 9 values representing what were intended to be exhaustive and mutually exclusive categories (though in many instances this proved not to be the case). Wherever possible, transcripts were coded by those who conducted the interviews, but for various reasons I ended by coding the bulk of the interviews myself.

A computer printout of frequencies was obtained in August 1979, and used for the refining of categories and elimination of coding inconsistencies. In November of the same year crosstabulations were begun, and further statistical analysis of an elementary kind followed early in 1980. All variables were analysed in relation to age, sex, and socio-economic status.

In the pages that follow I have tried to bring the old people of the Toowong survey alive for the general reader. I have given them names (chosen at random from a telephone book), and attempted to show the importance of the socio-historical context in which they lived for the old age they eventually attained. I have made much more use than before of interviewers' impressions of their appearance and personality, and also of the impressions I formed myself from those many hours of listening to their voices.

Consistent with the care in preserving the anonymity I promised them, I feel I owe them the utmost honesty in presenting their lives as they revealed them to us. It will surely be apparent that the ageist stereotypes of which they are a primary target do not fit these people.

Chapter 3: The Place, the Period, and the People

The place: Toowong in 1979

The city of Brisbane has spilled out from a site originally chosen as a "maximum security gaol for convicts too intransigent for Sydney to restrain" (Wood, 1971:9). The central business district is confined to a half square mile on the north bank of the Brisbane River, 12 miles from the mouth of Moreton Bay; it is enclosed on three sides by a conspicuous meander and on the fourth by a steep escarpment. Westward, the land is flat along the river but rises quickly in a series of broken ridges to the foothills fronting the Mt Coot-tha bushland reserve. A busy highway, lined with figs, bamboos, jacaranda trees, and eucalypts, now runs west along the river, parallelled a few blocks further in, first by the railway line, and then by another major road, which was formerly the route for one of Brisbane's earliest tramlines. Travelling west by any of these routes, the first suburb reached is Milton; the next is Auchenflower (closer to the river) or Torwood (in the foothills); both are included in the area officially designated Toowong.

The main Toowong shopping centre is situated where the highway curves away from the river, crosses the railway line, and continues up Toowong High Street, where long-established poinciana trees shade a nature strip in the centre of the road.

The old tram line takes a similar curve half a kilometre or so further towards the hills, and other shops have been built at this point, where the road veers away towards the big hillside cemetery on the slopes of Mt Coot-tha. In a valley at West Toowong, another minor shopping centre has been established. Paterson's timber mill is in operation just behind the Toowong railway station, and the studios of the Queensland branch of the Australian Broadcasting Corporation stand between the station and the river.

About half of the old people interviewed in this survey lived somewhere between the river and the cemetery. In Toowong, as elsewhere in Brisbane, high-income families tend to live on hills and low-income families on lowlands, a pattern well established by the 1870s. The pattern is complicated by the high status of comparatively low-lying riverside sites, and by the existence of the cemetery itself, which presumably detracts from the value of some of the higher sites. In many places the terrain is sharply broken by ridges and gullies; there are streets climbing up and down like switchback railways, and numerous two-level roads. Most dwellings are "free-standing houses featured by weatherboard walls and an iron roof, built on stumps" (Cities Commission, 1975:4); typically, they stand in well-tended gardens shaded by sub-tropical trees.

A common pattern in old-established, lower-income areas well inland from the river was for respondents to be found as clusters of near neighbours, each living independently. Usually they proved to be in frequent and friendly contact, and had known one another for many years. Recently settled areas had fewer residents of eligible age, but 31 respondents, usually among the more affluent, were found living in high-rise blocks of home units closer to the river. They had moved there within the last decade, often on retirement from a country property or from a larger family home elsewhere in Brisbane.

For old people Toowong seems a pleasant place to live, convenient to the city and with good shops, transport, and a council library equipped with large-print books. Cooling afternoon breezes are usual in summer, and very few respondents commented other than favourably on the climate. Winters are sunny and dry, with temperatures ranging from a high 22 to a low of 10 degrees Celsius at night; autumn and spring are slightly warmer, and despite some intermittent showers, skies are mostly blue. Summer maxima average 31 degrees Celsius and humidity is high; most of the average yearly rainfall (1312 mm.) falls during the 4 main summer months, December to March. Brisbane, tucked away in the south-east corner of the state, is normally outside the cyclone belt that plagues northern Australia, but it is no stranger to summer thunderstorms and occasional gale-force winds.

Immigration to Queensland by the old has been encouraged recently by the state government's abolition of death duties, but the great majority of those coming north settle, not in Brisbane itself, but in seaside resorts an hour or two away by car.

Toowong at the turn of the century

The name Toowong dates from the 1820s, when explorers reported hearing the Flinders cuckoo calling "toowong, toowong" in the creeks and gullies of the foothills of Mt Coottha. Later a ship's captain named Drew acquired land in the district and nailed a sign to a tree proclaiming, "This is the village of Toowong" (Gregory, 1977:5). By the 1890s, when the oldest of the respondents were still children, Brisbane was a city of some 100 000 inhabitants, ranking fourth in size among Australian cities after Melbourne, Sydney, and Adelaide, in that order.

The railway west to Ipswich, built in 1875, passed through Toowong. It was partly responsible for some decline in the suburb's status, incurred when an influx of lower-income settlers, many of them British migrants, poured into the colony during the booming eighties and were exploited by "avaricious speculators" who "divided estates into the maximum possible number of blocks of land" and built working-class housing on "Tiny allotments in narrow streets" (Lawson, 1973:100). Parts of Torwood were developed in this way, as well as low-lying areas close to the railway line and main roads. In 1885 the government passed the Undue Subdivision of Land Act, prescribing a minimum allotment size and width of streets. By the end of the eighties the boom had been followed by a slump, the flow of assisted migrants had been cut off, and little new building took place during the difficult and turbulent nineties.

The period

The 1890s, when most respondents were born, are usually seen by historians as "a time of radicalism, nationalism, artistic creativity and industrial militancy" (McQueen, 1978:10), and in no part of Australia was this more evident than in Queensland. The nineties opened with the seamen's strike and was followed by the shearer's strike in 1891, precipitating the emergence of the Labor Party. For Brisbane, and for Toowong as part of it, the nineties were marked by other dramatic events. An overflowing of the river in 1890 was followed by the record-

Toowong railway station in the 1893 flood.

breaking floods of 1893, which swept away both bridges linking north and south sides of the river and caused several deaths
as well as devastating loss of property. The oldest respondents,
if they had been in Brisbane at that time, gave vivid accounts of
the flood. One reported falling "head first in" and being rescued
just in time to save her from drowning; her mother gave birth
to a stillborn child and was removed from her home on a door
as water lapped onto the verandah. Another remembered
"larking about" with tins of jam and condensed milk from a
flood-devastated factory; others recalled houses floating down
the river, or haystacks with "a poor old chook" perched on one
of them. A third big flood occurred in 1896, followed
thereafter by a drought that lasted well into the first decade of
the twentieth century.

Natural disasters were matched by the man-made. In April
1893, a few months after the catastrophic flood, the worsening
economic depression culminated in the failure of 8 of the 11
banks in Queensland, causing the financial ruin of numerous
small businessmen and even some members of the elite. For
ordinary people, such as the parents of Toowong respondents,
times were hard enough to make an indelible impression on
respondents old enough to remember them. But socio-
economic antagonisms that began to make themselves evident
in the nineties were matched by countervailing forces encouraging cohesion, and none of these was more important
than a naive pride in being part of a great Empire, symbolized
by the solemn figure of the Queen. Some respondents
remembered celebrating her Jubilee with picnics and the
presentation of medallions; others remembered making purple
and black rosettes in mourning for her death.

The new century was ushered in by a referendum over
Federation, opposed by Queensland but carried by the rest of
Australia — a potentially divisive issue that did not arouse
nearly as much interest among respondents as their nostalgic
memories of Queen Victoria. It was demonstrably the end of an
era, and the greatest change of all was already casting ominous
shadows upon the international scene. Respondents were born
at the end of a long period of unprecedented peace; and they
faced a century of war.

The lives of respondents were first touched by war in the last month of the nineteenth century, when the Boers won three battles against the British, and Australians, who to that date had been unsure of their role in the conflict, suddenly decided that the safety of the nation was inescapably linked with British prestige. South Africa became Australia's first line of defence. Several respondents remembered contingents marching through Brisbane streets; the song "Goodbye, Dolly Grey" was remembered with nostaglia. One respondent recalled how the erection of a monument to a Boer War casualty in the little South Australian town where he was born fired his patriotic spirit for years afterwards. Another remembered helping his mother keep kerosene tins boiling to give the troops tea and sandwiches as they changed trains at the New South Wales border. The war stepped up the market for Australian horses, to the sorrow of some country-bred respondents who lost favourite steeds to the cause.

It was the First World War, however, that initiated most respondents into an understanding of the real meaning of war. For the men who served it was, if nothing else, a dramatic disruption of their normal lives. Of the 94 men in the sample, 37 per cent clearly indicated active service; 2 of these survived shipwrecks during the war. Many of the men had adventures to recount, and once started on the war, were reluctant to stop. For many it was a horrifying experience that haunted them with nightmares for years afterwards. A few maintained that they had enjoyed it, or at least had gained from it in some way. Several were wounded or gassed, however, and found that old war injuries had "come against them" in their old age. A well-known footballer was shot in the chest and told he would be a permanent invalid, but he struggled back to health and international status before disabilities returned in his eighties. One respondent reported, apparently without bitterness, that he had been gassed three times but was not eligible for a war pension because he had taken pride in never appearing on sick parade.

A similar range of feeling, though perhaps of less intensity, was evident among the women. A few enjoyed it; for example, one respondent came straight from a finishing school in Switzerland to serve as a volunteer waitress and scullery maid in a rest centre for troops in London, and she found the plunge from one world to another exciting and enlightening. She married one of the soldiers she met there, and came to Australia after the war. Two women, one in England and the other in Australia, worked in munitions factories. Nearly one-third of the sample said they were really not much affected, as nobody close to them went away. However, patriotic fervour was high, and acceptance of Allied propaganda unquestioning; some respondents, learning painfully after the war that one's own government could lie, were slow to accept the first accounts of Nazi atrocities. For most Australian girls voluntary war work was no more than a once-a-week affair, and offered little relief for the constant anxiety concerning friends and relatives who were serving overseas. Perhaps more than the men, they tended to look back on the First World War as a time of sorrow, making bittersweet the celebrations that came at its close.

Very few recollected the twenties as a time of prosperity. By that time most respondents were married and bringing up young families; on the whole they looked back on those times as only slightly less difficult than the great depression that followed in the thirties. Effects of the depression on Queensland were cushioned to some extent by the rural base of the economy, but 26 respondents reported that they or their husbands had been without work for up to 3 years at a time, and many more said their working days had been cut down to 2 a week or less, or that they had accepted substantial reductions in pay while continuing to work full-time. Only after the Second World War did living standards begin to approach today's. Respondents, almost without exception, had had a lifetime's training in frugality, and they tended to find planned obsolescence, and the throw-away habits of their descendants, quite bewildering.

The Second World War itself was, on the whole, much less notable for respondents than the first; the proportion of those reporting that they were not much affected increased to over half. By that time respondents were in their forties or early fifties; only five reported having sons who served, one of whom was 'still missing'. The Second World War was followed by war in Korea and then by the war in Vietnam; one respondent lost a much-loved grandson in Vietnam, but on the whole international conflicts no longer had much impact for respondents. A few were resigned to Armageddon, or feared it for their grandchildren, but the terror of war appeared on the whole to have been numbed by habituation. For most of the old people, the First World War overshadowed all others, and they were well aware that in this respect, as in so many others, Australia has to date been a "lucky country".

Between and since the wars, the respondents have seen an uneasy peace, marked by economic boom and depression, and a giddy pace of technological change that has kept gathering momentum since their childhood days. The magic lantern gave way to the moving picture show; gas lights were replaced by electricity; the telephone became a commonplace; the arrival of a "motor-buggy" was no longer something to rush outside and gape at — soon people ran to look, instead, at the miracle of a biplane droning across the sky. As respondents married and set up homes of their own, the richer among them began to acquire refrigerators instead of cool safes; wireless was invented; in America there were machines for washing clothes. By late middle age respondents had learned to deal with plastics and television and all the accoutrements that combined to make life more comfortable and more complicated than it used to be. In 80 or more years of living, all respondents had taken part in a period of unprecedented social change and, to some small degree, had themselves been responsible for the directions of that change.

The people

The criterion for inclusion in the survey was having been born in the nineteenth century; the youngest respondent eligible for the survey was therefore one whose birth-date was 31 December 1899, and a woman precisely of that age was in fact included. As the criterion for eligibility included those who would turn 80 during 1979, ages ranged from 79 to 97, the average age being 83. There were 245 octogenarians (defined as aged 79–88), and 67 nongenarians (89 +). For a more even distribution, the sample was divided into 169 "younger cohorts" (aged 79–84), for whom the average age was 80.5; and 143 "older cohorts" (85 +), with an average of 88.8.

In the sample 94 were males, 246 were females — a male-female ratio of 1:2.5. In all Western populations there is a progressive linear change in sex ratios from birth throughout life. In Queensland, 106.4 males are born to every 100 females, but the lower life expectancy of Australian males (68, compared to 74 for females) results in a marked female excess in the later years of life. Women not only live longer than men, they tend in our culture to marry men older than themselves, so that the probability of widowhood is very much greater for women than for men. Eighty-three per cent of those who had been widowed were female, while sixty per cent of the still-married were males. Of the 43 respondents who had never married at all, only 2 were male.

As a corollary to women's longer life expectancy and greater susceptibility to widowhood, residential patterns were also markedly different for the two sexes. Not only were women more likely to be living alone, they were also more likely to be institutionalized. However, the large majority of both sexes were living independently in the community, usually in some sort of family situation.

The ethnic composition of the sample reveals the homogeneity so typical of Australian society until the end of the Second World War, when large-scale immigration began from places other than the British Isles. Seventy-five per cent were Australian-born, and most of the rest came from Britain; only eight people were from other parts of the world: two Russians, three Germans, one American, one Dutchwoman, and one Pole. Only five of the immigrants had been resident in Australia for fewer than fifty years. The main flow of British emigration to other parts of the world took place between 1853 and 1880, and the parents of respondents, rather than the respondents themselves, contributed to Queensland's share. By the time most respondents were born, economic depression had persuaded the government that assisted immigration would only add to unemployment and the numbers of people seeking relief rations; it was not resumed until 1899.

Most respondents were born in Queensland, and almost all the rest had lived in Queensland for 50 years or more. Of the Queenslanders, 42 per cent were country-born, 27 per cent came from large provincial towns such as Rockhampton and Toowoomba, and 31 per cent were born in Brisbane — at least 11 people among the latter actually in the area now known as Toowong. A further 13 per cent came from other parts of rural and urban Australia.

In a sample so similar ethnically, religious affiliation could be expected to fall within a rather narrow range. Thirty-four per cent of those from whom this information was obtained belonged to the Church of England; 33 per cent to various Protestant denominations; 19 per cent were Roman Catholic; 11 per cent claimed no religious affiliation; and 3 per cent coded as "other" included Russian Orthodox, Jewish, and Seventh Day Adventist members.

In assigning a measure of socio-economic status as many indicators as possible were taken into account. Occupational criteria included father's, spouse's, and the respondent's own. Educational criteria were also important — not only educational standard and years of schooling, but the type of school attended were considered. Lifestyle indicators such as ownership and type of dwelling, financial situation, and source of income were also considered, although as already mentioned, questions concerning financial standing prompted so much resistance that the effort to assess it precisely was abandoned. The upper stratum included all tertiary-educated professional people, 3 of them titled, and those of managerial status or minor professionals, amounting to 26 per cent. About 44 per cent were judged to belong to the middle stratum; these included teachers, clerks, tradesmen, shopkeepers, farmers, salesmen, and small businessmen. The lower stratum sometimes had similar types of occupation but with educational and lifestyle differences that suggested a lower status, often revealing a very variable occupational background in which mining, droving and small business enterprises might be combined. Together with those whose main lifetime occupation (or spouse's occupation) had been as labourer, unskilled factory worker, or domestic servant, the lower stratum comprised 30 per cent of the sample as a whole.

The profile of a "typical" respondent emerges as an 83-year-old Australian-born widow living independently in the community, usually with some other family member, and probably belonging to the middle socio-economic stratum. Mrs Tavey, tall and slim with china-blue eyes, lived with her 64-year-old daughter in a pleasant high-set home which they jointly owned; she was typical in all except one respect. She was 94 years old. An abridged version of the transcript of her interview is given below.

No, I don't mind telling you how old I am — when you get beyond the 90 stage you get less sensitive about your age. I was born in August 1884, in Ashfield, Sydney. There was one boy who died in infancy and I had two sisters, both considerably older — I was the youngest in the family and I was born very late in my mother's life. My father was a building carpenter in the early days. He earned quite a lot of money, but unfortunately he was an Irishman and addicted to drink and very liberal with everybody. He eventually had a fall from a building and that caused his death. He was probably in his forties. Mother never talked about it very much. Mother didn't die herself till she was well up in her eighties. She was a very sweet old dear, and she went out of her way to do kindness for everybody. She was a maternity nurse, and when my father passed away, she used to go out in the country and nurse. My sister married at 17 and my home was with that sister. Mother came home at intervals. But I remember she used to make the most delicious rice puddings — lovely creamy ones, not these hard baked things.

I lived with my sister in Bathurst, and I went to the Congregational church because it was the nearest. Besides, the minister was our personal friend. I grew up with his family. I went to school in Bathurst for six years, and I got to the top grade — in those days it was Class Six. I got a certificate. The headmaster wasn't strict at all; he was very popular. He used to come out and play games with us — rounders with the girls and cricket with the boys. There were one or two boys that were a bit noisy and used to get into trouble occasionally, and sometimes they were caned in front of the girls, which of course was very infra dig for them! (LAUGHS) I think it was the best punishment they could have had, caned in front of the girls.

When I left school I went home to help my sister. By this time she had six children, and I was the one who mothered those children because my sister — well, she had a very good voice and she was very socially inclined and very nice-looking — and very spoiled! You know, her social life — she went out a great deal while I mothered the kids. I did love them, and I grew up with them. I was only — I think about four years older than my eldest nephew, and we grew up like a family. I was like the eldest sister.

I always read a great deal. That was my favourite occupation, if I could get five minutes away with a book, I did so. I liked Dickens — I remember the first book I ever enjoyed was David Copperfield, and I think Scott — I don't recall any magazines, I don't think there were many magazines on the market. But all sorts of books I used to read. I loved novels, especially love stories, being very romantic — I was very fond of the boys and they were fond of me! (LAUGHS) I had lots of boy friends. We used to go to Sunday school together, and church together, and walk home — we used to have little dances and sing-songs, and that sort of thing.

My periods didn't start till I was about 16. I didn't get a single word of warning from anybody older. It was always kept a deep dark secret — anything in the sex line or — anything about sex was taboo. How stupid, when Mother was a nurse! She didn't tell me until I was about 16 and then she told me the facts of life and she told me to be a good girl, but she didn't give me very much help about — how to keep out of — on the straight and narrow! No, my period didn't come as a shock, I think I gathered from different — sources — schoolgirls — the wrong source really. I gathered that it was — it was all rather —

I went to the Technical College in Bathurst and then I got a job in an office in Sydney. My mother was nursing at Collington up here in Queensland. By this time she was in her sixties, and she was asked to take a housekeeping job with the officers of a milk and cheese factory; she was asked to take charge of their quarters. But she needed someone to help her, and she wrote and asked me if I — so I went up, and my husband was the assistant engineer up in the factory. I was 24 or 25 I think — he was a little younger than me, a year and a half. I was 27 when we got married. My sister was living up here in Brisbane and I stayed with her for a while and we attended the Wharf Street Congregational Church, and that's where we got married. I sang in the choir there. I was married there in 1911, the old church on the corner of Wharf Street and Edward.(?)

My husband was born in Bendigo, and he came up here, took a job at Collington — his uncle was the managing director of the factory there. He had his diploma in engineering or whatever it is they had to have those days — certificate I think it was. And then he joined the Brisbane tramways — he went there in 1912, just at the time of the strike! It was a big general strike, I don't remember how long it was, but some considerable time I think. Everything was in an uproar in Brisbane. I couldn't tell you what they were striking for — what do they usually strike for? Better conditions or for more money —

He was in the tramways for 38 years. He was a qualified engineer and he got three pounds a week for a start! When I look back on it now I don't know how I managed. He was a very good man. He had a quick temper, but he was a wonderful husband. No, he didn't help in the house, but he did all the outside chores, painted the house, and — and if I wanted anything done inside he'd do it for me, he painted the kitchen — and I've done that myself in my time, too. I think my married life was the happiest time. And when I was with my young family and we were all happy and carefree — that might have been — but my married life was very happy. He was a very considerate husband. And what he had he endowed me with. If he ever earned any overtime, he always bought me something. He kept us supplied with chocolates. (LAUGHS) Every Friday night he used to always bring home a little packet of chocolates or something for us, even though he was only earning three or four or five pounds. And even as late as his last years, I think he was only earning 800 a year when he was a qualified engineer.

My daughter wasn't born till after I'd been married three years. I had a premature birth, you don't call that a child, do you? I would have liked more children, but my husband — he'd had a very unhappy experience in his early days, he lost two of his cousins in childbirth, and I think he was always terrified. I had rather a bad time, but I had a very good doctor, that old Dr Marks, he was a wonderful doctor. You were in hospital in those days not for four days as you are now, but for a whole fortnight and three days I was in hospital, until I was completely well. And at the rate of two pounds five shillings per week! I had rather a — painful time, but I won't go through it, my daughter doesn't like that sort of thing brought up —

Birth control? (LAUGHS) I was always under the impression that if you kept away from the fire you didn't get burnt! No, I had no difficulties at change of life, none whatever. I was well into my fifties, 52 I suppose. I started very late, sixteen, and I went on till I was 52, and then it just — faded away. That was all. No difficulty at all. I never had any troubles down there.

My husband died of a coronary 14 years ago. He didn't retire till he was 67, because they kept him on temporarily. I think it was a hard blow for him when he retired, because he was wrapped up in his work and he was very conscientious and he didn't mind working — oh, 24 hours at a time! Sometimes he'd be away all night before he came home, if there was a job to be done, he'd stop there and do it. But he didn't find it hard to adjust — we had a garden, a very nice rose garden out in front, and he did a lot of work around the house. We had a deep gully in our backyard then, he filled all that up, all by hand mind you. He did a lot of cementing, he was always busy with something.

The First World War? It was a very trying time. I had a favourite nephew who was killed at Gallipoli. He had a beautiful voice and he used to keep all the men entertained in his battalion — he was only 19 and full of life. He used to pop his head up to have a look out, and he was warned about that, but one day he — a sniper got him.

The depression years didn't affect us very much, my husband was working — we were living here. We've been here since 1923. My daughter was growing up. She had passed her Junior and she had an extension scholarship to go on with her Senior, but she was tired of study and — she took up commercial work, and she got a job without very much difficulty. We had a little bit behind us. We were buying our home, which was a bit of a slug — this house only cost 750 pounds, but that was out of a 3-pound-a-week wage, dear, so it took a bit of gathering together. But we managed.

In the Second World War I went into Red Cross down here at Auchenflower and I also did a course down at the local hospital — Fermoy. We had a sort of station down here at the local church preparing for any bombing or anything like that, to take people in who were injured or without homes. I don't know whether I was actually in charge of that but it seemed that it just drifted on to me! (LAUGHS) We made mattresses.

I was always an outdoor lady when I was nimble enough to — I loved going places and doing things, and usually I rose to the top. I was captain of our tennis club, and when I went into Kindercraft, I became everything excepting president, which I refused. When I was young I went ice-skating and dancing. I loved dancing — in fact, I won a waltzing competition once, up in the country. I played tennis just with our local ladies, they're nearly all passed away now. We had the most sumptuous lunches! Up till my seventies I played tennis.

I've been here 65 years. Yes, we've owned it now for many years. I have no other source of income excepting my pension, which I've only been receiving the last four years. Until then I managed on our life savings. No, finance isn't a problem at all — we manage very well. My daughter has her superannuation, and between us we divide our household expenses. My daughter left her job to take care of me when my sight deteriorated, and I'm very grateful for that. I'd like that mentioned and put in, because not many daughters do that sort of thing. And she takes good care of me — sometimes more good care than I really want! (LAUGHS) I say, for goodness sake let me alone and let me — paddle my own canoe, but — (LAUGHS)

Yes, we have given some thought about going into a home — a church home. But since my sight has deteriorated, these last two years — I can find my way about my own little domicile better than going into — anywhere else. And besides, it's — You know, $30 000 to buy a — it's a lot of money! I've never owed — our house was the only big debt we ever had, I had to go without many things to get a home, and having done that I wouldn't enter into any other — I've never bought anything I couldn't pay for. And besides —

I have quite a lot of visitors. My Kindercraft friends very often, quite a number of people, and — I've always cultivated my daughter's young friends, they come here and we have pleasant evenings. And there's my transistor, which is a great friend to me! I'm able to listen to the various things that go on, and hear what's going on in the world. You've got to keep up with the times, haven't you! I don't like wars and rumours of wars, and I hate to hear about these unfortunate people who are refugees from their homeland, you can imagine the conditions on these boats. But there's little I can do about it, can I? And I watch cricket.

Lonely? (LAUGHS) Well, occasionally. When my daughter — I do encourage her to go out and meet her friends and that, but — I'm always very happy to see her home. Bored? I don't know what it is to be bored. I think there's something wrong if you get bored. No, I don't go to the Senior Citizens. I have friends who belong to it, I know all about it, but — (PAUSE) I can amuse myself — at home. We go out — my daughter has a car — she takes all the poor old bodies that can't get out from the homes. We have several friends in homes, you know. We take them out for the day and take our lunch out. Yesterday a blind friend came over and she had lunch with us. My daughter had to go for her and bring her back — that's the sort of girl she is! (LAUGHS)

Politics? I think I'm more interested now than I ever was, but — you can't get to the bottom, they're all so evasive, you can't get to the truth of the matter, can you! I don't think I've changed my vote. I vote Liberal. But I'm just commencing to wonder how Fraser — how he got into that position, for a start. Well, I know, of course, but I've really lost faith in him. I think he's — rather weak, really. I think Bob Hawke's — I admire him, I think he's a very clever man. As for Joh — (LAUGHS) I think he's a bit of an evader too. Mind you, I think he's a good man. It strikes me, Caesar's wife's got to be above suspicion — a man whose private life is not above suspicion, I don't think his public life — I think one influences the other.

I'm both for and against the Aboriginals. Now when I was first up in Collington there was a camp not very far — and the first time I encountered them there were a lot of figures walking about in pink flannelette nightgowns, a boiling hot day — Aboriginal women. They had strings tied round them, or a bit of rope or something, others were trailing them in the mud. I just couldn't understand why the government had supplied them with pink flannelette nightgowns in the middle of a tropical summer. Why didn't they give them pink dresses instead of these nightgowns? And I was always a little bit — on their side, because I thought they were — misled, mismanaged. Of course, some of them were exceedingly dirty, some of them wouldn't work if they could get out of it. And yet a woman that used to come and do the washing for me, Rosie her name was, I couldn't speak highly enough of her. They — when they're good they're very very good and when they're bad they're horrid! (LAUGHS)

Asking me what I think about nuclear power — well, my scientific knowledge isn't sufficient for me to say. I think it has to be very carefully handled and until we really know the pros and cons I just wonder if we should go on with it.

I don't belong to any church, but I go round and visit at them all. And try to find out from one place or another what the answer is to the universal questions. At the moment I'm — there's nothing very important, it's just — hanging — well, I'll say hanging on to life.

Just — making the best of things. Which to me is a very frustrating business, my eyes being so bad, because I've always been active, able to do things for other people which I can no longer do. My daughter belongs to St Andrews and I take an interest in that. And I go with her to the Guild occasionally and I meet some very charming people in there.

Life after death? Well — (PAUSE) I really can't answer you that question. I sometimes wonder, and — I haven't got to the bottom of that question really. I haven't answered it to my own satisfaction. I believe in God and I believe in the universe and — but I wonder about the meaning of life. I just wonder sometimes. I wonder when you hear about all these dreadful cases of poverty and — man's inhumanity to man — if — there isn't very much in it after all. You hear of good things being done, but unfortunately the good deeds seem to be outweighed by the bad ones. Or are they?

No, I'm not worried about dying. (PAUSE) I'm just going to simply slide down and go to sleep.

I don't mind being 94, not if — (LAUGHS) if you could give me — I say to my doctor, if you've got a pair of eyes lying around the place that you could give me, I'd be as happy as Larry! He thinks I'm a scream. As for being 20 again — with the knowledge I've got now, yes. I would — oh, I don't know that I'd alter my life very much. But no, I wouldn't want to live to 100. All my friends say, oh, get a letter from the Queen! I say, I'm not going to let the Queen know anything at all about it. She's not interested in me, it's only a matter of — duty on her part. This thing's thrust in front of her and she signs it. It doesn't hold anything at all for me.

The best advice I can give people is, do what you can for other people — when you can, as long as you can.

At 94 Mrs Tavey was no stranger to bereavement, disability, and frustration. She felt moved to protest, sometimes, against a devoted daughter's ageist determination to do too much for her. Life had lost some of its savour, and old age had not brought her to any mythical haven of serenity and certitude about the "universal questions". But to describe her — or the multitudes of others like her — as rigid, helpless, and senile, or any of the other attributes commonly considered "typical" of extreme old age, is to reveal at once the blatant falsity of ageist stereotypes concerning them.

Mrs Tavey's old age was the cumulative result of her life as she had lived it in its social and historical context, from childhood on. The chapters that follow will take up other people's stories, seeking commonalities, and points of difference too. To a variable extent, most respondents had succeeded in resisting pressures to conform in their old age to self-fulfilling ageist stereotypes, and the clues both to success and failure must lie somewhere in the past.

So I shall begin part 2 with memories of childhood.

Part 2   The Drama of Living

Chapter 4: Childhood

My mother was fairly poor when my father died, she only had this mail contract; she got 40 pounds a year to run it. She used to make a little bread and sell it here and there. We usen't to wear boots and shoes because we couldn't afford it, except to Sunday School. We had to go to bed at sundown, we wasn't allowed to roam the nights at all — when it got dark we had to go to bed. We lived very bare. We used to have bread and dripping, and I had pet goats — we lived on goat, and they're lovely to eat, too. We used to ride them, and they used to draw the cart along for us, we used to cart our own water from the creek in those days. We milked our own cows, and we had a lot of chooks. . . . I had a real happy life as a child.

I remember flying a kite and it was all paddocks — Father making me kites. I always had to have a dog, and they were always getting poisoned or lost. I was very fond of dogs, having no brothers or sisters. Then my father bought a home with lots of trees, and big gardens, and a cow and a horse. It was only about two and a half miles from the Post Office — a big old place which is still extant. And my pride was that I would climb every tree in the garden. My mother was very good. At that time — families were much more strict with girls. There were a lot of things that ladies didn't do — but I remember saying that I'm not a lady and I never will be a lady! That was like keeping your nails clean and wearing gloves, and having your stockings pulled up and not around your ankles and that sort of thing. I used to get three marks every day, one for doing homework, one for wearing gloves to school, and the other for doing exercises in the morning.

In many respects the childhood of Toowong respondents was very different from the kind usual today. The oldest respondents were born in 1882, the youngest in 1899; so the 24 years from 1882 to 1906 cover the period when they were young children (if early childhood is defined, rather arbitrarily, as the time from birth up to and including 7 years of age). They were born in a period of accelerating change, and one of those changes was a reduction in the number of children born to the average family.

Family size

Marital fertility began to decline in the 1880s and by the 1890s had been reduced by 20 per cent (Game and Pringle, 1979:6), although by today's standards it was still high. Among respondents the two- or three-child family of origin was a rarity, and nearly two-thirds had five or more siblings, while seventeen per cent had nine or more. The rapidity of the change is shown by the fact that the eight-year average difference between the "older" respondents (85 +) and the "younger" respondents was enough to reflect it: older respondents were more likely to have come from a large family. The reduction was also markedly linked with socio-economic status. Nearly three-quarters of the lower stratum, compared with less than half of the upper, had five or more siblings, with the middle stratum about halfway between the two.

Mr Todd, aged 86 at the time of interview, had come from a family of "seven or eight brothers and a couple of sisters". He was born out west, where his father had a team of horses and did all sorts of labouring jobs.

> Sometimes we wouldn't see Dad for three months. We didn't have much food and stuff like that. We were pretty poor when we was kids, just scraping to get along. Mother was having a hard time with the money he sent in. She used to grow some vegetables to — keep us going, and we used to shoot kangaroos, emus. . . . I've eaten possum, quite good eating too, like a rabbit. We'd eat anything.

Mrs Dolan had known similar poverty on the tiny Irish farm where she was born; there were ten in her family, but five died in early childhood. Mrs Neall, also country-bred, was from a family of 12.

> You had to live off the land. It was hard at times, in the drought. My mother couldn't read or write, but she was a great woman, you know, in her day. She used to go out washing for people, two shillings a time, but mostly she worked on the farm all day, no housework, it didn't bring anything in! All the time with the fowls and the chickens and feeding the pigs and all that. We weren't allowed to iron, that was wasting time! (LAUGHS) And us kids — there was a — an outhouse, you know what I mean, but us kids, we weren't allowed to use it, we had to go down the paddock to — you know! (LAUGHS) But it didn't do us any harm.

And apparently it hadn't. All 12 survived to a good old age. At 85 Mrs Neall was petite and energetic; she had a much-lined, sharp little face and twinkling eyes. She had gone out to service at an early age and done "all sorts of jobs", and she always regretted not having been able to complete her schooling. Eventually, however, she married a builder and became relatively prosperous. She had three children, and in her old age her seven grandchildren and four great-grandchildren had enlarged a family that was the centre of her life. Apart from being slightly deaf, her health was excellent.

Mrs Parsons, aged 84, came from a very different background. She described her father (a civil engineer) as a Shakespearean scholar:

> We were brought up on Shakespeare — and *The Rise and Fall of the Roman Empire* — and Dostovesky's *Crime and Punishment*, I read that at the age of ten! All that part was good, but father was so very severe — the old type of Englishman — really he quite lost the affection of his children. My brother used to call him "Old Tribulation'!

He certainly seems to have had some eccentric ideas on the bringing-up of children. At breakfast they were only allowed to speak in French. "If we wanted to go to the pottie," she said with a laugh, "we had to say, 'petite affaire', or put up our thumb, 'grande affaire'!"

Mrs Parsons spoke of being "moderately comfortable", but the household included a cook, a housekeeper, a nurse girl, and a "jobbing man", and few respondents could look back on a childhood so well-provided-for materially. Poverty was much more usual, though seldom as severe as that experienced by Mr Todd, Mrs Dolan, and Mrs Neall.

Middle-status respondents were more inclined to speak of the financial situation, as Mr Ensworthy did, as being "Never really short of anything, but — ". According to the interviewer, at the age of 80 Mr Ensworthy "smelled of soap", but was casually dressed, with bare feet. His face was much-scarred with what he called "doctors' fancywork", marking the removal of skin cancers incurred during his outdoor life as a survey officer for the State Electricity Authority. He was born in Wales, where his father was a schoolmaster; he was the eldest of three children and came to Ipswich in Queensland at an early age, but had been living in Toowong with his wife since 1929. Their one child was married and they had three grandchildren. Nowadays, their only income was the old age pension, and though he "couldn't splash it around", he considered it was enough:

> If you're careful, that is. I've painted the whole of this house inside and out — lined that front room there, put in those windows. We've got a new colour TV set, and we've carpeted the whole of that passage just recently, and the house re-wired, new vacuum cleaner, new wall heater, new refrigerator. And we pay cash for everything.

Miss Hannan was also from a middle-status background. Her father was a postmaster and she described their financial situation as "just ordinary"; there were five in her family. In adult life she worked as a clerk in the Taxation Department, until her retirement at the age of 60. She had never married because "the fellow I was keen on was killed in the Great War, and I couldn't be bothered with anyone else after that". She had had poor eyesight all her life, and at the age of 83 was in a nursing home — "a diminutive person", the interviewer said, "sitting beside her bed minding everybody's business". She was said to have an acid tongue and was not popular with the nursing staff.

Analysis of interviews revealed that differences in socio-economic status were linked not only with family size, but also with different styles of upbringing. These reflected the age-stratification system of the time.

Stratification by age

By age-stratification I mean a system of inequalities of rights and duties, privileges and deprivations, power and powerlessness, defined by the formal and informal rules of Australian society according to the particular *age*-stratum to which the individual happens to belong. In the childhood of respondents, more so than in our society today, rights and privileges increased with age. Aries contends that in the nineteenth century family life became child-centred for the first time (1973:31), but this was certainly not evident in the Toowong interviews. Children had no rights other than to be fed and clothed, and for these they were expected to be duly grateful. "Teasing" of children by older siblings and other adults (especially uncles) appeared to be an accepted pastime; it was apparently regarded as not only legitimate but amusing to deceive, frighten, frustrate, bewilder, and bully the young.

There were two conflicting myths concerning childhood current at the time. The first typified children as angels come to earth, whose natural goodness must not be sullied by premature contact with the evils of the world. Sir Joshua Reynolds' extremely popular painting, "The Innocence of Childhood", epitomized this myth. At the same time children were depicted as vessels of original sin. Religious dogma insisted that the "main duty of parents and educators was to eradicate . . . [innate] depravity" (Caldwell and Richmond, 1967:3). "Spare the rod and spoil the child" summed up the prevailing ideology of child-rearing.

Mrs Parsons, the daughter of "Old Tribulation", was not alone in stressing the severity of her upbringing, though it was particularly evident in the upper stratum to which she belonged. In the sample as a whole, two-thirds said that their upbringing had been "strict but fair", or "too strict". By "strict but fair" they usually meant that prompt obedience was exacted, and disobedience punished, often corporally; "too strict" usually referred to unduly heavy punishment inflicted for arbitrary reasons.

Middle-status Mr Ensworthy reported an upbringing that was "normally strict — what you'd expect from a schoolmaster, no mucking about!" Similarly, Mrs Leigh spoke of being "fairly strictly controlled, compared to what they are now", while Miss Hannan recalled her father as "a very fair man". In a lower social stratum, Mrs Neall's strong-minded illiterate mother used to make sure they "jumped to it — not like today — she only spoke once!" Mr Todd confessed to "copping it a bit", as did Mrs Dolan in Ireland, though more from a "brutal" schoolteacher than from either of her parents.

Not surprisingly, it was lower-status families like Mrs Dolan's that exacted most of their children in the way of work:

> You milked the cows, and you put the milk in a big tub for the cream to set, and then you had to churn it, and they used to take the butter into town and sell it there once a fortnight. And we had to cut the turf — you've got a certain kind of spade that you cut the turf in pieces. It's very soft, you could put a finger through it, but believe me, it's a back-aching job! And you have to spread it out to dry. All through the summer you had to take a piece of turf to school, towards the winter you know. And all sorts of other jobs — I had to harness up the horse when I was so little I had to get a chair to stand on. . . .

In Mrs Neall's Australian childhood, the round of chores was no less constant:

> When the corn crops are in, you're husking there and shelling, and you crack corn for the chickens. And we had to get the fruit off the trees in the orchard, and dry them in the sun — you couldn't buy fruit or vegetables, if you couldn't grow them you did without. Even the dogs had to work and find their own food — they got a drink of milk after we'd done the separating, that's all. . . .

Mr Todd lived in a tent most of his childhood. His schooling was intermittent and finished at the age of ten, and long before then he and his brothers were trapping and shooting kangaroos and koalas for their skins and bringing the carcasses home for food. At 86 Mr Todd was in excellent health, although he was living in a hostel for old men. In keeping with his early life, he was a firm believer in outdoor activity and exercise: "I don't want to be no bloody cabbage! If you lay about all day, well, naturally you must deteriorate! No good to me."

Whether or not they were expected to be of economic help to their parents, children in all social strata were regarded as subservient to adults, including older siblings. Even those who had few set chores to do were expected to do their elder's bidding at a moment's notice, and at other times to keep out of their way. Many respondents mentioned, as Mrs Leigh did, that children were "to be seen and not heard".

In addition to stratification by age, there were other authority patterns more prominent at the turn of the century than they are today. Especially significant for respondents — their lifelong career and eventual old age — were the power differentials between the sexes.

Stratification by sex

The whole question of the internalization of gender roles has sponsored an enormous literature. The women's movement has concentrated so heavily on female subjugation that it tends to neglect some of the essential dialectics of sex-role socialization, especially in earliest infancy.

Femaleness and power, to reward and to deprive, must be one of the primary associations made in infancy, and for nineteenth-century infants would be made even more significant by the nearly universal practice of breast-feeding. In accordance with the custom of the times, it can be assumed that respondents were born at home, not in hospital, and the figures, voices, personalities impinging on their consciousness must have been overwhelmingly female. A doctor (male, of course) was probably present for the confinement, but was unlikely to be called in thereafter for anything but a life-threatening illness. A bearded parental face might occasionally appear above the infant's cot; but the most significant of significant others would initially have been female rather than male.

But this early female ascendancy was soon replaced by the prevailing belief that men were "naturally" the dominant sex. To identify the main source of authority in their childhood, respondents were asked whom they remembered as being "head of the house". Half the sample saw their father as household head, and for those who, like Mrs Parsons, remembered him as "too strict", he was definitely what Baumrind (1973) calls an authoritarian rather than an authoritative figure. Middle-status Mr Ensworthy never doubted that his father was head, and Miss Hannan was equally sure about hers, but Mrs Leigh had "never even thought about it — my parents seemed to work together always". This more egalitarian pattern was reported by about a quarter of the sample, most typically by the middle stratum, while upper-status fathers were the most patriarchal of all.

Mrs Neall's hardworking mother "definitely ruled the roost", and represents about 23 per cent of the sample. Some of these were forced to take up the reins because of the father's early death, an event that Mrs Dolan remembered very clearly:

> You know how they lay out people on the table, with candles each side, that's in my mind now. And my big brother said to me, "Kiss him". Well, I kissed Father and it was like kissing a stone, and I yelled!

Recent anthropological studies of the roles of women cross-culturally have revealed a variety of ways in which women achieve, "even in situations of overt sex role asymmetry . . . a good deal more power than conventional theorists have assumed" (Rosaldo and Lamphere, 1974:9). Certainly in the Toowong transcripts overt acknowledgment of women's subordination to men was notably lacking. However, differences in what was considered suitable behaviour for the two sexes were clearly evident, and proved a pervasive element in the way respondents were brought up. As Bardwick and Douvan point out, "dependent behaviour, normal to all children, is permitted for girls and prohibited for boys" (1971:182).

But emerging more clearly from the interviews is the *rejection*

To be a boy was to be granted a freedom to take risks . . .

of dependence by both sexes, which was encouraged for boys and firmly discouraged for girls. To be a boy was to be granted a freedom to take risks which the girls often envied and sometimes emulated, if they could evade the protective supervision they found so irksome. Boys could go swimming in deep waterholes; girls were not allowed to go swimming at all. Boys could ride spirited horses; girls, usually, only an elderly hack. Boys were expected to be outside most of the time; middle- and upper-status girls in particular were supposed to take care of their complexions by venturing outside only when wearing big hats. Boys could "give cheek" and (occasionally) get away with it; "boys will be boys" excused a range of behaviour considered altogether too "forward" for girls.

These role expectations had profound consequences for the whole life-course of respondents, including their eventual old age. From infancy onwards boys were encouraged in a problem-solving confrontation with events. Girls, against their own better judgment, were encouraged to believe that they were delicate little creatures best advised to shrink from challenge and to accept the "protective" authority of others. On the other hand, though they were systematically taught to avoid rather than to confront events, girls did learn other skills denied to most of their male contemporaries. They were thoroughly versed in the domestic arts and, at the same time, in the importance of maintaining networks of relationships which encompassed the men but expected little of them in the way of overt acknowledgment. Event-confrontation by males, event-avoidance by females, network-maintenance by females, network-neglect by males — these were patterns established in childhood that continued throughout their lives and had observable effects on their old age.

Network-maintenance

Mr Todd was a practical man with a range of manual skills, but he was not very skilled in maintaining family relationships. There were hints in his interview that there had been "plenty of women" at various times in his life, and this may have been why he had been parted from his wife for some years before her death and had come to live in a hostel. He had lost touch with most of their six children. Nor were cooking and cleaning in his repertoire; he would have been all right in a tent in the bush, but in the city he needed someone to "do" for him. The hostel gave him food and shelter and a degree of male companionship when he wanted it. He played billiards, did a lot of walking, and joined in any outing that was offering; he was too self-sufficient to be lonely.

Miss Hannan, in her nursing home, was probably there for much the same reason as Mr Todd was in his hostel — some inadequacy in the "feminine" skills of network-maintenance. Her eyesight, though poor, was probably better than that of 94-year-old Mrs Tavey, whose ties with her daughter were so close. Never-married respondents had usually managed to maintain close links with a sister or brother or a friend, or even more usually, with someone of a younger generation, such as a niece. But Miss Hannan was a loner. "I'm sick of friends", she said. "I'm a straight-out free person."

Mrs Dolan had never had children of her own, but she maintained a warm relationship with her step-daughter, whom she lived with "half and half" (she liked moving round, travelling interstate and visiting distant friends). Mr Ensworthy still had his wife to maintain their network of relationships for him. Mrs Parsons, Mrs Leigh, and Mrs Neall all lived alone. Only Mrs Neall, however, who in objective terms was closest to her family, admitted to ever feeling bored or lonely, and this was more in relation to a vivid past than in complaint about the present.

> It's good, but it's — empty, see. Everyone's gone. That's the only thing. You miss them, like, in the evenings, when — they come in for their tea, and kids coming home from school throwing everything everywhere! [She laughed, rather wistfully.]

Event-confrontation

In spite of her family-centredness, Mrs Neall was in no way a passive person. The interviewer described her as erect and spritely, with a good sense of fun — but a little shy. An initial shyness on the part of lower-status women was frequently mentioned by interviewers; they lacked the abounding self-assurance of a Mrs Parsons, or the quieter confidence of a Mrs Leigh. Higher status brings with it the more "masculine" conviction, even among women, that events can be confronted and successfully moulded to the individual will. Lower status brings experiences that persistently underline the lesson that life-chances are determined by distant others and that authority is fundamentally oppressive. Mrs Neall was a capable and courageous person, as she proved in her account of her life, but though she welcomed the female interviewer without qualms, she admitted to being timid about male callers: "The man who came for the gas this morning, I didn't know at first what he — he wore a beard. I get scared when I see beards. I don't mind living alone, but —."

No male respondent would have dreamed of admitting that he was afraid of strangers, though probably almost as vulnerable to any threat of robbery or violence. Among women, especially lower-status women, it was not uncommon.

Miss Hannan, on the other hand, gave the impression of being afraid of nobody. She was unpopular at the nursing home because she refused to conform to the stereotype of the "good patient", who did exactly as she was told and pretended to be happy about it. It seems likely that all her life she had preferred masculine event-confrontation to feminine network-maintenance, and now she was paying the price for non-conformity by being labelled with the ageist/sexist stereotype of "cranky old maid". Mrs Parsons and Mrs Leigh had combined network-maintenance and a degree of event-confrontation in a socially acceptable mix; Mr Ensworthy was still confronting the small events of his life in a typically masculine manner; perhaps less typically, so was Mr Todd.

Mrs Dolan, coming from a lower-status background, had events thrust upon her and on the whole had accepted the challenge; but in one respect she revealed a fear of authority that was not surprising in view of the way she had been brought up. In her case the authority she feared was the church. A Catholic, she had married a Protestant:

> . . . and there was such a to-do, I was so hurt. I don't suppose I should say — Is that [tape-recorder] still on? Oh dear! This won't get back to them, will it? Because I — Well, I'll tell you this, I never forgave them really, because he was a good man and — I think there should be just one religion. I think if they'd just all get together and — (PAUSE) Who *will* be getting hold of all this?

All these people varied in looks as much as they did in personality. Mrs Dolan was squarely built, with blue Irish eyes and a fair, soft skin crinkled all over like tissue-paper. Mrs Parsons was also rather stout, but her firmly moulded face, framed by thick wavy white hair, had scarcely a wrinkle; only the fact that arthritis dictated the use of a walking stick betrayed that she was not twenty years younger than she looked. Mr Todd was spare, tanned, and a little stooped. Mrs Leigh was rather tall and angular, and she obviously took considerable care with her clothes and general appearance.

None of them was without at least some of the problems commonly associated with old age. All of them, with the possible exception of Miss Hannan, were frequently assured that they were "marvellous" for their age, and tended to believe themselves that they must be exceptional.

But they were not. They were typical for their age. Like most, they simply failed to conform to ageist stereotypes.

Chapter 5: Education

Toowong, in the nineties . . .

We had to walk nearly three miles to get there. Mr Smith was there as headmaster — he was elderly, but Charlie Campbell, he was very nice, he was a pupil teacher — just a tomboy like any other. And there was Miss Reeves, and Miss Abercrombie. . . . We had mixed classes. You had drill before you went into school in the morning. The bell would ring and then you'd all have to get in class and then they had drill and you'd march into school. The boys had separate drill to us, they'd do that sort of thing, exercises, while we'd be doing sewing classes. The school didn't supply many games, we just had our own. We did skipping and hopscotch, and we had long grass — we used to play in that long grass, tie knots in it, let one another fall over, tripping people up! We used to have Arbor Day, we had the whole day off school to make gardens. When Queen Victoria died the Council put on a big shivoo down at River Road, we had dinner and tea there, a real picnic. My Dad was really a runaway sailor and they were forgiven when the Queen died.

In the country, 1903–1912

We rode our horses to and from school and kept them in a horse paddock during the day. The desks were long benches, they could accommodate up to six, and we sat on just plain stools. We had to sit up straight, and put your arm round your work so that nobody

saw what you were doing. We used slates mostly — very much
the three Rs. . . . The girls and boys played cricket together, and
rounders, and we had one ball game we called Brandy, someone
with a rubber ball would stand at one end, and the rest of us would
run from one end to the other and he'd try to hit us with the ball
and if you were hit with the ball you were out, and — Yes, girls
too, we all played them together. We used to play singing games
— What's one? Roger is dead and laid in his grave — You all got
round in a ring and sang that.

George Naylor and Elsie Harwood have been Australian
pioneers in the psychology of ageing, and their work on the
learning capacities of older people has won international
acclaim. Though they have not used the term "ageism", they
have been active in publicizing their conclusions that "the
acceptance by the elderly of suggestions relating to their incompetence may have contributed as much to observed "aging"
as any actual, measurable decrease in capacity for mental function" (Naylor, 1974:49) — a clear indictment of one important
factor in ageism. Similarly, Dr Harwood points out that "the
findings of longitudinal studies have shown that a great many
people do not significantly deteriorate until the 9th or 10th
decades" (1977:4). Since Professor Naylor's death Dr Harwood
has continued with the work they had undertaken together,
and in 1980 she presented a method of scoring intelligence in
old people in terms of an "Age Resistance Quotient" in which
"Values above 100 imply a resistance to age which is propor-
tionately above average, while those below 100 signify the
reverse" (Harwood and Naylor, 1980:6).

But age itself — the passing of years — cannot be resisted
(excepted by suicide). It is resistance to *deterioration*, not
resistance to *age*, that Harwood and Naylor are measuring. No
doubt some deterioration is genetically programmed, but
nobody as yet knows how much, and it is illogical to assume
the case proven when (as Harwood and Naylor themselves
point out) even the best established "facts" of biological ageing
are so seldom universally true. Clearly ageism, in the sense of
self-fulfilling ageist stereotypes, contributes to deterioration
rather than to continued development. Ageist attitudes

encourage "routines that can be performed almost habitually, with a minimum of problem-solving and decision making", and discourage "continued mental exercise (and, indeed, exertion) [which] is the key to mental longevity" (Harwood and Naylor, 1974:51).

In the world in which Toowong respondents grew up, education was thought of as confined to the early years of life and was regarded as synonymous with "schooling". With one possible exception, all of them were literate and numerate, and most were the children of literate parents who, like the respondents themselves, grew up in a society where the mid-nineteenth-century trend towards universal schooling had finally been registered on the statute books. This occurred in England in 1876, and a year earlier in Queensland, which was the second of the Australian states to legislate for free and compulsory education (Ruzicka and Caldwell, 1977:21).

The degree to which children (or their parents, on their behalf) were able to avail themselves of free education at the end of the nineteenth century depended very largely on where they lived. A few respondents came from Central European nations, and from Ireland, where fees were still exacted, but the great majority were educated in Australia; in Queensland, fees for "non-vested" schools were eliminated in 1870. Queensland's Education Act of 1875 provided that schooling should be compulsory for all children "not less than six nor more than 12 years of age for at least 60 days each half year" (Wyeth, 1953:127), but the compulsion clauses were not actually put into effect until a quarter of a century later. Rankin points out that in Victoria in the 1870s only half the enrolled children attended school on any given day, and although the proportion gradually increased, it did not reach 60 per cent until 1901 (Rankin, 1939:123, 129). This was reflected in the recollections of respondents, some of whom reported going to school only when there was not much work to do at home. Altogether, nearly a quarter left early because of family circumstances, and slightly more than half left at 14 or 15, which usually (but not always) coincided with the completion of primary school. A further 24 per cent were 16 or older before leaving school, but this did not invariably indicate higher education. Several repeated the highest primary school class, in some instances because it was the only educational opportunity open to them and they were reluctant to leave. The latter were sometimes retained as pupil teachers, whose recruitment was the mainstay of the Queensland teaching profession at the time.

In 1874 competitive "Scholarship" examinations were introduced, intended to equalize opportunities for the gifted poor so that they could join the children of more fortunate strata in sharing the benefits of a grammar school education. Originally confined to tests of arithmetic, grammar and geography, the Scholarship dominated the educational scene for many years. Children who went to school in other Australian states, and certainly those educated in Britain, were exposed to a wider range of subjects and of teaching methods, but in general the differences in educational opportunities were not marked.

Common to all educational experiences was an emphasis on a biological model of human behaviour, coupled with blatant ethnocentrism. The belief was widely held that societies evolved according to Spencer's maxim of the survival of the fittest. Victorian England, at the head of a great Empire, was therefore demonstrably the fittest to lead the white races in their subjugation of lesser breeds. Within societies, the same principle was believed to apply: the fittest rose to the top, the less fit achieved appropriately subordinate positions, and the least fit eliminated themselves.

Fitness to survive in this unending struggle had moral connotations: people could *choose* fitness, and those who did not do so lacked moral responsibility. Economic fitness (the most important kind) was proven by choosing thrift and hard work; physiological fitness was proven by choosing cleanliness and avoidance of excesses; mental fitness was proven by close attention to lessons; religious fitness was proven by knowledge of the Bible. Yet underlying this strand of voluntarism was a deeper fatalistic base: choice in these matters was predetermined biologically. People were much more likely to choose wisely if they had been born white and British, and not within the lower socio-economic stratum (the members of which were innately, and by definition, feckless).

The meaning of age and ageing was also interpreted in social-

Darwinistic terms. Old people deserved to survive while they could provide for themselves economically as a result of a lifetime of thrift and hard work; while they avoided unseemly excesses and kept themselves neat and clean; while they remembered the lessons of their youth, and accepted the Biblical warning that if "by reason of strength" they lived beyond three score years and ten, they must expect nothing but "labour and sorrow". The chronological meaning of age was thus firmly linked to a biological meaning of decay. Further, only the young could learn: the biological model decreed a sharp decline in intellectual ability more or less coincident with the attainment of adulthood.

Evidence for the systematic inculcation of the biological model on which these attitudes were based is found in the Royal Readers, which were produced in Scotland and widely used throughout Australia. At first early Scholarship examinations were notably lacking in questions that made any reference to Queensland, or indeed, Australia (Goodman, 1968:71), but by the turn of the century local material included the article "The Aborigines of Australia". In this it was declared that their "appearance, mentality, and social institutions" warranted rating them as "one of the lowest races of the great human family" (1901:98). Ethnocentrism as blatant as this is underscored by innumerable other examples, some in what would seem to be quite unpolemical areas of knowledge. Even the description of the geography of "the Temperate regions" contains references to Europe, and in particular Britain, as "the cradle of those free political institutions which have developed the self-control and independence of man as a member of society" (Royal Reader, 1901:126). To be British was to be civilized, and to be civilized was to be self-controlled and independent.

Such overt and deliberate propaganda, building on foundations laid in early childhood, could hardly fail to have had a profound impact on the development of lifelong attitudes. It is to the credit of respondents that less formal learning experiences later led most of them to revise many of these notions. After being taught to despise Aborigines, in old age only 15 per cent appeared to do so, and 25 per cent were coded as being favourably disposed towards them; the rest were either neutral or ambivalent. Similarly, unquestioning patriotism, though still upheld if a direct question was asked, revealed an undercurrent of uncertainty. Most were prepared to concede that England had made many mistakes, to question the value of war, and to consider that Australia should act as an independent nation. However, the work ethic, which was also the subject of constant exhortation in their schoolbooks, remained very firmly entrenched, as did the conviction that biology was the major determinant of human destiny.

Formal education

For the oldest respondents, formal schooling began in the late 1880s or early 1890s and ended in the first few years of the new century; for the youngest, it began about 1904 and had ended by the time war broke out. Education was changing sufficiently for the experience to vary between older and younger cohorts.

Ninety-two-year-old Mrs Emerson gave a vivid picture of school life in the early 1890s in Toowong itself. She still remembered the names of most of the teachers. She had to walk three miles to get there, and because of shortage of seating only half the school could sit down at a time. Pupils stood for half an hour, reading aloud and reciting poetry, then sat down for the next half-hour on long backless forms at long desks for writing and "doing sums" on slates. In the alternating half-hours when they were required to stand, they had to toe a chalk mark, while a teacher came round to cane the legs of those whose feet had inadvertently edged forward. For more serious misdemeanors boys were caned on the hand, a penalty girls were seldom called upon to suffer. They were not immune, however, to being stood in a corner with a "fool's cap" on the head.

Mrs Emerson left school at 12 because "Mum was sick", and for the next 2 years she was busy looking after the family. At 14 she went to work packing biscuits into tins at 3 farthings a tin, and handed the money she earned to her mother at the end of the week. Later she was cook and housemaid in a country hotel, and later still, helped in private houses when women had their babies. She married a man who worked at the Toowong sawmill, who died of kidney trouble when the elder of her two children was ten. They had just moved into the house in Toowong where Mrs Emerson lives to this day.

Left a widow in the 1920s with two young children to provide for and no government aid of any kind, Mrs Emerson went out to do washing and ironing by day and at night supplemented her meagre income by sewing. Overtired, and alone except for the two children in bed, Mrs Emerson became a prey to unaccustomed fears, including a fear of the dark. They were dispelled by what she remembers as a religious vision:

> I used to always watch for the morning star, then I'd know it would soon be daylight, that was a relief. And one time, there in the sky, shining, I saw — not just one star. I saw the Cross. And I felt as though — I felt I hadn't been grateful enough for all that the Lord had done for me; I hadn't even believed properly, and it came to me just to give it over to Him. I'll never forget that morning. I got down on my knees and I did ask the Lord to help me through, and He did. Ever since then I've put my trust fully in the Lord. I've had that faith ever since. It's a marvellous thing, a marvellous feeling.

At time of writing Mrs Emerson, now 97, is still living, alone, in the house she keeps as immaculate as ever. She tends a remarkable array of pot-plants and a fair-sized garden; her grandsons mow the lawn for her and her daughter, who lives in a distant suburb, insists on doing the washing. With her wavy white hair, shy, sweet smile, and bright dark eyes, she is still a good-looking woman, and a highly intelligent one. Network-maintenance comes as naturally to her as breathing. It is delightful to see her great-grandchildren and their little friends come running to "Ma-ma" to be enfolded in her warm embrace. Never one to seek confrontation, she has dealt with quiet courage with events as they have happened, retaining values she believes have stood the test of time, adapting to new ideas as she sees fit. Nowadays she wears a hearing-aid and a Vitalcall pendant, and intends to stay in her own home until she dies.

Mr Pollitt was another of the older cohorts, 89 at the time of interview. He was born and reared in England, the son of a London machinist in a torpedo factory. He went to what he called a higher elementary school, and remembered learning French from a Frenchman who noted down mistakes for which they were caned after he was gone. Another of the older ones, Mr Trevor, was brought up in the Australian bush; he and his five brothers and one sister were too busy helping with the work to have much time for schooling. He was shepherding turkeys out in the bush from the time he was four years old; altogether he went to school for about 13 months and most of the time, he said with a laugh, "I wasn't there!" His parents thought he would have plenty of time to get educated when he was older, but apart from looking over his brother's shoulder when he was doing his homework, the opportunity did not arrive until a three-months' illness put him in bed, and with the aid of an old Bible and a dictionary, "taught myself everything I know".

The children of upper-status fathers were the only ones among whom a majority proceeded beyond primary school, and 17 per cent of these went on to tertiary level. Sex differentials were weaker than expected: 32 per cent of the females, compared with 40 per cent of the males, advanced beyond primary school.

Schooling was not confined to conventional institutions. Miss Alder was a volatile old lady who, at the time of interview, was having driving lessons and hoped to get her licence before she turned 83. In her childhood she was taken away from the small private school she attended, because her father (whom she described as a brilliant engineer, mathematician and inventor) was not satisfied with what she was learning. Thereafter she sat on his knee every night with a slate and a piece of chalk and received his personal instruction:

My father was over-zealous to bring me up correctly, and he was extremely strict. He wanted me to be ladylike, feminine, but at the same time practical — I had to know how to sew and cook, but in addition, I had to know how to use tools. On Saturdays, instead of going out playing I would be down turning the lathe and making little doorknobs out of ivoryboards. I was never educated for anything in a business career because he said that young ladies didn't go into business — but I managed a business in Sydney for five years, an art studio. You don't have to go to school to have general knowledge.

Mrs Henry might well have made the same comment. Brought up in the country, when she was seven years old her mother had a haemorrhage of the lung, and the care of the house and four younger brothers became the seven-year-old's responsibility. There had never been time for formal schooling, but in a career that included volunteer nursing and keeping the books for her husband's butchery, she had acquired an enviable fund of knowledge. A tall, buxom, quiet woman, she was very different in appearance, personality, and background from dimunitive Mrs Clements, who made up for her lack of inches by her forcefulness and sense of drama.

At the time of interview Mrs Clements was living in a rather shabby flat in an old converted house, but the lounge room was full of beautiful antique furniture. She was wearing old torn slacks and a blouse with sleeves rolled up; her feet were bare, and her long grey hair untidily pinned up. She said she was "born with a silver spoon", and had first been to school in England, accompanying her importer-exporter father on his travels. But when she was 10 he died: ". . . and I had to go to this scrappy Sydney public school and mix with kids who weren't my class. And I had a bitch of a mother!"

Eighty-year-old Miss Eadie's experience was more usual. When she was young she went to a country school, riding a horse to get there and taking a bread-and-dripping lunch, which she used to augment when she could with a piece of cake bought by doing other children's sums. In her old age she was quiet and composed; the interviewer mentioned her neatly-groomed hair and well-tailored slacks with matching blouse. But in her childhood she seems to have been somewhat unruly. She and one or two other girls made up the numbers for play-ing cricket, and on one occasion this led to an argument in which she was challenged to fisticuffs by another girl. They duly battled it out after school before a considerable audience

Slightly more than half the respondents insisted that they were very happy at school.

until they were interrupted by a warning that the police were coming — "So we all got on our horses and went for our lives!"

Slightly more than half the respondents who gave an opinion at all insisted that they were very happy at school, but among the rest there were some Dickensian incidents reported — one respondent had seen an enraged teacher break a boy's arm. But on the whole respondents spoke respectfully and sometimes even affectionately of the teachers they had known, who plainly provided models reinforcing the doctrines set out in the text-books. Rationality, forethought, the avoidance of excesses, and adoption of hygienic modes of living were promulgated as marks of civilization and progress, the heirs to which were uniquely white and Anglo-Saxon. Authority, at school and at home, was hierarchically ordered in line with genetic endowment, which conferred upon males superior abilities and therefore an inborn right to lead. Learning consisted of absorbing a finite number of facts, and although adulthood marked the end of all possibilities of development, adults had absorbed more facts than children and were therefore entitled to unquestioned power over the young.

Much of all this had to be unlearned, and in the course of their lives the Toowong respondents proved capable of doing so with admirable selectivity.

Further education

Though the majority finished with formal education as soon as they left school, a sizable minority did what they could to acquire extra skills and knowledge. Miss Eadie won a scholarship to a secondary school in Brisbane, but her parents could not afford to let her continue it for more than one year. After that she became a pupil teacher at her old school and eventually, more or less by accident, made teaching her career:

> In those days you took what you could get — I didn't like it much. I think today I would enjoy it because it's not so stereotyped; there's more communication between the children and the teacher — or there should be. But in those days you had to have your pupils sitting up with their arms folded, not speaking, and getting 100 per cent for tables and mental and spelling. . . . I hear people going on today about children not being able to spell, but I think it's better today. In those days it had to be — copperplate, and — I've seen some schools where the children are very free and also very good!

Obviously Miss Eadie was one of those who had done some thoughtful unlearning.

Mr Pollitt, one of the older respondents, had gone on branching out into new areas of knowledge most of his life. After leaving primary school he became a "trade lad" in the arsenal where his father worked. In spite of working a 52-hour week without holidays, he went to the Polytechnic 3 nights a week and passed an examination that won him an apprenticeship available to only one "trade lad" in a thousand. He was married before he was 20, and in the early years of the new century he and his wife came out to Australia as assisted migrants.

He earned his living variously as a fitter and turner, pattern maker, oxywelder, coppersmith, and draughtsman, then obtained a diploma in engineering at the university in his spare time, and eventually became a teacher, and head of his department, in a technical college. At nearly 90 he was living alone because his wife had arthritis very badly and was in a nursing home; and in spite of the many skills he had mastered, domestic ones were not among them. His clothes were stained and torn; unwashed dishes cluttered the sink, and he confessed that his bed was unmade. Three times a week he drove to see his wife in a bayside nursing home, but in spite of his obvious devotion to her he had not been very successful in taking up duties in what he regarded as a woman's domain.

Miss Alder, whose father had insisted that she learn the use of a lathe and other tools, had made good use of these "masculine" skills throughout her life, and had shown an ability to acquire others as occasion called for it. When the Depression caused the closing of the studio she was in charge of in Sydney, she set up a guest house and tackled household repairs among her other duties until she collapsed from overwork. For a time she was on the dole, but later she inherited a little money and dabbled in aviation — without getting as far as obtaining her pilot's licence. After the war she came back to Brisbane, bought a small house, and set about improving it, doing everything herself — "even to the excavations!" — and eventually selling it for many times what she had paid for it.

Now in her eighties, she was living with an older sister and an assortment of cats and dogs in a house they jointly owned and kept in impeccable order. Her feet, she said, had "died — there's no feeling in them", but this did not appear to be a hindrance to her in her driving lessons. She was planning to buy a little car of her own and was excited at the thought of all the places she would then be able to explore.

Just as eagerly as Miss Alder, Mrs Clements plunged back into an equally varied past. Her early attempts to acquire an education had been hampered, she said, by her "bitch of a mother's remarriage and production of a new baby every year", leaving the eldest daughter to wash the nappies. She had to hide her school-books under the ironing board so she could study them as she worked. She won a scholarship to a commercial college and topped the year for her typing speed, but made very little use of these skills. Instead, she threw herself with typical fervour into ballet dancing and, later, production. From the interview it was not altogether clear whether she had been married twice or three times, but she had two sons who had done well in the world and several adult grandchildren, all living in Brisbane.

Opportunities for further training through formal education was mostly the preserve of the upper stratum — the barriers to tertiary education were formidable. However, not all of those who received little formal education were handicapped by this in later life. Mr Trevor, who had taught himself to read when he was sick in bed, was, in his eighties, a prosperous property owner, and pointed with pride to the considerable library he had collected over the years. But for many of the respondents — especially the women — the only way to supplement their education was a taste for reading.

On the whole parents did not encourage reading for either sex. Two middle-status women said specifically that they were supposed to fill their spare moments by darning stockings or doing other handiwork and were not allowed to read — it was regarded as a waste of time. One avid reader confessed that she thought that it had its dangers — "It makes you doubt the Bible". Others who loved reading, like Mrs Emerson, could find little time for it in middle life because of the exigencies of earning a living, and when old age gave them more time for reading they could find no enjoyment in the "filth" of modern novels. But there were some women who turned to books on historical, biographical, or geographical subjects, and some men who studied technical and lay-scientific works; thereby they continued their education into old age.

Education and old age

The biological model of ageing decrees that old age is not a time for learning. Stereotypes of inflexibility ("You can't teach an old dog new tricks"), memory failure, and general intellectual decline are used to justify the notion that educational potential is inversely proportional to chronological age. Such definitions of the situation have a built-in propensity for self-fulfillment: inflexibility is rewarded by the comforts of routine, absent-mindedness is excused by being just what is expected, intellectual decline is encouraged by relaxation of effort and withdrawal from stimuli that can sometimes prove disturbing. But as Harwood and Naylor point out, "Unquestionably, the biggest obstacle to learning in later years is the belief that one is too old to learn" (1974:51).

For Toowong respondents society, with rules of behaviour built into it, was "out there" when they were born, like the air they breathed; and again like the air they breathed, they took it in, internalized it, initially without question. Society, as "breathed in", has defined old age as a period of inevitable decline. Old age is stigmatized, a devalued status, as Irving Rosow (1974) puts it. And the old themselves accept the devaluation and the stigma. There are few things more conducive to poor performance, in any sphere, than a self-image of oneself as a poor performer.

Added to these damaging expectations — the subjective dimension of old age — there is the objective situation of the old as characterized by loss. Mr Trevor had lost his wife only three months previously, and had not yet found much point in the activities he had enjoyed when they were shared. Miss Alder had lost friends more congenial to her temperament than the reticent elder sister with whom she lived. Mrs Emerson had lost her acuity of hearing and a certain amount of her mobility: "My legs tangle sometimes", she said with her shy smile. Mr Pollitt had lost the opportunity to practise his many technical skills. Mrs Henry had lost the sense of purpose she had enjoyed when her children were young. And although most of them had problems that they were dealing with constructively, these problems tended to be of a kind defined by society as inherently insoluble. As one distinguished geriatrician (Whitehead, 1978:198) says:

. . . man is a problem-solving animal and without facility to have problems to solve, goes into a decline. Our society encourages and forces the elderly into becoming non-problem-solving beings.

What we don't use, we lose. To retain our faculties, we must use them, and to use them, we must have a stimulus to use them. A healthy and intelligent 10-year-old deprived of physical exercise, intellectual stimulation, variety of social contacts, and close emotional ties would not remain healthy and intelligent for long. Yet for old people, close emotional ties are commonly — even inevitably — severed by bereavement; social contacts of any kind tend to be reduced, often both in quantity and quality; intellectual stimulation may be entirely absent; opportunities for physical exercise are limited. It is remarkable that in spite of all this, *most* old people manage to deal with their problems and achieve a degree of development — in the sense of improvement, the acquiring of new skills, and successful adaptation.

Most of the deficits accompanying old age are more social than biological. They tend to be built into the social situation of the old — especially the very old — but they are certainly not built into their genes. Therefore, they are amenable to change.

To varying degrees it is apparent that the Toowong respondents were aware, at some level of consciousness, that their difficulties were more socially than biologically deter- mined. They persisted, against all the odds, in learning, adapting, dealing with problems in the light of a long ex- perience without rejecting the possibility of new solutions. Mrs Emerson, for example, was aware that living alone when one's mobility is restricted poses other dangers besides physical ones. Not only did she accept the latest technological aids — at 96 years of age she filled in a form indicating that she was interested in the concept of *developmental* ageing.

Most of these people were accustomed to being told that in their mental alertness and willingness to continue learning they were different, exceptional for their age. But they were not.

In their weaknesses, as in their strengths, they were reasonably typical of the rest of the Toowong respondents, and probably of the rest of that extremely heterogeneous group — the very old.

Chapter 6: Work

In the depression I finished up working at a cannery down here at Milton, it was terrible, the pineapple used to eat the skin off your hands and everything, your feet were all sore and bleeding — the pineapple juice, it was terrible. When you're handling tins with the raw edge, putting pineapple in, eventually it cuts the gloves and the juice seeps through into your skin. Cannery work's terrible. After that I worked for a biscuit factory for nearly twenty years — I loved working for the first people that owned it, but they sold out, and the new owners, they were very strict. I started off printing containers, they used to buy them blank and you had a rubber roll and you put the wording in, the name of the biscuit and the date and everything in red ink, you had to roll each side of that, you mustn't have any smudges on it or anything. . . .

I was apprenticed to a jeweller. . . . You know a jeweller's bench? They're all cut out, you know, and underneath they have a peg where you do your filing, and underneath there were leather pouches made and that caught all the filings, the silver filings and that sort of thing instead of going on the floor. But my eyes played up, making these little fine silver chains, so I went on to a farm up at Nanango, milking cows and riding horses and that — That suited me. I had a good time up there. But then I got a job in a grocery store and people started bringing me brooches and things and I finally started a little shop. I moved to Brisbane in 1924 and I taught myself watchmaking, from a book — and there was a man round at North Quay, a doll repairer — all the kids had celluloid dolls in those days. And he wanted me to be a receiving depot, and I did, and then — Well, instead of disappointing the kids, you know, I started repairing these dolls. They used to come with the legs and arms off and that, and I made different tools, I was pretty handy, you know — I could whip a pair of legs on with new elastic in about two jiffs! And it became the major job. . . .

Mr Best had been in the railways all his life. "Was my work — satisfying?" He looked rather bewildered as he repeated my question. "Well . . . I couldn't tell you that. You'd have to ask some who — I always tried to give satisfaction."

He had risen to be an A-class signalman:

> I was a signalman for quite a number of years, and the best thing about it was — Well, you had several men over you, but you done quite a bit on your own, you just told them what you done and they'd know it was OK. . . .

Such a degree of autonomy at work was rare in Mr Best's situation, and he thoroughly appreciated it when it came his way. The railways, he said, had been his life. Long after his retirement (he was 86 at the time of interview) he still took an intelligent interest in the technicalities of transport systems, old and new, and visited the Railway Institute one evening a month for the chance to talk shop with old workmates. But the concept of work satisfaction was foreign to him, and to other respondents in all strata. Many took pride, as Mr Best did, in doing a fair day's work for a fair day's pay, and if they stayed with one firm or organization over a long period, they developed a sort of loyalty to its interests. But the work itself was seldom questioned for its value either to the individual or to society. They seemed to regard a pay-packet, or the opportunity to earn one, as less of a right than a matter of good fortune. Work, as they saw it, was simply a necessity.

So the chief impression gained from an examination of the transcripts is of the changes that have taken place in the meaning of work itself in an increasingly affluent society. The objective reality of the work situation for most male respondents probably consisted of repetitive, ill-rewarded occupational tasks; they had been inured to hard work, sometimes from early childhood: one spoke of having a bucket strapped round his neck while he milked a cow because he was too young to hold a bucket between his legs. Such experiences were commonplace for more than three-quarters of lower-status respondents, female as well as male.

Respondents first began to try out their own interpretations of the roles described as "earning a living" 60, 70, sometimes 80 years ago, and the type of work first undertaken was closely linked with socio-economic status in old age. More than half who began life as labourers or domestic servants were still coded lower status at the time of interview. They worked in factories of various kinds, in sawmills, on the roads or in the railways, or driving carts delivering anything from coal to papers. Most handed their first pay-packets over to their parents, even after they had left home. Ninety-five-year-old Mr Treacy, for instance, reported that he went to Glasgow and earned money as a sideshow wrestler:

> I could wrestle any man up to 15 stone as easy as I could drink that glass of water. Every time I wrestled I got good money for it, and I used to send it home to my Mum and Dad in Ireland. . . .

Starting work on a farm or in some sort of clerical capacity apparently offered opportunities for occupational mobility, for a considerable majority of those coded 'upper-stratum' in old age come from such a background. In Australia in the early years of the century one worker in three was employed in the primary industries (Cohen and Black, 1976:25), and even in towns and cities, work patterns were linked to seasonal rhythms dictated by the production of wool, wheat, sugar, gold, and meat. Shearing, harvesting, cane-cutting, droving, were not year-round occupations; for the lower stratum, the slack months had to be filled by fencing or rabbit-trapping or a spell in the cities on the wharves. Lowenstein concludes that in Australia "casual work had always been the norm for a large number of working people" (1978:10).

The century began with the continuation of a continent-wide drought of unparalleled severity, reducing the livestock in Queensland by almost two-thirds and resulting in hard frosts, even in northern areas, which had disastrous effects on the sugar-cane. This prolonged the effects of the 1890s depression, making work hard to get and wages low. Though the proportion of trade unionists was higher in Australia at that time than in any other part of the world (Alexander, 1967:10), defeats in the strikes of the previous decade had dispirited the movement. There had been, in McQueen's judgment, "at least two volunteers ready to replace every striking unionist" (1975:210) which Shann (1948) considers was due to their poverty rather than to their will. The workers were persuaded that their best interests lay in pressing for compulsory arbitration, which was in fact granted in 1904. It was followed, in 1907, by the famous "Harvester judgment" of Mr Justice Higgins, setting a minimum wage for Australian men of two pounds two shillings a week, calculated as adequate for the "normal needs of an average employee, regarded as a human being in a civilized country" (Tew, 1951:124).

The masculine role of economic provider was unchallenged at the beginning of the century, and ensured that there were no males included in the category "never worked for pay". A few had never, or only occasionally, worked for wages or a salary; one claimed that he had begun his independent career at the age of 9, droving a mob of bullocks from near the Queensland border 600 miles south for sale in Sydney. The tendency for frequent changes in occupation, very evident among their fathers, became less common with the gradual evolution of more settled working conditions. For male respondents, the most usual occupations were the middle-status ones of farming, clerical work, teaching, selling, and small businesses of many kinds.

But an analysis of the main lifetime occupation of the sample as a whole reveals "home duties" as the main component. In view of the fact that three-quarters of the sample was female, this is not surprising. Nevertheless, female respondents did go to work, and in considerable numbers, especially before marriage.

Female work-roles

The Harvester judgment of 1907 made no provision for women
workers, although they were already a significant part of the
workforce. For example, the 1901 census report quoted by
Encel et al. (1974:71) lists the proportion working in "manufac-
turing" (presumably factory workers) as 23 per cent.

Factory work was the first job of about 12 per cent of female
respondents in the Toowong survey, including Mrs Turvey. At
82 she was almost as broad as she was long, "waddling as she
walked", the interviewer said; she had small twinkling eyes in a
broad face, and a ready smile. She had worked in a tailoring
factory in England for half a crown a week, and after she came
to Australia on the *Union Castle* she went to Plumridge's
chocolate factory in Brisbane, and complained that the girls
who worked there seemed "commoner" than those in England.
Next she went to a pyjama factory in the same area, where she
earned 12 shillings and six pence a week but had to take a
month off without pay at Christmas time — there were no
unions to look after the rights of women workers.

Mrs Purlson, whose father was a carpenter, found a job in a
printery:

> . . . and I thought I was made, because I was earning money! Not
> that the wages were much, but it was a job. I thought I was very
> clever to have it — it all helped the household. I remembered
> changing the — These sheets, they had varnish on, and you had to
> watch you didn't get stuck in it. If you weren't careful flipping
> them over you caught it round the head.

For many respondents the first job was part of some family
enterprise, and the girls, more often than their brothers, were
expected to provide their services without the formality of
wages. Several girls took part in the incessant round of duties
associated with dairying; others helped in the family shop, or
took over the housekeeping so that their mother could do so.
The 1911 census revealed 5000 women whose occupation was
"shopkeeper" at that time (Encel et al., 1974:22). Housekeeping
duties in the family home were almost never paid, a fact that
still rankled with 87-year-old Mrs Land:

It was our parents' belief that the children should do the work. I think Mum and Dad made the biggest mistake of their lives when they — I was 22 and never earned a penny and none of the others under us did either. Now I think that was very, very wrong, because in a way it makes slaves of the children. . . .

If undertaken for others, however, household duties were a source of meagre income. About one-third of female respondents had their first experience of paid work in some sort

About one-third of female respondents had their first experience of paid work in some sort of domestic capacity.

of domestic capacity, if waitresses, cooks and the one barmaid are included along with less formal occupations such as "looking after the children". Mrs Tuvey had taken up domestic work after her factory jobs, and did not give up till she was 70:

> I was hanging out the clothes one day and I thought, I'm a blooming fathead, working this hard when I'm 70! And I went straight in and said to her, look, I'll finish here today and after that —

Mrs Manning had persisted even longer — until she was 75. She had begun work as a private domestic on a Queensland cattle station at a time when, according to McQueen (1978:43) the usual wage was 10 shillings a week and the main complaint was the long hours. But Mrs Manning had no complaints; she described her first employer as:

> . . . lovely, a real lady. She used to show me quietly how to make our beds the way she wanted them and all that sort of thing. I was 14 when I started there, and she — She asked me about my periods and I said I didn't have them, and she said when I did to come and tell her, and I did. You just made diapers, just tore up a sheet, because you couldn't buy anything here till later years, really.

She later married a cook and did "housekeeping work" all her life. At 82 she was thin and lively, with a wrinkled sun-spotted face and carefully permed white hair. She lived in a tiny house described by the interviewer as "extremely tidy and neat"; it had been left to her by a former employer who had appreciated her high standards. She had lost a son as well as her husband, but maintained close ties with her three remaining children, whose family troubles were the subject of a considerable part of the interview. But she had no doubt what it was that "kept her going": "I reckon work helped me a lot, even when the children were small. I had nobody to help me, you did everything yourself — I still got plenty to do. Work is my salvation."

At the other end of the social scale, some female respondents seem to have sought paid work before marriage in preference to housework, although few put it as explicitly as Miss Blessington: "I had to do something — I couldn't stand just loafing about at home. I've never been interested in housework! (LAUGHS)"

Stenography had only recently been added to nursing and teaching as a suitable occupation for the daughters of gentlemen; only the middle or upper strata could afford to pay the fees required for business college training. The city stores also restricted their intake of new staff to the relatively well off by requiring an unpaid training period of up to six months. In all, only 20 per cent of female respondents had never worked for pay, and although no strictly comparable figures seem to be available, the fact that 80 per cent undertook paid work before marriage seems to be an unusually high proportion for Australian girls of that era. But the question has never been thoroughly investigated. Perhaps economic necessity and some degree of feministic independence made the work-before-marriage pattern a common one earlier in Australian history than has so far been acknowledged.

Once married, two-thirds spent the greater part of their lives as housewives, but a few had managed to combine a career with marriage. Mrs Vann, for instance, had had commercial training in Melbourne and came to Brisbane to start a very successful stationery business before the First World War. At 89 she was still the managing director, though she no longer went to work every day; widowed and childless, she lived with a housekeeper-friend.

But Dr Odell was the outstanding example. She had had five children and her doctor-husband was still alive. At 84 her own practice was flourishing, and she had numerous other medical and political interests which kept her name before the public and fully occupied her time.

Most career women, however, had remained unmarried. Miss Blessington had had a successful commercial career and dreaded retirement, but managed to invest her savings so well that financially she was better off than ever. Miss Glenn was an architect. The elder Miss Alder had been the matron of a well-known hospital and during the Second World War had attained the rank of colonel. Miss Willers had had 'a nice little dress-making business'. Work before marriage might have been a commoner pattern than is usually thought, but most female respondents conformed to sex-role expectations by giving up work on marriage and devoting their lives thereafter to network-maintenance. The event-confrontation mode involved in working outside the home was usually chosen by the unmarried.

Women may have found it easier to obtain work, because from about 1911 onwards the employment situation improved. Overseas borrowing stimulated the extension of railway networks and other construction industries, and assisted immigration was revived on a larger scale than before to cope with employers' requirements. At the same time, fertilizers, new strains of wheat, and new farming methods were bringing marginal lands into production; Miss Affleck, who at 92 was in the chronically-ill section of the general hospital, said that she had been a farmer most of her life, until her nephews had taken over from her.

Protectionist policies also encouraged the growth of secondary industry, and though the outbreak of war brought some interruption and re-direction, on the whole it stimulated rather than retarded economic growth. Certainly it greatly encouraged the employment of women (at lower pay) in a much wider variety of occupations. After the war they were expected to go back to their kitchens to make way for returned soldiers, for whom the employment situation was not promising.

The Depression

McQueen asserts that "There are good reasons for seeing the whole of the inter-war period as a depression in Australia" (1978:122). Certainly there is plenty of evidence for the claim by some respondents that they had known nothing but hard times till after the Second World War. Mr Reston, who at 82 was described by the interviewer as 'still a ladies' man — likes to charm', was "in softgoods — I had a job in a warehouse" before the war. He spoke rather bitterly of his reception there on his return:

One thing that sticks in my mind is the day that we came home from the war. Three of us from the firm came back the same day, and I remember the manager telling us how thrilled he was at the wonderful job we soldiers did, but of course we had to face up to the fact that we weren't as qualified commercially as the ones who'd stayed behind, and they only could give us three pounds a week. I had a commission then, I was earning over a pound a day in the army, and to come back to that! The other two boys told them what to do with their three pounds in good Australian language, but — Jobs weren't easy to come by, you know. So I stayed on.

In 1929, when most respondents were in their thirties or early forties, Australia was plunged with the rest of the world into sudden economic depression. After the Wall Street crash Australia was among the countries worst hit by the fall in export prices and the withdrawal of overseas capital, and economists are still debating the proper course of action for governments at the time. Theodore, as federal treasurer, proposed bold initiatives of credit expansion, but his thunder was stolen by Lang's more radical proposals. Both were rejected by a premier's conference, and orthodox deflationary tactics were adopted.

Of all the Australian states, Queensland was least affected; in 1932 unemployment peaked at 18.8 per cent, compared with 34 per cent in South Australia (Lowenstein, 1978:13). Nevertheless, about half of the Toowong respondents recalled it as a time of great anxiety. It was also a time of political and social turmoil, but the response of those on whom the burden fell was overwhelmingly one of "endurance, not revolt" (Lowenstein, 1978:11), and this was reflected in the transcripts. Prices for primary products were so low that some reported leaving the land because they were unable to pay the interest on their over-drafts. The ordinary working man was even worse off. Mr Alton, for instance, said that he had been out of work for three years in the Depression: "We just survived the best way we could. Nearly broke the wife up. I used to go crook at her; I used to say to her, you have no sympathy for a man, just abuse!"

Conditions for the granting of "sustenance" required realizing on all assets except a house, attending a depot at a regular day

and hour, declaring their continued unemployment and destitu-
tion, and signing for about seven shillings' worth per person of
bread, groceries, meat and milk (Bland, 1968:102). Relief work
was also available, usually a day-and-a-half a week, working on
the road for a payment of one pound twelve shillings.

Not all were as severely affected. For a favoured few like Mr
Notting, the Depression proved an opportunity for advance-
ment. The son of a coalminer, he first went to work as a
barber's assistant in Bendigo, but when a big department store
opened there he went down to try for a job. "I'd only got in a
few paces and I saw a man there and said, 'Excuse me, sir, I want
to see the manager.' He said, 'I'm the manager, sonny — what
do you want?' 'My mother sent me down to see if I could get a
job, sir.' 'Oh, she did! What's a hundred ha'pennies?' I said,
'Four and twopence, sir.' He got me by the shoulder and he
called out to a man there: 'Smithson! Smithson! Give this boy
something to do.' I started work straight away. I've always been
good at figures."

Being good at figures helped him rise to section-manager by
the time the Depression came, and this, combined with a
certain ruthlessness, gave him his big chance:

> My section was prospering, but we had too many old codgers in
> it living on their past reputations. By degrees I eliminated a few of
> them and then the others began to come round. . . . We did so well,
> I was offered other jobs, name my own salary —

He joined the firm he stayed with till his retirement as
managing director. At 82 he was healthy, active, and as forceful
as ever.

Clearly, the brunt of the Depression was borne by those who
could least afford it, while members of the upper stratum were
to a large extent protected from its worst effects, presumably
by power, influence, and the extent of their economic assets.
As usual, middle-status respondents were between the two
extremes.

More women than men said they were not greatly affected
by the great Depression. To some extent the female role
appears to have cushioned them against the stressful impact of
economic events in the wider world. Presumably social expec-

tations for participation in the workforce predisposed the men towards event-confronting patterns of behaviour which made them see the Depression as a personal problem, to be dealt with as best they could if a judgment of personal failure were to be avoided. For the women it was apparently of less immediate relevance. They had been brought up to give their energies to network-maintenance, so economic realities were seen more as a test of endurance than as a challenge to their sense of self-worth.

All strata recovered sufficiently from the Depression to continue building the economic requisites of a moderately comfortable old age. None of the respondents was financially destitute, homeless or habitual drunkards, drifters, or gamblers. Whatever their socio-economic status, they were alike in that they tended to husband their financial resources, staying out of debt, gambling only very moderately, and doggedly maintaining what assets they could.

Work in old age

The norms of age-stratification in Western society euphemistically define old age as "time to take a well-earned rest", and in most cases compel people to retire. Retirement is a modern invention, confined to high productivity societies, and for many gerontologists its connotations are overwhelmingly negative. Hendricks and Hendricks list some of the structural characteristics of modern high productivity societies which make retirement necessary to their functioning — for example, urbanization and the technological advances associated with it; the compulsory education systems that bolster both, and ensure the obsolescence of tradition-based skills; and the absorption of the workforce into industries where self-employment is an anachronism. All these are best served by mandatory retirement at a given chronological age, with pension schemes of one sort or another to ease acceptance (1977:67).

But old people themselves do not necessarily share the gerontologists' view that retirement is an imposition of "compulsory unemployment" (Comfort, 1976:6), or "a traumatic break with past involvements" comparable with widowhood (Lopata, 1972:276). Three-quarters of the men in the Toowong study stated unequivocally that retirement had been no problem at all. The question of whether people do or do not want to retire is complicated by socio-economic status, hidden variables such as job strain and degree of autonomy, and whether the attitudes expressed are prospective or retrospective. Most retired people maintain, in the face of the evidence, that their retirement was voluntary, and the reasons given are overwhelmingly concerned with health (Shanas, 1968:328); but financial status and the availability of pensions are significant factors both in a decision to retire and adjustment to retirement when it does take place.

For the old people in the Toowong study, reflections on retirement were retrospective rather than prospective, despite a few who asserted that they had never retired. Certainly Dr Odell was as fully involved with her career as she had ever been (and still is at time of writing; she is now nearly 89). Mrs Archibald, like Mrs Vann, had remained on the board of directors for a business she had continued after her husband's death. Mr Reston said he still maintained control of his cosmetic firm, and Mr Trevor said the same about his grazing properties, while one of the old men at the hostel, a former carpenter, owned a block of flats and held himself fully responsible for its maintenance. Others, like 84-year-old Mrs Wood, did part-time work to augment their pensions.

A sharp drop in income after retirement of the main breadwinner is a universal phenomenon in industrial societies. During the 1970s, old age pensions were made payable without means test to all aged 70 and over, and the rate was increased to $106.40 per fortnight while the Toowong study was in progress. Additional income, often in the form of interest on bonds or bank savings, was probably more prevalent than was reported: several studies state that under-reporting of financial resources is common amongst old people. As already mentioned, the first Toowong interviews soon established that finance was a topic that respondents tended to define as too personal. Mrs Clare, for instance, who was otherwise quite forthcoming, said testily: "I'm better off now than I have been the biggest part of my life — that's as far as I will go. I think these questions are very stickybeaky."

In deference to these attitudes, in assessing financial status it was decided to rely on information about whether there was a source of income ("small" or "good" in the respondent's own estimation) additional to the pension that all respondents received. In 1978–79 the guaranteed minimum wage for unskilled workers was $120.50 per week — more than twice as much as the weekly equivalent for pensioners ($53.20). Long-established habits of frugality ensured that most people were able to "put something by" for recurring expenses such as rates and electricity, though house-painting (a major expense of weatherboard homes) and repairs were sometimes seen as rather worrying. However, beyond some complaints from all socio-economic strata about the high cost of living now compared with in their youth, few respondents said that finance was a problem to them, and these few were almost entirely confined to those in the middle or lower strata who had to pay rent. Mrs Wood — described as "healthy, trim and active-looking, looks nothing like 84! — was one of these. She said:

After the 26th I'll be paying $42 a week in rent, because the rates and everything have gone up and the landlord just painted it all and carpeted it. I said, "You've only been improving your own property!" But still and all — The youngest daughter keeps on saying, "How are you going to manage, Mum?" And I say, "Just by being thrifty." But I make about four wedding cakes a year. I did one before Christmas. I rang the pension people and asked if I could do that and they said yes, as long as I didn't make a welter of it. I only had a fortnight to make the cake and ice it — it was a bit of a rush, before Christmas — but that — The cakes go towards my telephone. If I can make enough just to pay my telephone, my gas and electric light, I'm happy. I'm very careful the way I shop. I don't buy a lot of meat that's got bones in, that way you're paying for the bone. I don't buy a lot of luxuries. I get my apples and oranges, and one sponge cake a fortnight. At Christmas time, one of the daughters, her and her children, they always put together and give me a hamper, and that helps a lot. But otherwise I do all right. I manage. But the youngest daughter, she worries, worries, worries.

Every day she rings me — "Mum, are you managing all right?" She says, "I don't know how you do it!" Well, I say, I've just got to.

The financial vulnerability of females is a commonplace in the literature. Presumably savings dwindle with the years, and the longer life expectancy of females accentuates this process, especially as they almost invariably have lower incomes throughout life. In the Toowong survey, more women than men were solely dependent on the government pension, but usually the high rate of home ownership made finance less of a problem than it was for rent-paying Mrs Wood. But even Mrs Wood was "managing all right" in her own estimation, and she was justly proud of the weddings cakes she made. She showed the interviewer some photographs of them, who reported that they had "absolutely exquisite icing with fine detailed flowers and curliques".

Nevertheless it was plain that whatever the rewards of the work role, all but a small minority were glad to be done with it as their lives drew to a close. This minority consisted solely of former housewives, for whom retirement comprised gradual reduction in responsibility for the comfort of others. Although this decrease in duties was welcomed by some ("I can do what I like when I like — I don't care if the cupboards aren't clean!"), it was regretted by others for whom work-ethic values became a source of derogatory self-images in their final years. Most were able to find satisfying substitutes for work in hobbies, family relationships, religion, or voluntary work; many gave a lot of their time to the Red Cross, the church, or other activities that embodied service to others. Activity per se was highly regarded, but *useful* activity was the ideal. Now that Miss Willers no longer had a dressmaking business, "I do these coat-hangers — yes, they are nice, aren't they? As soon as I finish one I start another. I do them for the stalls."

Many still felt useful while they could knit for their grand-children. But Mrs Longward spoke for those who felt they had lived beyond their usefulness. Although she had only just turned 80, she had severe arthritis and looked very frail; "I'd like to die tomorrow", she said, so softly that it was difficult to pick up the words on the tape. "I'm only a — nuisance to people." She paused to gain her breath. "They're terribly good to me, but still I — I can't do anything. I'm so useless. I help get the tea at night, that's all I do."

Male respondents, who had survived the stresses and strains of workforce participation and the resulting confrontation with events, seemed better able to adapt to a loss of the work-role than those who, like Mrs Longward, had given their lives to network-integration yet could not resign themselves to accepting the services they had rendered others.

Service to others was not confined to females. Mr Derrick had begun his working life selling motor-bikes in the first few years of the century; at 89 he retained his lifelong interest in motors and drove his own car *delivering* Meals on Wheels to people mostly younger than himself. Tall and stooped and troubled by a hernia, he continued his work for Meals on Wheels till he was 92.

There is no more persistent element in ageist stereotypes than the denigration of the old as "unproductive". In the Toowong sample a few former housewives in poor health had accepted this judgment as part of their self-image. But most respondents rejected it, and with good reason. Mr Derrick and Dr Odell might have been exceptional, and so, in her own way, was Mrs Wood and her wedding cakes; but very few of the Toowong respondents — even the oldest among them — could justly be labelled "unproductive". In most cases it was not age, but illness, that forced unproductiveness upon those who could not meet the standards set for them by society — and by themselves. The rest contributed to their own households and to society in general by adherence to a work ethic they had internalized so long ago that it continued to structure their lives into extreme old age.

They worked at their own pace and for their own purposes; but only a few of them (mostly in institutions) bowed to the edict that they must not work at all.

Chapter 7: Leisure

Well, we didn't have much time for — play, exactly. We milked the cows in the morning and then we walked three and a half miles to Pullenvale School, and then we'd come home and do the same thing in the afternoon, then we'd have our homework to do while Mum and Dad was over on the hillside, cutting wood, so we didn't have much — You just made your own fun. As we grew older, my father and mother used to go to dances with us. They always liked company, they'd have the neighbours around, they'd come to our place and we'd have a dance in the kitchen. Mother would go into the paddock and get those big creeping vines, and lap them round the beams in the kitchen and made it look a bit nice. We had the old accordion, the old style one, and the concertina. My eldest brother and some of my cousins, they played them. Every Saturday night we'd have a dance and a sing-song. No hard drinks those days. Some would recite and others would do a bit of acting. My brother was a very good actor. He used to dress up and — You know, act the goat a lot. And we used to go riding a lot — end up at a dance. Or take a sulky and away we'd go. . . .

I used to play with my brothers — cricket and football, it wasn't competitive like it is now. The boys had their gymnastic things, the parallel bars and punching ball, and I'd have a go at it with the boys too. The girls did mostly skipping and rounders and things like that. And then we'd have — there were Sunday School picnics. You'd have a bus take you out to a paddock somewhere, and the teachers would get on the swing, and they'd have long dresses on and they'd pile the dresses round the bottom so the dress wouldn't blow up. Different to these days! (LAUGHS) . . . Later on in life I played tennis . . . Nowadays I — sew, and read — I like fiction, I like love yarns! (LAUGHS) Yes, I watch TV. And we're always having visitors. The people 4 houses down, we play Scrabble, they come here one week and we go there the next week . . .

The British sociologist Stanley Parker argues that work and leisure are best considered together as joint time-and-activity dimensions along a continuum from constraint to freedom (1971). On retirement, the balance does not shift as radically from constraint to freedom as might be supposed. Parker recognizes "non-work" constraints on time, consisting of activities requiring attention to physiological needs and non-work obligations. In old age these activities may expand to fill the greater part of the day, leaving little more free time than formerly for what the people concerned regard as true leisure.

Toowong respondents had been brought up to regard leisure (in the sense of "play") as peripheral to everyday reality. The leisure-patterns they had constructed over the years were built out of "scraps", as it were, of time and interest left over from the serious business of living. By the time they reached old age most had modified those interests, while others had intensified them. On the whole, sex-role differences in leisure were less evident than might have been expected, and where they existed, seemed to be linked to indoor/outdoor, solitary/gregarious polarizations that persisted into old age.

Childhood

At the turn of the century the injunction to be "seen and not heard" applied at table and in other situations of contact with adults, but children who were not actively engaged in some set task were expected to keep out of their elders' way. Perhaps that was the reason so many respondents were convinced that "kids had more fun in those days". The contrast between adults

"Kids had more fun in those days."

and children was much emphasized, and the children relished what freedom they could snatch to "make their own fun".

The long walks home from school that were so common was one such cherished opportunity for freedom from adult supervision. Mrs Emerson chuckled as she recalled slipping and sliding down the hills on the grass, sometimes tying knots in the longer grass so that others would trip over. Boys climbed trees and caught possums and shot down birds with a shanghai; boys and girls alike hunted "lobbies" in the creeks. In the towns boys built billy-carts to go hurtling down the steepest slopes, and joined with the girls to run out into the streets when flocks of bats flew over. They threw their hats into the air and called:

Bat, bat, come into my hat,
I'll give you a slice of bacon!
If one won't do I'll give you two,
And set your head achin'!

In the schoolyard both sexes played I Ackie and Bedlam and Red Rover, but marbles was strictly a boys' game, and skipping strictly for girls. Playing with dolls was exclusively feminine, and girls were adept at elaborate string games; hopscotch was mostly for girls just as tops were mostly for boys; both sexes played "jacks" with old bones. A surprising number of girls from all social strata played cricket, and a few claimed that they had played football with the boys.

Male respondents seemed to have a particularly keen memory for the games they played at school. Mr Perry described three of them:

Boys would play what they called Bump the Barrel. You'd stand up in the front against the wall, and there'd be a row of two or three with their backs down, like that, and you'd see how far you could jump on the other fellow's back. . . . You could get under the school when it was raining, you'd peg this knife off your nose or off your chin or your shoulder, spinning the knife — like that — and it'd stick in the ground. The one who got through all the things that you had to, they'd win. And we used to play Buttons. We made this hole in the ground, about that big deep and about from here to the bed up there long and — You'd toss a lot of buttons up and nip them into the hole, see?

Three different versions of the game called "Buttons" were reported. It was played in Britain as well as in Australia, and apparently by both boys and girls.

Respondents' assertions that they had more fun than modern children may represent nothing more than nostalgia. On the other hand, dependence on their own resources must have helped to encourage the self-sufficiency so highly valued at the time, a self-sufficiency most tried to maintain into extreme old age.

Family entertainment that included adults was mostly home-based, and began to play a more important part as respondents grew from children into adolescents.

Youth

In many homes the making of music was a major source of entertainment, and musical instruction of some sort was a commonplace. It was not restricted to the rich; McQueen asserts that the piano was "the pinnacle of working-class aspirations" (1975:118). It was transported across the ocean and carted hundreds of miles inland, and girls in particular, if their parents had any ambitions for their becoming "nice young ladies", were expected to practise their scales daily. Some had also had to learn the violin; Mrs Smythe said wryly that it had been "belted" into her. For a few, music lessons were no drudgery, but a delight. One or two reported having their own family orchestras, and several who could afford no expensive musical instruments managed to have a wonderful time with the aid of a mouthorgan or even combs and gum leaves. Singing around the piano, a favourite middle-status entertainment, was augmented with recitations, shadow plays, and magic lantern shows.

But the favourite night-time recreation undoubtedly was dancing. Eighty-nine-year-old Mrs Clancy still remembered it with zest:

> We used to have a real good time at dances. You paid a shilling to go and the girls sat on one side and the boys sat on the other, and when the MC called the dance out, whichever fellow put his hand on you, you had to dance with him. There was one fellow used to like to swing the corners, and I said, if he does that to me, I'll swing him! If it's a square dance, I'll be one end of the hall and he'll be at the other before we're finished! And that's what happened! (LAUGHS) And every now and then there'd be dances held at — You know, the asylum. Anybody could go, but you have to dance every second dance with a patient. . . .

Others were more formal. When Mrs Day was growing up in England she went to dances that were "all no-nonsense, very circumspect", with both sexes wearing gloves and a great attention given to etiquette; her father was a civil servant. Formalities were observed in Brisbane, too. Mr Sturt had gone to dances in Toowong at which he always wore a two- or three-piece suit —

> We even wore those to the university, as a matter of fact. And at what they called the Assembly dances — the Austral Assembly — the girls strictly on one side and the boys on the other side and you had to carry out the formal approaches and so forth. No ready mixing at all.

Country dances seemed to be more exuberant, with groups of young men and women riding miles to the local hall and dancing to the strains of a concertina and a fiddle until the early hours of the morning before riding home again. There were surprise parties at people's homes, and impromptu dancing on the back verandah while others sang around the piano. Several mentioned dances on the T.S.S. *Koopa*, a large two-masted excursion steamer of 416 gross tonnage, licensed to carry over 1000 passengers. It arrived in Brisbane in 1911 and supplemented the services of the much smaller vessels *Beaver* and *Garnet*, which were also mentioned fondly by some respondents. Mrs Boulder had met her husband on the *Koopa*:

> It used to be two shillings for a night, about two hours' trip to Bribie Island; we used to have lovely times. I was selling tickets for the Red Cross, and I hate that, I don't like selling tickets. And this night — I had to go round till I'd sold these tickets, and he bought the lot, because he wanted me to sit beside him. That's where I met him.

But Mrs Payne was among those who had been brought up to regard dancing, and most other forms of entertainment, as intrinsically evil. She had not been allowed to go to "the pictures", either. This is an example of the "wowserism" which was a subject of popular debate in the first two decades of the century. John Norton, editor of *Truth*, claimed the coinage of the word, though according to Dunstan (1968) it seems to have been current since the gold rush days of the 1850s. Wowsers kept alive the spirit of Puritanism in the non-conformist churches; the ban on dancing was continued by the Methodists until after 1948. Dunstan lists ten major "evils" that wowsers sought to combat, including desecration of the Sabbath, strong drink, smoking, the theatre, dancing, mixed bathing, and cremation; and instances of these attitudes cropped up in several interviews.

For young people in the cities, motion pictures rivalled dancing for popularity. Toowong had its own picture-show, open to the sky and furnished with deck chairs; it cost sixpence to go in. But many thought of their youthful entertainment predominantly as daytime activities. Football and cricket were usually left behind with school, but one of the girls played interstate hockey and tennis. Lacrosse, croquet and sailing were mentioned. No one spoke of swimming or surfing. Sea-bathing was gaining popularity on Sydney beaches, although only night bathing was allowed until 1903, and the sexes were strictly segregated until 1917 (Dunstan, 1968:154). In southern Queensland the main surfing beaches were cut off by rivers and mangrove swamps, and no respondents mentioned being among the vanguard who popularized them.

The daytime activities most frequently mentioned were long walks, picnics, and tennis; and the latter two retained their popularity as favourite modes of entertainment in mid-life.

Mid-life

The tendency of respondents to report that they had no time at all for leisure increased as they recalled their adult years. According to 15 per cent of older cohorts and 6 per cent of the younger, this had been true even in youth; but for the majority of the sample, the responsibilities of work and marriage had relegated leisure further into the background. The polarization between indoor and outdoor modes became more evident, together with another dichotomy — between gregarious and more solitary pursuits.

For the gregarious, dances and theatre-going (usually to motion· pictures) remained quite high on the list as leading forms of recreation, and visiting among relatives increased in popularity. Among outdoor activities picnics were still popular, but now seemed to be undertaken for the children's sake, and the beaches as a destination were mentioned far more frequently. Mrs Rogers, for instance, who was the wife of 'an engine-driver in the pits', mentioned how they had bought a little house at an isolated spot on the coast:

> Before that we used to go down in a cart, the whole lot of us, and my brother would drive us down and my husband went down in a boat with all the eatables. We had to take enough eatables down for a fortnight. We hung the bread on a tree in a bag, and we dug a big hole in the sand for the butter, covered it well over. I cooked on two big fires, a fire going on underneath. I cooked plum puddings and steam puddings and — (LAUGHS) And we had plenty of fish and crabs — and oysters. We'd stop a fortnight down there. As soon as the children got their breakfast, they'd disappear. I don't know where they all went, right up the beach somewhere and made sandmen and things. We went down there every year, and as they grew up they brought their sweethearts home, and the children started to come in — so they all had a good childhood.

At 89 Mrs Rogers was almost blind and living with her daughter, but she still liked to be with people — especially her family. She was eagerly looking forward, she said, to the party they were planning for her ninetieth birthday. On the other hand Mr Leslie, although he shared a liking for the outdoors, preferred to take off by himself. In mid-life he was one of the few who retained an earlier predeliction for long walks. He had often walked the 20 miles from Brisbane to Ipswich and caught the train home, or if he had a week-end to spare, he would take a haversack and a sleeping-bag and set off further afield. He recounted getting caught in storms and minor adventures such as waking up one morning covered in cow-dung, and laughed with an infectious enjoyment at these long-ago happenings (at the time of interview he was 93 years old).

For the gregarious, tennis remained a favourite sport across a surprisingly wide social spectrum. Mrs Day had taken up tennis when she came to Australia, and Miss Glenn, one of the first women architects in Australia, had played "just social tennis, of course" most of her life. But so had Mrs Clancy, whose husband was a shop assistant, and even one or two from a definitely working-class background. They clubbed together to hire a court and played "hit and giggle" one afternoon a week while the children were at school, and in some cases started friendships that remained with them into old age.

Those who preferred more solitary occupations began in mid-life to develop the hobbies that occupied them in old age. For many of the women it was reading. Though respondents' parents did not, on the whole, value recreational reading very highly, it was considered more seemly for girls than for boys, and in later life few men found time to read more than a newspaper. The women, of course, were equally busy, but the avid readers among them managed to retreat occasionally to the world of fantasy provided by a novel. Usually they were romantic stories woven around themes of network-maintenance, while the newspapers read by men reflected their interest in confrontation with real events.

Mr Rhodes was one who had been too poor and too busy for entertainment during childhood and youth. During a varied career as farm-hand, sawmiller and motor mechanic, after marriage he went to the far north of Queensland, selling oil. It was a strenuous life:

> You had the territory, it wasn't an hourly rate at all, you had to produce something from the territory, and figures — they were your only master. My territory covered from Greenvale to Cooktown up to Normanton and everywhere in between. There was one mile of bitumen in the whole of the territory. To get down to Port Douglas in those days, to get down the range — you only had rear-wheel brakes; you see, the range was so steep that it was necessary to tie a couple of trees on the back of the car to get down. You were actually pulling the two trees down and down and down this steep range. In the wet weather you had chains on almost continuously. . . .

But in the midst of all this it was also necessary for Mr Rhodes to make contacts after hours. Naturally both gregarious and athletic, he took up golf as he began to prosper, and eventually became president of the local golf club. Later he joined a service club and other voluntary organizations. In many respects he was typical of respondents who had attained middle socio-economic status by their own efforts, and tailored their leisure activities to advance their work. As they grew older, golf was likely to give way to bowls; and some of the women tennis players, too, gave up tennis for bowls. The preferences of a lifetime set the stage for their leisure patterns in old age.

Old age

From a life-span perspective, behavioural modes associated with eventfulness and network-maintenance influenced the type of leisure respondents chose in their old age. Those who had devoted least energy to network-maintenance were apt to find solitary modes of entertainment, whether as active hobbyists or (if they had usually sought to avoid eventfulness) as passive spectators of the activities of others. Those who had devoted their lives to maintenance of kin or friendship networks, or both, and who had typically preferred the stimulus of confronting events, did their best to maintain gregarious contacts even when faced with disability. Several respondents who seldom left their homes had roster-systems for keeping in touch with friends by telephone. Mrs Clancy, for example, alternately rang or was rung by particular friends on pre-arranged days of the week.

Socio-economic status was important for the structuring of gregarious leisure pursuits in old age; 60 per cent of upper-status respondents belonged to voluntary associations ranging from sports to church organizations, compared with minorities of the lower (37 per cent) and middle (42 per cent). The advantages of upper-status membership — which were likely to include better health as well as private transport and other facilities — helped these respondents to carry on with gregarious leisure activities longer than most. The gregarious, like Mr Perry (whom the interviewer described as looking about 60) tended to be vigorous and healthy, their success in social relationships probably contributing to both. But if illness or disability occurred, they were more inclined than the solitary to lapse into a resigned passivity — like Mrs Day, who quite typically attributed the change to her years rather than to her arthritic knee: "Oh, I used to go out a lot, I used to be a great one for — But I can't get around now. When you're old you sort of — lose touch."

There were many variations in these patterns, of course. Intelligent many-sided people like Miss Glenn or Mr Rhodes, to mention only two, cannot be neatly pigeonholed as gregarious or solitary, indoor or outdoor oriented. Both Miss Glenn and Mr Rhodes were tall and held themselves very erect; Mr Rhodes measured himself under the shower-rail in the bathroom every morning and was still the same height, six feet one-and-a-half inches, as he had been in the army in the First World War. On his retirement he had taken up bee-keeping and cabinet-making as hobbies, but when he and his wife moved to a unit in Toowong he decided that neither was suitable for his new domicile. So he adopted his wife's hobby of tapestry and soon became very skilled with his needle. This was a major change of style for a man who had to that date accepted that sewing was only for women. But Mr Rhodes was a flexible man. He maintained gregarious links with church, lodge, and the bee-keepers' association, and joined the local senior citizens' centre and its concert party, becoming a singer for the first time in his life at the age of 83.

Miss Glenn had substituted bridge for tennis, though she still took long walks because she liked the open air. She, too, was a hobbyist:

> While I can use my hands I'll never be lonely. I enjoy all sorts of — wood-carving, for instance. I can look around this room and think, I did that . . . and that . . . and that. . . . See that gargoyle? Someone said the other day, "Oh yes, one of the ancestors!" (LAUGHS) And pottery and — the curtains, the mats. The curtains are a bit interesting, really — those are made of paper. You can't have heavy curtains if you like to see out.

Most respondents had found cause to modify their leisure-patterns as they grew older. Mr Leslie had modified his long walks by supplementing them with bus trips to a terminus and walking about from there, sometimes as often as twice a week: "Down to Sandgate, that makes a nice trip — and I see all the pretty girls!"

Modification was demonstrated by people who asserted with pride that they had played tennis "up till just a few years ago" — and were now among those who took pleasure in bowls; or the eager picnickers of yesteryear who still liked to drive out into the country; or the movie fans of the 1920s and 1930s who followed "The Young Doctors" on television. The gradual transition from active to passive modes of entertainment was probably shared by the majority of the Australian population regardless of age, but was no doubt more apparent for respondents and their contemporaries than it would be for younger members of the community. To some extent, increased passivity was undoubtedly a realistic response to failing energies. The degree to which failing energies were a *result* of increased passivity is impossible to estimate, but age-stratified norms dictate such passivity, and most respondents could be expected to conform to leisure norms as they did to those concerned with work.

There were some, like Miss Glenn and others, who had intensified rather than modified their former leisure pursuits, sometimes to the point where a former part-time hobby, indoor or outdoor, had now become a focus of existence. For many, like Mrs Clancy, an interest in gardening was particularly likely to have intensified over the years: "If I get a fit of the miseries", she said, "I just put me hat on, and out in the garden I go!"

The prime example was Mr Sturt, who was actually a professional horticulturist who still gave radio talks and wrote a weekly newspaper column on the subject. He was 84 and looked exceptionally fit, but he accepted the myth that a nursing home would probably be his final domicile: "I'd hate it of course, but I'd have to — accept it. You've got to accept that you deteriorate. Of course at the present time I — But no doubt I'm gradually deteriorating, you've got to accept that."

A majority of respondents, except among the institutionalized, stated firmly that they never felt bored. As one old lady put it, "Only the bores are bored!" But in the two nursing homes, the hostel and the hospital, boredom emerged as more of a problem than loneliness. Mrs Smythe, for instance, had been in a nursing home for nearly 12 months and had in no way adjusted to it. She said she was "bored, oh yes, bored — thoroughly fed up!" On the other hand Mrs Payne, who was also in a nursing home, managed to do a little fancywork in spite of severe arthritis, and said resignedly that she was quite happy there. She had elected to go to a nursing home for the familiar reason that she "didn't want to be a burden on the family". She had been there five years.

In keeping with their lifelong socialization, respondents tended to accept restrictions on their activities as solely due to biological ageing. They made no allowance for ageist norms that prescribe a drastic reduction in physical and mental activity, and in doing so accelerate biological decline. It seems to be true that modern societies move at a pace that is uncomfortable for most human beings to sustain. People of any age who are freed from a strict time-schedule tend to relax into a slower mode of being. The luxury of taking one's own time is a frequent and much-appreciated accompaniment of old age. But it has its dangers. Too often, routinization sets in, reducing challenge and impoverishing the environment of stimuli to a point that may be as dangerous, in its own way, as the risk of hypertension or heart attack.

People who live to be 80 or more tend, on the whole, to have found a balance between activity and rest that helps to keep them alive. But societal norms about activity in old age seem to be excessively cautionary. People like Mr Rhodes and Mrs Clancy, Mr Leslie and Miss Glenn, have had to set their own activity targets and strive for them against the weight of public opinion. They and the many like them deserve more encouragement than usually comes their way.

Chapter 8: Sexuality

No, my mother didn't warn me about menstruation. Mother was extremely reticent — not a sound from Mother! I never remember, never, in all my life — even when I was a married woman — I never remember Mother mentioning any — saying one word about anything intimate, certainly not about anything to do with sex, never! And now they teach all about abortion and incest and all that! When we were growing up, our — outings — they were only very — conducted sort of things. But then I went away teaching, away up north — my uncle gave me a revolver before I left, it seemed — the wilds, you know. While I was up there some old chap, a farmer, he took a shine to me, but — I was what the old lady I boarded with called a "proper"!

My mother used to say, if you have a baby to a man, that's the gutter for you! So every man was putting me in the gutter potentially, or my fingers would drop off with — leprosy, gonorrhea. Fear is a great saver and I think there should be a bit more of it these days, but not to the extent — Fear was my guideline. But then I met my first husband, and my life was a bed of roses and excitement. He was a Dr Jekyll and Mr Hyde. He'd go up to the altar to preach, but let the little choir-girl go up to him and she'd be pregnant, women chased him like mad. He only went for the Simple Simons, he never had the sophisticated woman that I grew into — and believe me, I had good reason to be sophisticated. He was very handsome, a beautiful body — not that I noticed bodies — oh yes, I did! I parted from him after — it was a woman who worked for him. I'd forgiven him twice and — oh, it was an awful shock. So I broke into his office and tore up his records and everything I could find that — We parted forever then. I married again, but I'm a loner now. I've had so many romances in my life — and big breakups, the first husband and the second. Some really lovely romance that I probably wasn't entitled to.

In the Toowong survey sex-related questions concerned the age of menarche, birth control, childbirth experiences, and the menopause, and more general attitudes were explored by probes on opinions about permissiveness and life-styles among the young. Explicit questioning about sexual capacities in old age was not attempted.

Most of the old people were more forthright in answering these questions than had been anticipated. To be sure, the question about menarche, which was usually the first to crop up, sometimes drew a startled, "What a question! You don't think I'm going to talk about things like that, do you?"

Some answered the question in a scarcely audible whisper. A few made it plain that they regarded this area of human experience as offensive and muttered something about "sordid details". But most old people took the question in their stride.

Menstruation

The age of menarche was of theoretical importance because a decrease amounting to four-and-a-half months a decade is widely reported to have taken place during the twentieth century (Brundtland and Walloe, 1976:363). Means for different social strata show a two-year difference between upper and lower strata. In Oslo in the year 1910, for example, it was 16 for lower- and 14 for upper-status girls, usually explained as due to better nutrition. This is also the preferred explanation for the trend towards a general decrease in all socio-economic groups.

One hundred and nine female respondents were asked if they remembered the age at which their menstrual periods had started; for the remainder, the interview situation in some way precluded the question. When asked, 13 per cent could not remember or preferred not to answer the question, leaving 95 women who were prepared to give retrospective reports of the event. Admittedly, such data must be of a very tentative nature; yet the accounts they gave were often surprisingly detailed. Mrs Hobbs, for instance, was 95, and she remembered her first period distinctly, though it was 84 years since its occurrence:

> It came on at school when I was eleven! I had a dreadful time — embarrassing! Came on at school and there were lessons and we were sitting there in our places, and then we were to go out on to the verandah for another lesson, and after we got out there the teacher came out and said, "Who was sitting on a certain seat there?" And I said I was, and then she saw everything and I was so embarrassed — but she was very kind and gave me something to wear and all the rest of it. And then I went home that afternoon, and I didn't tell my mother, but I went and had a bath. But the next day I came out with spots all over the chest, and she was very nervous because at that time there was an outbreak of Hansen's disease, leprosy, and it seems that they came out in spots. She didn't want to tell the doctor in case they — But she got the doctor in and the doctor said it was just through having a bath at the wrong time.

An analysis of age at menarche by socio-economic status revealed status differentials that were, on the whole, consistent with the literature, though it was the middle rather than the upper stratum that best demonstrated the trend towards earlier menarche. Some aspects of upper-status lifestyles, such as encouragement of bird-like appetites and the wearing of tight corsets, may have tended to suppress menstruation.

Mrs Hobbs was coded as middle socio-economic status. She was the daughter of a Dublin merchant, and had been married first to the manager of a cane farm who died of typhoid fever on their honeymoon. Her second husband was "in the Main Roads", and she had been married to him for 43 years. When he went blind as a result of war injuries, she worked for a time as a librarian, though she had no specific qualifications for the job. At the time of interview she lived with her unmarried daughter. At 95 she was described as "straightforward and intelligent, neatly dressed with pearls, white hair in bun". She herself attributed her early menarche to being "a fat little thing, not tall, a dumpy, but very well advanced in growth".

Mrs Hobbs early menarche was atypical, however, in that she was one of the older cohorts, for further analysis revealed a slight but apparent cohort effect: 37 per cent of younger compared with 29 per cent of older cohorts reached menarche at 11–12 years. Norwegian re-evaluation of historical sources asserts that "the age of menarche . . . was essentially unchanged during the last century, but had a marked and dramatic fall after the turn of the century" (Brundtland and Walloe, 1976:363). The eight-year different between the average age of the two Toowong cohorts was apparently sufficient to reveal a similar fall in this Anglo-Saxon population. It is of interest that retrospective data requiring recall of the dating of a personal event, which would seem to be particularly subject to the dangers of imprecision, is nevertheless consistent with the literature regarding menarcheal trends. One old lady recalled the actual date — "The day we left England, 21st January 1911!"

Mrs Hobbs was not the only one to mention the restrictions commonly imposed during menstruation. Bans on bathing (upheld by the medical profession) and similar folklore seemed, in fact, to be the main thrust of sex instruction for girls. Thirty-one per cent said that their mothers had given them some nominal instruction, usually after menstruation had occurred. Mrs Green was one:

> We were down at Wynnum for the holidays. I was sleeping in the bedroom with my mother, and one morning I woke up and — (PAUSE) She said, get back into bed for a little while, I want to have a little talk with you. Then she told me. Oh, I wasn't going to have that at all, that was no good for me! Because I was a bit of a tomboy I'm afraid, I used to play cricket and football with the boys, and go swimming, and out rowing in the boats and one thing and another, and she said to me, "You won't be able to go swimming or out in the boat or anything" — and I was in a terrible state about it! (LAUGHS) I felt terrible about it. I felt awful about it for a long while.

Forty per cent were quite sure that they had received no warning at all, and several admitted to having been "frightened to death". One had hidden her soiled clothes and sobbed herself to sleep, convinced she had some fatal disease but unable to bring herself to mention it to her mother. Other girls, including elder sisters, were sometimes a source of information, but often of a very limited kind. When Mrs Renshaw was 13 her sister told her that before long she would lose some blood and would have to wear a napkin, then walked away, refusing to talk about it any more.

Respondents were also asked if menstruation had caused them pain or other difficulties. About 29 per cent remembered difficulties, and forthright Mrs Amies was one of them:

> I was sick every month, sick as hell. There was five girls worked in this store with me, and I was the only poor cow who had to go home. Every month — Oh, I thought it was awful! I'd come home and Mum gave me brandy and hot plates on my tummy. I used to pray I wouldn't have girls when I was married. I only had the one girl, and as it turned out, she was lucky, and her daughter too, they're all right. How do you get on?

Menstruation is no longer spoken of as "the curse", and Mrs Amies' daughter and granddaughter may have benefited physically from its re-definition as a minor inconvenience that requires little or no interruption of normal activities. Similar changes in attitudes to childbirth and menopause have occurred during the lifetime of respondents. Problems at menopause were reported less often than with menstruation; 71 per cent declared that it had caused them no trouble at all. Mrs Amies, who had had trouble with her periods, said she "went through change of life just like it was a monthly, not as bad as I expected really". Mrs Bird represents the very small minority who reported difficulties:

> For about the first three years it really was very trying. It changes your attitude. You get irritable, and — these hot flushes, they — You get very impatient, that sort of thing. A very difficult time, it really was.

In a study first reported in 1963 Neugarten et al. found that attitudes to menopause were more positive among those who had already experienced it than among pre-menopausal women. This suggests that its ill-effects have been exaggerated in the folklore, a possibility that is reinforced by Neugarten's findings that fears about menopause are less prevalent among women of higher education (1968:195–200). For Toowong respondents, the menopause was 30 to 40 years behind them, and the passing of years may have diluted memories of its discomforts. Negative expectations of the menopause are still built into social norms, and for women of the respondents' generation must have included potent self-fulfilling prophecies of biologically determined illness and depression. Yet there seems little reason to doubt that for most it was of minor consequence.

Given the reticence that prevailed during their early years, the candour on these subjects displayed by most respondents indicates their flexibility. Many were critical of the secrecy surrounding sex that they had experienced in their youth. Indeed, they and their contemporaries must have contributed in no small measure to the change in societal norms that took place during their lifetime. Among those changes was the increasing acceptance of birth control.

Birth control

At 85 Mrs Ridley was still a strikingly good-looking woman. She was tall, with large grey eyes and a firmly moulded face framed by naturally wavy hair, but she seemed rather frail, and said she had a lot of trouble with her legs. She did not elaborate as to the cause. The daughter of a Catholic undertaker, she described her childhood in a provincial town in vivid detail, and was very frank about her lack of preparation for married life: "Instead of telling kids where babies come from, we sort of learnt as we went along." She laughed. "You're stuck with it on your honeymoon; you don't know whether he puts it in your eye or your ear!"

She was one of several who believed until her own child was born that babies emerged from the navel. Learning about sex "as we went along" could lead to some ludicrous situations. One respondent recalled her mother whispering to her as she went off on her honeymoon: "You know, dear, when something stops — something begins!"

Nevertheless the emancipation of women from this sort of ignorance was already underway, and like other features of feminine liberation, received its greatest impetus from the introduction of increasingly reliable methods of birth control.

By the beginning of the century, when a few respondents (the oldest) were already married or considering marriage, a number of contraceptives were obtainable in Australia and were advertised in the press. In 1904 a Royal Commission was appointed in New South Wales to inquire into the falling birthrate, and evidence deplored the situation "when the wife defiles the marriage bed with the devices and equipment of the brothel, and interferes with nature's mandate by coldblooded preventatives and safeguards; when she consults her almanac, and refuses to admit the approaches of her husband at certain times" (quoted in Ruzicka and Caldwell, 1977:25). The "devices and equipment of the brothel" included quinine tablets, spring pessaries, sponges, spray douches, syringes, and condoms. Chemical abortifacients were also advertised. By the 1920s, when most of the respondents were settled into marriage, moral indignation was declining under the pioneering efforts of people like Marie Stopes, Margaret Sanger, and Norman Haire, and the Dutch cap and the Grafenburg ring had become available. Nevertheless, Mrs Ridley (who had only one child) probably represents the majority in the method of birth control adopted: "Oh yes", she said, "I wanted more children. But Daddy was the engineer!" She laughed. "He adored our boy, but he didn't want any more, so he played safe. I suppose I went along with it because I was very social, I liked going out. No, he didn't use contraceptives." Again she laughed. "He took the ticket half-way!"

There seemed to be some confusion about the meaning of the term "birth control". Mr Kent said: "No, we didn't use birth control. Except of course — I think we got some sperm-killer or something like that, otherwise we'd have had a big family we couldn't keep."

Mrs Claymore was 87 at the time of interview, bent-shouldered but with sharp blue eyes and a lively tongue. Like

Mrs Ridley, she said it was her husband's decision that they have only one child:

> He was down under the house when I was having the baby. Oh, the trouble I had! He could hear me. Going through that, he said, that was enough for him. No more, my hubby said, he said no more. How we prevented it? (LAUGHS) Oh well, we don't do it. And of course there was French letters. . . .

Although contraception remained officially discouraged by pro-natalist policies throughout the reproductive lifetime of respondents, the limitation of family size became very widely accepted as a personally and socially desirable aim. Withdrawal, the condom, abstinence — these were probably the three most usual means for achieving it, but knowledge of them was still unevenly disseminated, even in the higher social stratum. Mrs Burton, the widow of a university lecturer, was one of three women who admitted to having been pregnant at the time of marriage:

> And for the second one — we stayed apart. We had no idea of planning then, didn't know how to. We stayed apart for a time, I said I cannot have another baby until this one — I didn't know much about babies, poor child. There was 19 months between the first two, and after that — well, we'd learnt to plan by then!

The importance of celibacy within marriage as a means of birth control in the respondents' generation should not be under-rated. Quite a number hinted at it as a way of life and did not seem unduly distressed by it, though apparently for Mr Thurlby it rankled sufficiently for him to discuss it at some length during his interview. By then he was 90, and his wife had predeceased him. He spoke of her difficult confinement at the birth of their only child:

> And there's a reason why there's only one. Careless doctor. He was young and — I suppose it was a little difficult and he started cutting her about in such a way that she was never interested in sex any more after that. So there was only the one child. I think that doctor — I've got an exceptional history, I think. Not all been good. I had a very good wife and — we were very happy, she was a good businesswoman too. But I never could understand why my

wife chose a certain doctor, she had a choice of two or three and he
— Even the sister that was running the private hospital, she said to
me afterwards, Oh, she was so sorry the doctor made such a mess
of your poor wife. He sent for her when he realized my wife was in
trouble, with his — messing about, and making mistakes. You
couldn't blame her for being — She wasn't interested in sex at all
after that.

Mr Thurlby had been an insurance salesman, and absorbed in
the difficult business of achieving a good living in hard times.
From all the evidence he appeared to have remained devoted to
his wife; he was also a devout Christian, giving much of his
limited spare time to service to the church. It is, of course,
impossible to guess how firm Mr Thurlby remained in his
celibacy, but in his long interview he certainly gave the impression that he had accepted this as a cross he had to bear. Societal
emphasis on the right to sexual fulfilment was not nearly so
strong in those days.

On the other hand several respondents, in commenting on
the permissiveness of modern society, remarked that in their
own time pre-marital and extra-marital sexual relations had
been more prevalent than was generally admitted: "It was more
under cover, that's all", Mrs Pyson said. "The same sort of thing
went on, I know it did. But it was just — whisper, whisper, you
know, not out in the open like it is today. I think it's better out
in the open."

Mrs Nally, who was mentally confused and in a nursing
home, may have been one example of suppressed sexuality
manifesting itself in old age. She denied that she was 90, as her
records said: "Oh, I'm not! Sister made a mistake. Eighty I am,
I've just turned — People get things wrong, you shouldn't
believe everything you hear. I'm — just on 20. That's it. I've
just turned 20."

She went back to the past and re-lived a very strict upbringing:

I'm a good girl. I stay home and help my mother. I don't go out,
I'm not allowed to. Just down to the gate — Some cheeky thing
said, what does he poke into your inside, how does he — Does he
lie alongside and poke into you then? The cheeky thing! Some of
them around our way, I take no notice of them. You've got to do as

you're told and you must watch yourself, some fellows, the way they hang about you — One night — It was about a fortnight ago, I wanted to go down and post a letter, and there was a fellow outside of our gate and he was crouched right down, and he tried to grab hold of me, the dirty creature he was. I wouldn't like those fellows hanging around me like that. . . ."

Mr Kent was 92 and in full possession of his faculties. He was like Mr Thurlby in one respect — he had been a salesman. But in other ways the two were quite unlike:

I had a good wife and I recognized I had a good wife — she was a better wife than I was a husband. I wasn't always true to her, which I regret now. I do recommend to any young fellow, stick at home, never mind about playing about outside.

Beautiful, vivacious Mrs Ridley gave a guarded hint of infidelity in her own past:

Yes, I suppose it is a permissive society today, it's — well, it's up to them. I suppose, though, it's always been — I mean, if you go about — flirting — It's so easy to love. There might be someone — better — and you're attracted and you see him and have a flirt and — it always ends in disaster. Unless you're strong enough to know who you're hurting — you're hurting the man's wife or vice versa, and it's up to you to control yourself and avoid it. But it all depends on — And it's so easy to love. It's easy to love.

Mrs Ridley herself seems to have been easy to love. In her old age she had several close friends, and her sons and his family showered attentions upon her. Prickly Mrs Claymore, on the other hand, asserted her independence by criticizing all and sundry, and appeared to delight in quarrelling with her son and recounting the details to any who would listen. Most female respondents, however, had managed to build enduring affectionate relationships with both male and female family members, and for those who were still married, a deep mutual affection seemed to be the norm.

Whether that affection involved "sexuality" was never explicitly explored.

Sexual ageism

Today sex is commonly regarded as a sort of athletic performance, and people who are unable to match the performance
of a hypothetical 18-year-old are apt to feel much the way as
their grandfathers did if those grandfathers were unable to lift a
bag of wheat. Women, too, have come to accept that failure to
achieve an orgasm, or better still, multiple orgasms, is to be
something less than a woman. But that was not the way
Toowong respondents saw it. For most of them, to "fail",
sexually, was to fail, like Mr Kent, to keep one's sexuality
under control.

I have a videotape of an interview with a nonagenarian actress
(not in the Toowong survey) which I sometimes show to
students as proof of the potentialities of extreme old age.
Students are invariably impressed with her intelligence, her
humour, her warmth, her compassionate wisdom. They nod in
approval of her high regard for today's young people and the
new openness towards sex. But when she mentions, in passing,
that she does not regard herself as having being over-sexed,
there is apt to be some uncomfortable giggling. They are disappointed in her. Her personal non-commitment to the goal of
multiple orgasms is seen in terms of failure.

But she, like the Toowong respondents, was a person of her
generation. She led a full and busy life. Widowed by the
Second World War, she devoted her energies to her art, just as
most of the Toowong respondents had to devote their energies
to the serious business of earning a living. The idea of sex as a
performance, a test, a primary index of manhood or
womanhood, was not nearly as prevalent then as it is now.

In keeping with the times, there has recently been a surge of
interest in sexuality among the aged. Wharton's book *Sexuality
and aging* (1981) reports a computer search revealing 1106
research findings. Masturbation is commonly recommended for
elderly widows; polygamy for elderly men; and oral and
manual stimulation for everybody. These are liberating ideas
for younger generations as they grow old: by the twenty-first
century elderly couples may routinely make use of

Sexuality is an historically relative concept.

technological aids such as vibrators, and a widow might continue its use in tender commemoration of the past. But for the
Toowong respondents and their contemporaries any insistence
that such practices are preferable to their own is a manifestation
of sexual ageism. What you are doing (*if* you are doing
anything), it is implied, is not good enough. You must be
sexually active *in modern terms*.

An Australian article by Hall, Selby and Vanclay (1982)
defines sexual ageism as "social expectations that the aged do
not have and should not have sexual relationships" (1982:29).
But the essence of sexual ageism is more subtle than this. It lies
in the definition of what constitutes sexual relationships.

Elderly couples in the Toowong survey frequently shared the same bed, but they were not asked what they did there — and the question is irrelevant. It was quite obvious that many maintained a physical intimacy they shared with no other human being, but I regard it as unlikely that it included sexual intercourse in the sense appropriate to that hypothetical 18-year-old and his hypothetical partner. In any case, the majority, especially among women, lacked a partner. Though several of the elderly widowers had no qualms about indicating (as did Mr Leslie, who at 93 was still married) that they had retained an interest in "the pretty girls", for the women of the sample a corresponding sentiment would have been considered — by themselves — as inconceivable. The reluctance of widowed or never-married elderly women to admit to sexual interests may be due less to sexual ageism than to their early socialization.

Labouvie-Vief and Blanchard-Fields (1982) have cautioned us against accepting youthful thought-patterns as the standard against which all others must be judged. The same caution should be exercised in accepting youthful sex as a universal standard. There is a case for arguing that the relationship between that hypothetical 18-year-old and his hypothetical partner is deficient, sexually, compared to that between partners who have lived 50, 60, 70 years of their lives together. And for the partnerless of either sex, the values of a lifetime had accustomed them to under-emphasizing overt sexuality.

Sexuality is an historically relative concept, and multi-dimensional. It should not be prejudged solely in modern terms.

Chapter 9: Marriage

I met my husband at a dance. He took a girl to the dance and he fell for me. I didn't get married till I was 32. I always regretted I didn't get married before, but — we had a wonderful life, my husband and I. Well, financially — it was never flourishing, like — I mean — But we got through, we got our own home and everything. He was a window-dresser. I wouldn't say there was any head of the family, not with us two. As my son said when his father died, Mum and Dad never had a row. He died 14 years ago. Oh yes, he helped in the house; he'd do anything. He'd wait on you hand and foot, he'd spoil you if he had the chance. Only I don't like being spoiled. I think the happiest time of all was when we had our baby. But my marriage was very happy. There was a woman up the road and she used to come down to me with her tales of woe, and she said to me quite disgustedly, you never have a row! My husband had to retire because of ill-health — he had heart trouble — so he was only on the invalid pension, but we got through. Oh, I never had a job after we were married — it would have been a disgrace in those days for me to have a job.

I met my husband at medical school. He used to always come top and I was one of the middle ones. He didn't approve of me at all — a female medical student! But he got over that, and I always used to be seeing him on the way home. I used to get very bad periods — as time went on I used to take a day off because I had such rotten pain, and the next day I would find all my notes written out for me — without a word — you didn't discuss those things, of course.

He'd just hand them to me. Well, we finished our exams the day peace was declared, and we went to England, and we went all over Europe, did the grand tour just after the war. I got my trousseau in Bond Street — all the linen and stuff, and a beautiful wedding dress, handmade. . . .

In the nineteenth century Australian women were considered to be particularly fortunate because more of them were able to achieve their "natural destiny", through marriage and motherhood, than their British counterparts. In Britain there was a marked surplus of women in the middle and upper classes, and up to a quarter were denied the possibility of marriage. In Australia, at least until the 1880s, there was a surplus of men. Marriage rates, however, are extremely responsive to economic conditions. When these worsened dramatically in the 1890s, marriage rates declined in tandem. There was a gradual improvement in the first decade of the new century, interrupted by the First World War, which came at a time when the majority of respondents were in their late teens or early twenties and would probably have been considering marriage. The war and its consequences may help to account for the high proportion of female respondents who had never married.

Though the great majority of respondents (86 per cent) had been married at some time in their lives, only 23 per cent were still married at the time of interview, and there were marked sex differentials. Of the females, 12 per cent were still living with a spouse, compared with 55 per cent of males; a finding consistent with international research. Women born at the end of the nineteenth century married men who were, on average, three years older than themselves (Krupinski and Stoller, 1974:9), and their five-year advantage in average life expectancy helped increase the possibility that they would outlive their husbands. One of the many ironies of old age is that men, for whom network-maintenance was not a typical lifelong endeavour, were more likely to be sustained in their final years within a network they owed chiefly to a wife. Wives, on the other hand, were apt to find the networks they had concentrated on building disrupted by the loss of key members.

Marital happiness

Monogamous marriage was almost universally accepted by respondents as the most normal of all lifestyles. Mr Aylwood, regretting that he had not been able to marry until fairly late in life, pointed out that: "In those days, if you couldn't keep a wife you didn't get married. So I had to save up and — Married life is much better than single life."

For most, a half-century of married life had not dimmed the conviction that love was the proper basis for marriage, and that love could endure. Linking the notion of romantic love to the ancient institution of marriage is a fairly recent development even in Western societies, but judging from the interviews, it was certainly the accepted mode of mate selection in the first two or three decades of this century. Respondents chose their own mates, and the fact that the field was often a narrow one seldom shook the prevailing conviction that their choice had been the right one: "My wife was my first girl friend", Mr Sommers said. "She was the only girl I ever had. We've been married 58 years this year." He paused, then added with a touching simplicity, "And she still — loves me."

Mr Sommers was one of the large majority (over three-quarters) who assured interviewers that their marriages had been very happy, and this overwhelming consensus of marital bliss is in line with most other studies. Andrews and Withey (1976) concede that "a note of scepticism" is warranted: presumably people feel a sense of family loyalty that discourages admissions of marital discord to an interviewer. In the Toowong survey this might have been enhanced by the fact that most respondents were widows or widowers, looking back on relationships whose unpleasant aspects had receded from memory.

Whatever reservations need to be made in accepting respondents' assessments at face value, the fact remains that in what were often quite frank and informal discussions, a very large proportion of the Toowong respondents remembered marriage as a high point in their lives. Scepticism becomes an impertinence in the face of obvious sincerity, sometimes con-

"My wife was my first girl friend, the only one I ever had."

veyed by no more than the tone of voice. Other checks, however, were available. Asked later in the survey to judge the happiest time in their lives, nearly a quarter spontaneously mentioned "the day I was married" or "all my married life", or some other unequivocal reference to their marriage.

Sometimes estimates of the happiness of the marriage varied between partners. Ninety-three-old Mr Leslie was interviewed while his wife was "gallivanting around with her sister", as he put it. He summed up their relationship by saying enthusiastically, "We got on pretty well, always. We're still getting on pretty well!" When his wife was interviewed he himself was doing his share of "gallivanting"; he was the one who liked taking bus trips and walking around to see "the pretty girls". Mrs Leslie was much less definite about the satisfactory nature of their relationship, but she seemed to blame herself for its deficiencies and to locate them mostly in the past:

> I'd say that we had to go through a lot of — you know — I'd say I had to mature a lot. I was — I don't know whether you'd say it was a happy marriage, exactly. It ended up I — Well, perhaps you might say average, it could have been worse. But at least with respect for each other, put it like that.

Twice-married Mrs Flower was another one among the 15 per cent whose marriages were coded as "average":

> Well, the first time — I wouldn't say exactly happy, but — well, reasonable. After all, you're not romantically — Well, he was in bed that long, you know, and before that he was ill a lot, and you can't be forever in love all that time, right up to the end. I think I was happier the second time I was married, but just the same — well — Only spots of happiness, really. Here and there.

Forthright Mrs Gant was one of the four per cent who candidly admitted to an unhappy marriage. She said that she enjoyed having her bed to herself, and she had never been happier than since she had been widowed. But she never contemplated divorce, and in this she was typical of Toowong respondents. Permanent separations other than by death had occurred in only four instances, and only one of these had been formalized by divorce.

Some of the still-existent marriages, happy or not, had endured for a very long time. Mr and Mrs Rostov were one of 2 couples who had been married 71 years, and several had been together for more than 60. Ten respondents had been married twice, and thrice-married Mr Earnshaw felt that he had been particularly fortunate: "My dear wife is sitting in there listening", he said, and called out to her: "Come on out here and smile at me!" Mrs Earnshaw replied that she would do so later, and he went on to explain that she was his third wife. "I had ten happy years with a good woman, then I had thirty happy years with a good woman, and now this is the eleventh year, I think it is, with another good woman. I've been very, very fortunate."

And in most of the transcripts it was contentment that came through, sometimes less by specific comments than by the overall picture the reminiscences conveyed.

For some of the old couples still living together, the depth of their commitment was revealed by its selflessness. Mrs Sommers, looking lovingly at her husband, said that they had succeeded in always avoiding their first quarrel; and Mr Sommers, crippled and ill and obviously dependent on her for any happiness that was left to him in life, declared that he was not in the least worried about dying — except for one thing. "That is, as long as — as long as — May goes first. She'd be — lonely —."

Mr and Mrs Fredericks were both in good health. They were still grieving for their only son, who had died of cancer three years before. He had not married, so they had no grandchildren, but they had many friends in all age-groups. The interviewer reported that a two-year-old child wandered in from next door and began to play with saucepans, then climbed onto their laps with complete assurance before pattering off again. In spite of their loss, they lived comfortable and busy lives and looked much younger than their years. Mrs Fredericks spoke for both of them when she said: "Sooner or later there's going to be just one of us, and — Well, I hope it will be me that's left, and Tom hopes it'll be him. We wouldn't — I wouldn't like to think of him being alone. Really it'd be nice if we could just — go together, but of course that's —."

She shrugged her shoulders, sighed, then changed the subject

to more cheerful things. The interviewer described the two of
them as "a real Darby and Joan". They were much the same
age, and appeared to have built a partnership of trusting and
affectionate equality.

Authority patterns

In most cultures the convention that husbands be older than
their wives reinforces husband dominance, and this was certainly so for respondents in their families of origin. But respondents
did not simply replicate, in their own marriages, the authority
patterns they had accepted as natural for their parents. Instead,
they responded to changing historical circumstances by
building their own relationships on more egalitarian grounds.

During the nineteenth century there were changes in the institution of marriage, including legal reforms such as the right
of married women to the custody of children, and to the
ownership and acquisition of property. At the same time
technological advances such as electric irons and vacuum
cleaners reduced the drudgery of household tasks, and wartime
scarcities simplified styles of dress — washing-baskets were no
longer piled high with starched petticoats. The dispersion of
women through wider sections of the workforce enhanced the
possibility of a more equal partnership between husband and
wife; ideally, if not in practice, marriage was beginning to be
seen as such a partnership.

As with the family of origin, an attempt was made in the
survey to gauge authority patterns by asking respondents to
state who was "head of the house", and the answers reveal a
marked shift away from husband dominance in the direction of
egalitarianism. For both their parents and for the respondents
themselves, husband-dominance was reported most often in the
upper stratum, but the 66 per cent of these who mentioned their father as head had decreased to 39 per cent who
claimed this for their own marriages; and for the sample as a
whole only 29 per cent reported dominance by the male. Males
were more likely than females to claim egalitarianism (which

suggests a difference in its definition), but older and younger respondents thought much the same about the issue.

In their own marriages, the sharing of authority was said to be the norm by more than half the sample (57 per cent). Mrs Mackie, who in her eightieth year seemed rather tired and unsmiling, was one of that majority: "I'd say we were both head of the house. What I said he said, and what he did I did — all in together."

Mr Aylwood was also living alone; he had been a widower for 12 years. He laughed when he was asked who had been head of the house. "You mean was I the boss? Well, no! But then, she wasn't either. I suppose we were an exception, because if we had an argument we always made sure it was closed before we went to bed that night."

Mr Sommers had recently had a stroke and could not marshall his thoughts sufficiently to make a judgment on the matter. But his wife declared that he had been head: ". . . up till now. That's the way it ought to be, I think. But now I have to make all the decisions."

She sighed as she said it, but at 83 she was a bright and dynamic woman for whom some degree of event-confrontation and decision-making seemed to have been a lifelong pattern. Mr Sommers was only a year older, but his illness had shrunken his big frame and made one arm and leg almost useless. They were a devoted couple. They were interviewed at the same time but by two different interviewers at opposite ends of the room, and their eyes sought each other's constantly for mutual help and reinforcement.

Mrs Gant's case was very different. She was 92 and living alone, having been widowed for over 20 years. She made the most of her few inches by standing almost aggressively upright, and when asked who had been head of their household her answer came sharply: "Well, he'd have said *he* was!" she snapped.

> He was like that. Domineering. I remember one time I wanted to go south, I wanted to go down to Sydney, and he objected. But this house belonged to my mother then, and she said to me, this is my house and I'm your mother, so you go. She said, I'll look after the children. And the way he went on! But I went, you know. Some

women won't take it. You can't do this and you can't do that — It's a great thing to be able to do as you like. I appreciate every moment of it.

Mr Cole, aged 81, found the question amusing, as many men did. He called out to his wife in the kitchen, and she dutifully answered that it was he who was head, to which he agreed; but it was a jocular exchange. Ninety-four-year-old Mr Rostov was a little puzzled by the question, though not because of any lack of mental alertness. He had come to Australia from Russia in 1911, but still spoke English with a slight accent. After a little discussion he said it was something he had never thought about. His wife, who was 92, was losing her memory, but she still made her own decisions, among them a firm refusal to be interviewed in spite of her husband's attempts to persuade her.

It's a pity, she is the thinker, she writes books. She has books there in a trunk. No, not yet published, not ever now, I suppose, because now — But she wrote a book about Russia once, it was published. And writing in papers. But now she forgets sometimes even our Russian words and so forth. It's terrible — and I can't help her. But still she could tell you some things more than I can.

Mrs Flower spoke for the 14 per cent who saw the wife as the dominant partner:

My first husband was sick such a lot, I was the one who had to — He left it all to me. And then when I married again — My second husband was a commercial traveller and he was away a lot of the time. So actually I — I was always the one who made the decisions.

The division of labour also provided clues to authority patterns. Thirty-seven per cent of respondents said the husband helped with household tasks, but these were generally of a kind regarded as suitably masculine — chopping wood, mowing lawns, attending to repairs. Some, however, were more diversified. Mrs Mackie's husband could "do the washing, wash floors, anything" if she was sick or otherwise needed help.

Mrs Flower laughed at an old memory concerning her first husband: "You know what he'd do when I was going to clean up? He'd go and sit on the toilet for half an hour!"

Some who could afford it arranged for paid help, and Mrs Sommers was among these; she had had "a girl to come and help with the children". Only 2 per cent of the men, compared with 21 per cent of the women, remembered having employed paid help in the house at some time. This seems to support the contention that domestic activities are systematically devalued as unworthy of masculine attention. In later life, however, some men had had to acquire the domestic skills they had not learned earlier in life, and this was usually less because of widowhood than the necessity for looking after an invalid wife.

Mr and Mrs Jefferson were in this category. Both in their early eighties, Mrs Jefferson was totally blind and declined an interview. At first her husband did likewise. He stood at the doorway in singlet and shorts, twirling a handkerchief round his finger and saying he was too busy to talk, while Mrs Jefferson sat in the lounge-room listening to the radio. Eventually the interviewer was invited to sit on a verandah chair while Mr Jefferson explained his many duties, then went on to answer other questions at some length.

He had been a tram-driver until his retirement 16 years previously, and his wife was already losing her eyesight, so he had had to take over all the housework as well as the gardening. The interviewer noted that both were a credit to him. They had four sons and four grandsons and saw them frequently, but nobody helped him with the house or the lawn or anything else. He dismissed the idea of applying for community services. "I'm used to it", he said. "As long as you're together, you're all right. Mother and I are all right. We've got one another."

Forlorn old Mr Donat might have echoed such a sentiment. His wife had died only recently; once or twice during the interview he broke down and wept. She had been bedridden for nearly seven years before she died.

> . . . and I did all the nursing myself. Bathing her, feeding her — I did get the Blue Nurses in for a start, but after they left she'd say, "Would you mind giving me a decent wash — they never touched my underbody." And you'd have to prepare the room and tidy up after them, and you'd never know what time they'd come. And when they did come, all they did was a slum job! They told me once I ought to put Gwen in a home, and that's when I — Get

outside! I said. If you ever dare come inside again I'll have you arrested for trespassing! A home indeed! They're not *homes*. Oh, they're bathed and they're given something to eat, but the life is so — traumatic — People go senile in there! My wife wasn't the slightest bit senile, because I kept her at home. Talked to her, and — When my wife had her final illness, even the night she collapsed, I had wheeled her through to watch a show she liked on television. I used to try and get her up for an hour to stop static pneumonia, you see, from lying down all day. And she didn't sleep. Sleeping tablets, yes, but — I didn't sleep, either. For the last seven years I'd say I haven't had two hours' unbroken sleep.

Obviously network-maintenance and domestic skills were not confined solely to females, though that was the usual pattern. And Mr Donat was paying the price of his devotion by the very fact that he had outlived its focus. He confessed, weeping, to being "dreadfully lonely — I haven't got a soul in the world!" They had had no children and in their 53 years of married life appeared to have made few friends. Before retirement Mr Donat had managed a chain of grocery stores, but it was all too long ago for any contacts to remain. At 80 he said he was "nervy", but otherwise "too healthy by half" — the years that stretched ahead looked unrelievedly empty in a world where, he said, the attitude was, "I'm all right, bugger you!"

Singlehood

Eighty-eight per cent of the females and forty-five per cent of the males were "single" at the time of interview, either because they had never married or (in the majority of cases) because a spouse had predeceased them. The proportions are similar to those found in cross-national studies.

The impact of widowhood and other bereavement, and its ubiquity in old age, is a major threat not only to the happiness but also to the health of the old. Brown points out that studies of medical and census records have resulted in "good evidence that bereavement leads to increased risk of physical and psychiatric illness" (1976:308), and mortality due to coronary thrombosis and arteriosclerotic heart disease is particularly prevalent among widowers (Parkes, Benjamin and Fitzgerald, 1969). Bereavement is a life-event less amenable to control by event-confrontation than those in the work situation more typically faced by men, who appear to be particularly vulnerable to disruptions of a network they have not been trained to repair. A certain degree of anticipatory socialization may make widowhood slightly less traumatic for females than for males, but for both sexes, bereavement of any kind poses a crisis that may be of a life-threatening or sanity-threatening order.

After more than 20 years of widowhood, Mrs Mackie still found her loss difficult to accept. For many years, she said, she had "kept in touch with him through a very good medium — Effie was wonderful!" It had helped her, but Effie herself had been dead some years, and Mrs Mackie had been depressed by a lack of results with other mediums. Now she was no longer sure even whether she believed in life after death. "I don't go into it much any more", she said. "I haven't even been to church, not for months, I'm sorry to say. But I — don't go, that's all."

Mrs Mackie's depression may have been due less to a long-ago bereavement than to some as yet unrecognized disease-process. The linkage between disease and depression is well recognized but complex, and there can be no certainty as to which is cause and which is effect.

Lowenthal and Haven (1968) found that the impact of widowhood is reduced by having a confidant, and this is more usual among women. There was some evidence in the Toowong interviews of long-lasting friendships among women. Mrs Flower was "great friends — like a sister really" with the woman in the flat next door; they were "in and out of each other's places" every day of the week, in spite of the fact that there was nearly a 20-year difference in their ages. None of the men reported such a relationship.

According to the 1971 census, 10 per cent males compared with 6 per cent females had never married; but single males are less likely than single females to survive into extreme old age. This may help to explain the marked disparity between the sexes in the Toowong study among those who had never married: 3 per cent for men and 18 per cent for women. Many female respondents, but none of the males, seemed to consider that their single status required explanation. Some said frankly that they had not wanted to marry: "I didn't like children." The First World War had decided the matter for some; for others it was a matter of duty. But decisions to marry or not, usually made in youth, certainly determined lifestyle in old age in one important respect: the place where they were living.

An existing marriage is, not surprisingly, the best possible protection against institutionalization or having to live alone. As was to be expected, the never-married were over-represented among the institutionalized, but only slightly more so than the widowed. Similar differences were found by Shanas et al. in Britain and the United States, and they point out that these differences extend to other aspects of family status and structure. There is a marked inverse correlation between the number of close relatives and the likelihood of being committed to an institution:

> The basic reason why relatively more single than widowed persons are in institutions is that most of the latter have children; and the reason why more widowed than married persons are in institutions is that the former do not have a husband or wife to give them help and support at home. (1968:111–12)

However, the never-married in the Toowong sample (almost entirely female) were considerably less likely to live alone than the widowed. The fact that nearly 40 per cent of them were coded as living in a "family situation" points to the continuity of sibling bonds, or in one or two cases, the establishment of close bonds with other females unrelated by blood.

For most respondents, however, "singlehood" came only through the death of a lifelong partner — a crisis eased slightly by its long anticipation as the "natural" ending of marriage. In their marriages the women in particular had sought more companionship and equality than the preceding generation, while accepting sex-segregated spheres of influence as "natural" (i.e., biologically based). In doing so, they opened the way for their children, and more especially, their children's children, to expect a more realistic equality — at the cost, if necessary, of the permanence of marriage itself.

Chapter 10: Parenthood

I just had the one son, that was enough for me. I wasn't going through that again. I had him here, they didn't recommend — in those days there was just the Lady Bowen, they said it was a torture-house, so I had him here. When Hubby came back from the war, the people round here — they was all chums round here — they'd say, ah well, there'll be another one in about 12 months time, but I said, no there won't. All the others had kids but I didn't, not any more. My son — he's 64 now, he thinks it's a bore when I talk about the old days, he says he don't want to hear about the past. Oh, my son and my daughter-in-law, don't talk about them — I live just to torment them, that's what I do! I had this bad turn the other week, I went over to them for two days, and I can tell you, I was glad to get home. They don't talk to you! Treat you like an outsider! So I've just made up my mind that I'm stopping here when Christmas comes, if they ask me to go over there I'm going to say no, thank you, I'd rather stop here. Grandchildren? Well, Joan, she's the best of the lot, she's a lovely kid, but she's studying art now over in London. But David — I could poke him up the nose. Oh yes, there's great-grandchildren, David's got two kids, Susan's got two — but I never see them, they never write to me. . .

I met my wife in Brisbane, when I left Sydney and come up here, in between the two wars. I was a fair age when I got married, mind you — I was 50 years of age when I got married. I'm 95 now. We had four children, very very nice — three boys, one is a major in the Army now, and one is a bank manager. I managed to educate

For many respondents, parenthood was the central experience of their lives.

my children well, and that's all I cared about. I never let my wife go to work — nowadays, nearly everybody leaves home, they're working when they're married, their children at home — I can't understand it. The happiest time of my life was with my family. We were very happy. Look, here's some of my grandchildren. Them three together — they're very nice, I like them very much. This one here — making her first communion — a nice little girl, I love her — I love all of them. . . .

For many respondents, parenthood was the central experience of their lives. On the whole it was taken for granted as an inevitable and desirable result of marriage, but they were part of a generation — perhaps the first generation ever — that regarded the number of children they had as a matter for rational choice.

Size of family

Respondents came from families in which 5.77 was the median issue, and produced an average of 2.49 children themselves. More than a quarter were childless, which seems a startlingly high proportion compared with the wider population, where it tends to fluctuate around five per cent (Day, 1975:18). Structural analyses found almost no difference for socio-economic status and cohort membership, but the proportion of childless females was almost three times that for males. Part of this marked difference in childlessness between the sexes is explained by the fact that 18 per cent of the females had never married, compared with only 3 per cent of the males. The question remains whether childlessness may have been a deliberate choice for some of the women who did marry.

None of the respondents, however, said that this was a matter of choice, and by most it was deeply regretted. Mrs Wales was one example:

The doctor I saw said that inside I was like a little girl of ten, the womb never grew. After I was married — I used to go and see my sister, she had her boys, and — Oh, I'd come home that upset! No, we never adopted any. I kept on — sort of — hoping —

None was more definite about the value of parenthood than Mrs Fowler, who as the mother of two children was very typical of her middle socio-economic stratum. In her eightieth year she was still tall despite a humping of her broad back. Her olive skin was mottled with age-spots, but her brown eyes were keen and her voice deep and firm. She had begun adult life as a nurse and was no stranger to the confrontation of events — she had managed her husband's business after his death a few years previously. But far more congenial to her were the feminine skills of network-maintenance. Her happiest days, she said, were when her children were small:

> They were never any trouble to me, my children! In fact, I was rather jealous when they had to go to school; I began to feel I'd been done out of something. I really can't understand how mothers find their children a worry. I enjoyed them thoroughly. And it was the same when they were teenagers. . . .

She went on to describe a home-centred family life in moderately affluent circumstances, and though she spoke fondly of her grandchildren, she thought they had been "just a bit spoiled, in a way — more drink, and that sort of thing". But they and their parents all lived in Brisbane and were "in and out all the time — I wouldn't like to be too far away from them". On the other hand, she was quite certain she would not want to live with any of them. She had her own interests and her own circle of friends, and was an exponent of the preference Rosenmayr (1972) has called "intimacy at a distance".

Mrs Myles was equally devoted to her children and the values of family life, but her circumstances were very different. At 90, she lived with two of her daughers — or rather, as she said with a laugh, "They live with me!" She had many more children than any other respondent — 8 girls and 4 boys, and all 12 had survived into adult life. But Mrs Myles' own health had been chequered by numerous operations and no less than six nervous breakdowns:

> I had a nervous breakdown when I had change of life, and I got over that with treatment, and then about 18 months later I took another breakdown, and I sat for 6 weeks; I couldn't move my arms, I couldn't do anything! The doctor said it was caused through pyorrhoea in my teeth, so I had to get them out. . . .

It is tempting to speculate that Mrs Myles' breakdown might have been due less to pyorrhoea than to an unconscious protest against overwork. The interviewer described her as "very cheerful and agile"; she was knitting for Lifeline throughout the interview, and had been out the night before ". . . just visiting — but we were up a bit late".

The daughter of a labourer with 10 children, she had not had much time for schooling before going to work as a laundress, but her intelligence and the range of her interests come through very clearly on the tape. At 18 she married a man who "jobbed about"; they had kerosine tins to sit on in lieu of furniture and she took in washing to help make ends meet at intervals throughout her married life. Before his death her husband had acquired a bus and begun a suburban service, and when he died suddenly Mrs Myles drove it herself until her eldest son was old enough to take over. Like Mrs Fowler, Mrs Myles was quite capable of resourceful confrontation with events; but again like Mrs Fowler, her inclinations were for the traditional feminine skills, both domestic and interpersonal:

> The children were lovely; they really were wonderful. I didn't have trouble with them at all. The boys never fought with one another, and I think that's a help to a mother. We never had enough money, and I used to — worry — I'm a great worrier, I am. But we had such good times, we really did! We had weddings at our place, and christenings, we had welcome-homes, we had send-offs — and birthday parties — Oh, it was lovely, it really was! Yes, I do own this place, but it's not where we lived most of — I've only been here five years, the kids got together and bought it for me. It's nice, isn't it!

She paused in her knitting to look with pride around the modest little room. If at times in her life work and worry had combined to overwhelm her, she had managed to survive her twelve confinements, four major operations, and six nervous breakdowns to become a particularly energetic and well-adjusted nonagenarian, firmly integrated within a close and affectionate family.

The same could be said of 89-year-old Mrs Rogers, who lived with her daughter and was almost blind, but whose thin old hands were never still as she knitted for the latest great-grandchild. "What I need is glasses for my hands!" she said with a laugh. "But I manage. I don't do complicated patterns now."

She had had five children, and her own mother had been her midwife for them all. "I've been living with my daughter Betty ever since her husband died", she said, pausing as her fingers counted the stitches on her needle. "But every Tuesday I spend here with Edna, and every Sunday my son comes and takes me over to have dinner at his place, and my other son — he lives in Campbelltown, near Sydney you know, and I go down there once a year to see him and his family, in the plane, you know." She chuckled at the thought. "I like planes! I have another daughter up north, I fly up there sometimes too. I've got quite used to moving about. You know", she said thoughtfully, "when we first came down here, Brisbane seemed just a little bit unfriendly, after the country town I'd always lived in before. But I know the neighbours now, and wherever you go, people are very nice. . . ."

Family contact

There has been a great deal of international research directed towards analyzing the contacts old people have with their children, including the type and frequency of contact, number of children contacted and proximity in living arrangements. The Toowong data were much less precise, but it was found that the great majority (81 per cent) of those who had living children were in frequent contact with at least one child, and a further 7 per cent managed to maintain intimate contacts in spite of geographical distance. However, no systematic effort was made to investigate the quality of the interaction reported, which as Dempsey (1980) and others point out, is an extremely important factor for the happiness of the old people concerned. Those who talked at length about their children usually conveyed an impression of family ties that were close although not always free of conflict. Those who were more reticent, perhaps saying hesitantly that their son or daughter called in "when they can

— not every week, exactly", seemed to indicate a degree of estrangement. But the grounds for these judgments are admittedly inadequate.

Family relationships in old age are likely to epitomize the strengths and weaknesses of network-maintenance achieved over a lifetime. As Townsend puts it:

> With increasing age old people tend to find themselves nearer one of two extremes — experiencing the seclusion of the spinster or widow who lacks children and other near relatives, or pushed towards the pinnacle of pyramidal family structure of four generations which may include several children and their spouses and 20 or 30 grandchildren and great-grandchildren. (1968:256).

The word "pinnacle", however, suggests a prominence and power that does not appropriately describe the structural position of even the most thoroughly integrated old people in today's world. Their age did not bestow on Mrs Rogers or Mrs Myles any hierarchical ascendancy; they seemed to be treated as beloved equals, and to accord others a similar affectionate respect. Mrs Fowler, living alone and with more resources at her command, may have had some influence in a wider sphere, but maintained links with her children and children's children in many ways as close as those of Mrs Myles, Mrs Rogers, and the others among the Toowong respondents whom they represent.

Eighty-nine per cent of Toowong respondents who had had children themselves also had grandchildren, and the extension of the family to a fourth generation — a twentieth-century phenomenon which in its frequency is unique in history — applied to well over half.

Mrs Fowler considered her great-grandchildren rather spoilt, and in this she was not alone. "They get too much too easily, that's the trouble", she said. "They break it the next minute. They don't appreciate things at all."

Similar criticisms were sometimes directed towards grandchildren too. But on the whole grandchildren were quite favourably regarded, and were usually exempted from criticisms often levelled at other members of their generation. Mr Dinsey, for instance, who had had a hip replacement and a stroke and was a more or less permanent resident at the general hospital, summed up the opinions of many respondents regarding the modern generation: "The modern generation are too lazy and too weak and they get their money too easily. They're not prepared to work, to strive." He paused, then went on to make another fairly typical remark: "My grandchildren aren't like that, though. They've done all right for themselves."

Grandchildren, and in particular great-grandchildren, offer a visible sign of continuity into the future, and provide the possibility of affectional links with younger generations. Such possibilities, however, had to be actualized by shared activities based on something more substantial than the thin thread of family obligation. A middle-aged daughter was commonly the instigator of these activities. But their perpetuation depended on the ability of the old person to maintain them, and that ability depended in turn on modes of relating to other people built up over a lifetime.

Mrs Blake, for instance, was not particularly interested in her descendants. Aged 84, she was in a nursing home, and was one of those whose disengagement from activity seemed to be due less to physical impairments than to lack of motivation. Asked about grandchildren, she shrugged her thin shoulders: "All they do is — Oh well, they call in occasionally, to show you the new baby and that. I forget their names, half the time."

For Mrs Parsons, on the other hand, the relationship was of a very different quality. The same age as Mrs Blake, she lived alone and was vigorous and articulate; her face lit up at the mention of great-grandchildren:

> My little great-grandchildren, they just think I'm Christmas! Old Ga-ga, they call me. They just think I'm marvellous — they hurl themselves with joy upon me! [She smiled]. All that sort of thing — You take the sweets that old age gives you.

But for some, parenthood had brought heartbreak in old age. Mrs Arkins had just been admitted to a nursing home because the son with whom she had been living, her only child, had had a sudden heart attack and died. Early in the interview she broke down, and for some time could not go on. To be left childless through death that seemed cruelly untimely was a bitter experience she shared with one or two other respondents, and becomes increasingly likely in the tenth decade of life.

At least 15 per cent of respondents referred to the death of offspring in childhood, maturity, or, in some cases, old age. Eighty-seven-year-old Mr Bertram said that he had had four children, two boys and two girls, but there was only one still alive, and he was living in Melbourne. Both his daughters had died of cancer, though Mr Bertram himself had survived an operation for cancer of the transverse colon no less than 54 years before. "They took it out of me and it healed up and everything went well", he said. "But I'm a bit handicapped now from losing my leg. It was thrombosis — went black. And then I had to have the prostate taken out of me. But I've got over the things that I've had, and I feel that God has been kind to me. I know I've got as thin as blazes, but otherwise my health is pretty good. Still. . . ." He paused, rubbing his chin thoughtfully.

> Since Mum died — And so many of my friends have passed on. I'm getting lower and lower, if you know what I mean. The people I used to know — Oh, I go out quite a bit, the Senior Citizens, and the Masonic, and the neighbours are good. And I spent Christmas in Melbourne, as a matter of fact, and my son's wife, she wanted me to — But this is my home. It's not that I'm lonely exactly, but — Well — [He gave a wry smile]. I don't mean this in any bad way or anything like that, but I wouldn't care if I died right now!

Only five per cent of those living in a family situation complained of loneliness, but surprisingly the highest scores for "never" feeling lonely were among those who lived alone — perhaps because it was a lifestyle that appealed to them or to which they had adjusted satisfactorily. At the same time, people living alone were more inclined than those in any other residential group to say they were lonely "sometimes". It was those who were in nursing homes or in hospital, surrounded by other people, who had the highest scores for feeling lonely "often". Townsend (1963) distinguishes isolation from desolation, and perhaps it is desolation that best describes the emotions people in nursing homes were trying to express when they replied to questions about loneliness.

Structural compensation

One adaptation to a reduced family circle that may occur in old age has been defined by Townsend (1968) as "structural compensation". By this he means the re-activation of sibling or other bonds to compensate for bereavements. This was evident in the Toowong sample among widows and among the never-married, and in a surprising number of cases, the re-activation was not with the siblings themselves but with the offspring of siblings.

Miss Sylvester was 82 and was interviewed at her niece's house, to which she went almost every day. She was the seventh in the family of ten, the daughter of a cemetery caretaker, and she and one brother had lived with their parents until both had died. After the brother's death some ten years before the interview, she took in university students as boarders. One of them was with her all through his undergraduate training in medicine, and when he left she "hadn't the heart" to find somebody to take his place. But she insisted that she enjoyed life:

> I like being the age I am! I've always been contented. Now Betty [her niece] she's inclined to worry. But I've got nothing to worry about! I keep busy, and I'm very well, and Betty — She's very good. Betty would always look after me if I did get sick.

She certainly looked well. The interviewer described her as: "Very neat and trim and attractive. Looks all of 65. Short thick grey hair. Nicely made up, good skin. Smart blouse and skirt. Friendly. Looks the active type — but a bit timid."

From her interview that timidity emerged as an undercurrent throughout her life. She had clung to her parents, her brother, her nice boarder, now her niece, keeping physically active in her house and garden but socially somewhat restricted. She had never gone out to work, and her one adventure had been a holiday in the north of Queensland with her bachelor brother. She had set a pattern of event-avoidance early in life and followed it through to her eighties.

Her niece, too, had never married, but had a job of some

kind in town. They went to church together every Sunday, and Miss Sylvester divided her time between her niece's and her own home in an adjoining street. "They both need painting", she said with a little sigh. But to the interviewer the niece's was immaculate, and it was difficult to imagine Miss Sylvester's own house being any less so.

The relationship she had established with her niece was a particularly close one. Other women who lacked children of their own had built links of only slightly less intensity with younger-generation relatives. Usually it was a niece; in one instance, just a friend; and in another, a nephew who came to mow the lawn and enjoyed a whisky and soda with his lively old widowed aunt. Many of them recognized the importance of such links as insurance against the almost universally dreaded fate of having to be admitted to a nursing home.

Male respondents, less skilled in network-maintenance and domesticity, had not availed themselves of such a strategy. Even when close ties had been maintained, as in Mr Denton's case, there was often pressure for acceptance of what the family perceived as a "safer" environment. From Mr Denton, aged 83 and afflicted with angina, the question about nursing homes brought a strong reaction. "Oh, don't talk of that subject!" he said, his hand instinctively reaching to calm his heart.

> That's the greatest trouble at the present time. My daughter feels that I should be in a home, not here, but I feel — This is my home, and while I've got my faculties, as you can see, I hope to stay here. But she's not very happy about it. She's a wonderful girl. She lives at Indooroopilly, and she shops for me and does quite a lot for me. And I get Meals on Wheels — and I always have spares, you know, in the house. On Saturday and Sunday I have to cook my own, but I reckon I cope very well indeed. I get home help once a fortnight. And if the old heart gets a bit — dicky — Well, these tablets, they do the trick, you know!

He slipped one under his tongue.

The myth of desertion

Part of the stereotype of old age is that modern families have deserted the old and thrust them, willy-nilly, into nursing homes, where they are neglected or forgotten. But Mr Denton's daughter — and others like her — can hardly be blamed for worrying about a parent who insisted on living alone in spite of infirmity and (in some cases) a degree of domestic incompetence. Though he did not say so, it is likely that Mr Denton's daughter could not have made room for him in her house without seriously disadvantaging other members of the family; and in any case, for Mr Denton as for many others, living in somebody else's house was an option even less attractive than the prospect of a nursing home. The notion that the old long to live with the young, and are prevented from doing so by the selfishness of the latter, is a myth as false, and almost as prevalent, as the nonsense that most of the extremely old are institutionalized. The facts are that in Australia, where institutionalization rates are higher than in most places, 82 per cent of people aged 80 and over are living, like anybody else, either in a family situation or alone. Living with children increases with age, especially among women, and in the Toowong sample nine per cent were in such a household.

Sociological theories of the family have been greatly influenced by the functionalist model. This postulates a mobile and relatively isolated nuclear family, consisting of two generations only, as having evolved in Western industrialized societies in response to the needs of industry and the emotional needs of family members (Parsons, 1954). Marvin Sussman challenged the model as early as 1959 on the basis of empirical evidence that a modified form of the extended family continued to exist and to maintain important caretaking functions for its members. Since then all research, Australian as well as international, has confirmed that industrialization has not seriously eroded the continuing importance of kinship throughout the lifespan of contemporary Westerners — although a multi-generational household is, and as Laslett (1976) has pointed out, probably always has been, rather rare.

These are uncomfortable facts for proponents of Kalish's "new ageism", (1979), who seek to advance the cause of the aged by stressing their disadvantages. But they are facts nonetheless.

This is not to say that family relationships in old age tend to be close and lacking in conflict. They vary — just as much as do family relationships between any two generations and in any period. But even when they are close, they are bedevilled by the stereotypes of ageism. In this view, "poor old" Mr Denton has no *right* to choose to go on living alone — it would be so much more comfortable for his daughter, who truly loves him, if he were safely in custody somewhere.

The right to make their own decisions — to be treated as adults rather than imbecile children — is a right which ageism can too easily tempt families to withdraw from the old.

Chapter 11: Politics

Yes, I'm interested in politics — in a general way. No, I've never changed my vote, not really. Mr Fraser's a decent living man, he's all right, and so's Mr Anthony, another country fellow — and Petersen too, all live decent clean lives, give them that. But they're all from the country, they've all been — Their parents started with nothing, they've worked hard, and as these boys grew up they'd be more farm-minded than — They'd be sent to boarding-school as the people had the money, and — Well, boys come from boarding-school still not politically minded or trained, and yet we've got three of those types — I vote Labor, as a matter of fact. When Whitlam was in, well, he was a lawyer, living in the city, he had a good brain, and his wife, she was well educated — They were well educated people and citified, with a full knowledge of what was going on. Now we have three — nothing wrong with the men personally, but their knowledge is not enough to manage Australia. As for land rights — well, I definitely say that before any whites came here the Aboriginals owned Australia, and they have every right to have their natural grounds whichever section they were living in. I think that no coalmine — and particularly outsiders, it's outsiders who are the ones that are doing the coalmining and digging up the sacred sites and — Comparing the brains of the one educated in the European style and the poor old nigger, the black, that's only been brought up on the land and grubbing for his food — he hasn't got a hope! I reckon it's wicked! And yet old Petersen seems to think it's quite okay!

Well, yes, I am interested in politics, I am now because I've got time to read about them. I'm consistently Country Party, you can't break me out of it. Though I'm disappointed in Fraser some ways. Fraser represents the city, I'm a countryman, but it all hinges on economics. If the city man's carrying our economics, I'll respect him, but the country man at the present time is carrying the economic burden. If it wasn't for him, we'd be living in poverty. We're all mixed up in politics, we've all got a part to play.

Lawson's *Brisbane in the Nineties* describes the city as one in which "the most extreme Labor party in the colonies emerged as a force and confronted the most conservative government" (1973:79). Lawson goes on to argue that such a picture exaggerates the "militancy, unity and level of class consciousness among the rank-and-file unionists" (1973:82), but there can be no doubt that Queensland was the scene of much political ferment at the time when most respondents were born.

In the first few sentences of her interview one old lady mentioned the emergence of the Labor Party:

I was born in Barcaldine, my father had a team of horses there. He used to camp under a tree in the main street, and that's where the Labor Party was born. There's a plaque there now. I knew the man who put it there. They put it there after the shearer's strike. . . .

All respondents had lived the greater part of their lives in a society where at least minimal participation in the political process is compulsory, for failure to vote has been punishable by a small fine since 1925. In Queensland women's suffrage was granted in 1905 — nine years later than in South Australia, but still well ahead of Britain and other parts of the world. However, universal franchise was not attained until 1967, when Aboriginals were granted the same entitlement as whites by a federal Act of Parliament.

Aitkin says that the origins of interest in politics lie in childhood socialization and the first experiences of work and adult life (1977:35). For most respondents these early experiences took place in stringent economic circumstances and within authoritarian structures, perhaps explaining a tendency for some respondents (all of them female) to regard any form of official authority as omnipresent and an object of fear. They would exhibit alarm and regret for having voiced criticism of the government, political leaders, the unions or the church. They would ask that their remarks be deleted, and nervously pursue the issue of what might happen if their views "got back to" any of these vaguely apprehended sources of power. Perhaps a fear of rowdy consequences contributed to this mild paranoia. They considered that a woman's role was to keep the peace, as unobtrusively as possible. They thought of politics, as Mrs Guildford did, as an annoying activity too often engaged in by argumentative males: "To tell the truth, I hated the sound of politics", she said. "It always meant an argument. I just dreaded politics!"

But Mrs Guildford's view represented only one segment of the Toowong respondents. In political as in other attitudes, they were no less heterogeneous than the population as a whole.

Interest and participation

Aitkin comments on the remarkable similarities between Western democracies in the political behaviour of their electorates, and groups Australian voters into three categories: the active, the audience, and the uninterested (1977:19). These are readily distinguishable among respondents. Miss Waters, aged 83, was one of the minority who "couldn't be bothered with politics"; indeed, she took this to the extreme by saying, "Just tell me who I'm supposed to vote for and I'll do it — I just don't follow it at all."

Mrs Rich was in the same nursing home and at first she, too, said that she was "not a scrap" interested in politics: "Politicians are a lot of damn fools!" She laughed, looking quizzically at the interviewer. "And after all, I ought to know — I married one!" Then she went on, more seriously:

> My husband was an accountant, and then he got into Federal Parliament — it was his whole life. In those days I took a keen interest, I'd go with him wherever he went. But I never made speeches, or anything like that. I was always against that. It's not a

woman's place; it's a man's place. But I helped him, and I enjoyed it very much. Very much indeed. I liked that type of life, going to garden parties and — getting dressed up, all that sort of thing.

They had had no children, and at 87 Mrs Rich had a heart condition that warranted nursing care. She had a private room and some of her own furniture, including a sewing-machine:

> I've always been fond of sewing, it's a hobby really. I make most of my own clothes. When I came here I made up my mind — Well, I wondered at first how I'd fit in. So I decided that I·*would* fit in! And I have. I like it quite well now.

Further on in the interview it emerged that she still listened regularly to political debates. She was coded as "moderately interested" — part of the majority Aitkin calls "the audience". They were a majority (59 per cent) for the Toowong sample too, but analysis by socio-economic status revealed that this mild level of interest was much more prevalent among the upper than the lower stratum.

For the small group coded as "very interested", socio-economic and sex differentials were negligible, though the slight variations that did occur were all in the expected direction — i.e., favouring greater interest by the upper stratum, younger cohorts, and males. According to Milbrath, "The finding that men are more likely to participate in politics than women is one of the most thoroughly substantiated in social science" (1965:135). However, for the Toowong respondents socio-economic rather than sex differentials were much more important in determining levels of interest. It is not difficult to find representatives of Aitkin's "active" minority among the women.

Mrs Connors, who had been born in Barcaldine, was 88 at the time of interview and could still be considered an "active" member of the party that had first emerged there. She paid her dues and attended meetings "when I can"; the son-in-law with whom she lived was a union official and it was evident that politics was the major topic of conversation in the household. But it was equally evident that Mrs Connors was a woman of her generation in that network-maintenance took precedence even over politics. One of her daughters had married a man of different political persuasion, and Mrs Connors spoke at some length of her efforts to ensure that this should not affect family relationships adversely:

> It's a bit awkward sometimes, you know how it is with men, they can't — But Marjorie and I, we won't let them. Not when they're in this house. We get on well, we all get on well together. It's just — sometimes —.

Mrs King was at the other end of the political spectrum. Her face lit up at the mention of politics, and she at once declared her keen interest. She and her husband, who had retired from medical practice, had made the spacious riverside unit where they lived an official headquarters for a right-wing organization actively engaged in supporting the white minority then in power in what is now Zimbabwe.

Party affiliation

Though respondents were not asked to state the party they supported, many readily volunteered this information, or in the course of the discussion provided unmistakable clues to their identification with a particular party. From 1957 until time of writing Queensland has been governed by a coalition of the Liberal and National Country parties; the latter is headed by "Premier Joh" Bjelke-Petersen, who has a considerable following as a strong, self-made man. Though Queensland is the only Australian state ever to have voted in a Communist member of Parliament, and for nearly 40 years was considered a stronghold of Labor, a factional split in 1957 destroyed Labor's power base, and at the time that interviewing took place, the party was in disarray not only at the state but at the federal level also. Analysis of party affiliation revealed a strong conservative bias, but there is little reason to doubt that this reflected a right-wing swing throughout the country and had little or nothing to do with the age of the respondents. Sixty-eight per cent of respondents indicated that they were Coalition supporters, while thirty-two per cent voted Labor. Party affiliation was closely linked with socio-economic status, and most had voted the same way all their lives.

Mrs Donohue was a staunch Labor supporter, but at 87 she doubted the wisdom of "getting all tingled up about that sort of thing". Her husband had been "a beggar for politics"; he had collapsed and died at a Labor party meeting 11 years before. Two sons had also predeceased her as the result of heart attacks. She was living with the last of her children, a 60-year-old bachelor for whom she displayed the same selfless devotion previously noted among some married couples: "I don't worry about dying for myself", she said. She was a bright little person who laughed easily, but now her eyes clouded.

> But I'd like Bert to go before me — that's the only thing. I worry about his welfare. He'd have to go and live with somebody, he couldn't do for himself, he's always been used to — He might go off like the others did, but if he got sick, I'd like to be still — I'd like to see he had all the attention he wanted, if he — That's the only thing.

Mr Sellars was one of the majority who supported the Coalition. At 82 he lived with his wife in a well-kept home and a garden that occupied much of his time; he played bowls once a week and belonged to one or two other clubs. In his account of his career as a stipendiary magistrate he displayed an excellent memory for events and their dates, and in his old age maintained a keen interest in current events. He owned his home, but had not applied for a pension: "I get superannuation, and if you apply for a pension it goes on to your taxation and you rob Peter to pay Paul, no point in it. I'm eligible, but there's nothing to gain by applying."

Mr Sellars' reckoning may have been faulty in this respect, but he was a man of definite opinions and did not change them easily. He had never wavered in his support for the party that he considered best represented his interests, and in this he was like most other Toowong respondents — and most other Australians. As Mrs Connors said perceptively: "I suppose your politics — your religion and your politics — I suppose you get it from your parents, your grandparents, your husband. I suppose you get it and you always stick to it."

But though this is true for the majority, there are others who do change their vote — and among Toowong respondents these amounted to 23 per cent of respondents who answered this question. Thirteen per cent had changed once — in most cases, during the big swing away from Labor in the 1976 elections. But 10 per cent had changed their vote "frequently".

For Mrs Hurd, aged 81, the change to a more conservative political affiliation may have signalled a personal liberation. She had changed her vote after the death of her husband: "I always voted his way — now I vote the way I like!" She laughed rather apologetically. "I'm a great one for the senior citizens and — other clubs too. They do a wonderful job, and they're not Labor. I get sick of politicians and the way they talk and talk and talk. I like to see some good done."

Eighty-nine-year-old Mr Glenister, on the other hand, had been a swinging voter most of his life:

> I'm not a know-all one way or the other. It's a job to pick and choose. I helped vote Fraser in, but I'm sorry I did now; I think I'll make it Labor next time. There've been some mighty good Labor governments. But there've been some mighty good other ones too. You've got to give it a lot of thought. . . .

Mr Glenister was not ideologically set in his ways. He was one of those who voted on issues.

Political issues

Berelson et al. (1954) and Parsons (1959) are among those who have distinguished two separate levels of political support: on the one hand, a broad ideological position (generally represented by party alignment), and on the other, specific issues on which attitudes were more loosely structured. Toowong respondents were asked their opinions on four topical issues of general interest: strikes, Aboriginal land rights, nuclear power, and conservation. Beneath the rhetoric, the official policies of the major Queensland parties are polarized. The present government has introduced anti-strike legislation (ineffective in practice), links land rights with apartheid, favours nuclear power, and regards conservation as secondary to industrial development. The Labor party (officially, at least), takes the opposite view on all counts.

(a) Strikes

The first big strike directly experienced by the 110 respondents who were in Brisbane at the time was the tramway strike in 1912. It developed around the right for tramwaymen to wear a union badge. The general manager of the tramways at the time was named, appropriately enough, Badger. He was an American with authoritarian attitudes and a deep distrust of unionists, and he was supported in his stand by a government led by Digby Denham, of similar sympathies and personality (Costar, 1978:106). Sixty-nine per cent of the one hundred and

The 1912 Tramway's strike was remembered by most respondents who were in Brisbane at the time.

ten respondents had definite memories of the event. They included Mrs Donohue:

> Black Friday they called it: A terrible lot lost their jobs. I know my sister and I went in this day and we went up to the Trades Hall and we heard Doug Bowman; he was speaking to the people from the Trades Hall and he was saying, Look, they're filling the police up with rum and they're going to raid the people. He says, get home, get home for your lives, as quick as you can, because there'll be a lot of people hurt. Well, we thought we'd get home; so we did, we got away. But it was rotten what they did, you know. One friend of mine, he was a railway guard, and he'd been to Tasmania for his holidays; he didn't know anything about the strike, he got off the boat and — Everything was quiet! There was nothing, nobody moving around, no trams running. He got as far as Albert Street and a policeman's tearing at him with a baton! They used to have the trees with a guard around them those days, so he got up one of these trees, and the policeman socking into him with a baton! He didn't know what for or anything else. That's how they were. I think they were half mad, I think it was true about the rum.

Mrs King's sympathies lay elsewhere:

> I remember my Uncle Norman was coming home with a loaf of bread for his sick wife. And they chased him, they saw he was a — a capitalist, you see — so a lot of the mob chased him. And he dropped the bread. Everything was in very short supply, and his family had to go without. So he went to a shop and bought a revolver and he carried that afterwards. He wasn't chased again. But he'd have used it! They got very nasty.

Mr Glenister, the swinging voter, gave few clues to where his sympathies lay:

> I went up George Street when the big melee was on up at the top, saw the hairpins going into the horses and all that sort of thing. There was nobody killed to any great extent, it was just — It was just about the trammies wanting to wear a badge, that's all.

Mr Drew was 93. He lived with his 92-year-old wife and a 60-year-old daughter; he had come out from England in 1908 and made his living as a carpenter, retiring at the age of 72. In speaking about the 1912 strike, he seemed to side with the government:

Mr Badger was the manager of the tramway company; he was a Yank, but I believe he was a good employer, paid them well. But they formed a union and the union wanted to get a badge and this uniform — he said no, I'm supplying the uniform and you won't wear a badge on it. And there was a strike for six weeks. They hired a lot of special constables. I've seen the police out with fixed bayonets! I remember that quite well. They used to ride them down on horseback, the police with fixed bayonets and — any reliable citizen, they gave them a badge, he was a policemen.

He paused. "All the years I worked", he said proudly, "I was never in a strike."

The strike lasted five weeks and fizzled out without the unionists having made any gains whatever. A leading organizer of the strike was a railwayman named Fred Hanlon; 36 years later he was premier of Queensland and attempted to suppress the 1948 rail strike with tactics similar to those used by his adversary, Denham, in 1912 (Costar, 1978:114).

Respondents spoke of other strikes — particularly the building strike in 1928 — in which some of them had been involved, and 36 per cent thought that "strikes are the only lever you got" and were mostly justified. But the majority of respondents, particularly the women, had a very poor opinion of strikes and strikers. Mrs King blamed them for most of the evils of society, and Miss Waters thought that strikers ought to be gaoled.

(b) Aboriginal land rights

Another political issue receiving wide attention at the time of interview was the question of Aboriginal land rights. No treaty was ever negotiated between Aborigines and white Australians, and their claim to land has only recently begun to receive attention, at least in the federal sphere. The Queensland government opposes change. In 1971 it passed the Queensland Aborigines Act, which with its associated by-laws and regulations has been widely criticized for contravening the Universal Declaration of Human Rights. By-laws and regulations vary in different areas and are replete with petty restrictions, such as requiring permission for owning a hot water jug or other electrical equipment, and requiring that the (white) manager approve the dress of any person going swimming or bathing.

Asked to express an opinion on an issue which, on the whole, had not aroused their interest, 41 per cent of respondents retreated into the position of saying they were "not sure" or "don't know much about it". However, 19 per cent indicated complete approval. Among them was outspoken Mrs Hope: "Yes, I feel strongly about that. It's their land and we took it from them. I certainly think they should have rights to their land."

Fifteen per cent were equally definite in their opposition: "If the white man hadn't come here", said Mr Drew, "they'd still be savages. They did nothing for the country. They'd been here for hundreds of years and did nothing with it, and they're blaming the white man for everything."

A further 25 per cent gave opinions coded as "qualified" approval or disapproval. Mr Glenister was doubtful whether they could use the land "properly" if they did get it, but thought they should be given the chance; Mrs Guildford thought they should be allowed to live the way they always had, without interference but not necessarily with rights that would compete with the white man's. Mrs Donohue pointed out that they are human beings: "They come into the world the same way we do; they go out the same as we do. If they get educated they'd be as good as anyone. But we got to get them educated — haven't we? I mean before we hand over —."

On the whole, the upper stratum (several of whom were landowners, or had relatives and friends who were landowners in country areas) disapproved of Aboriginal land rights more often than the landless lower stratum.

(c) Nuclear power

In Australia trade unions have taken a stand against uranium mining, and the whole question of nuclear power is a lively political issue. Nevertheless, 42 per cent of respondents declined to express a definite opinion, usually on the grounds of the scientific complexities involved. Nearly a third qualified their opinions in some way; 14 per cent expressed complete approval, and 12 per cent disapproval. Probably because so many people thought that higher education was necessary to deal adequately with the issue, females and the lower stratum were most inclined to say they were "not sure".

Mrs King was "all for it": "I really am! If we don't do something about it, they'll take it from us, there's nothing surer." She did not elaborate as to whom she meant by "they", but she had earlier made in plain that she saw Communists, both foreign and home-grown, as an ever-present danger to the Australian way of life.

Mrs Hope, on the other hand, was on the opposite side of the fence. "Nuclear power? I think it's wicked!" she cried. Then she paused to make a reluctant qualification:

> Well, in itself it is and it isn't, if you know what I mean. If it could just be used for necessary purposes — But that's not the way things are. There's too much war business goes along with it. And if America dabbles in and starts another war. . . .

There followed a tirade against America and its foreign policy. The wife of a chief engineer for an international shipping line, Mrs Hope had spent much of her married life in Hong Kong, acquiring a tremendous respect for Asian peoples and an intolerance of America — especially its involvement in Vietnam — that amounted to a burning hatred. Tall and thin, with an eager, freckled face and a forceful way of speaking, she was now widowed and living alone. Her one child, a son, was unmarried and was overseas on business. As anti-American as Mrs King was anti-Communist, in personality and manner of speech the two were not unalike. Apparently different life-experiences had decided their political preferences for them at opposite poles.

(d) Conservation

Respondents were also asked their opinions on conservation, defined, where necessary, as resistance to the sand-mining of beaches (a topical issue), and general approval for the principle of preserving the countryside as well as old buildings. A well-known historic building was at the time under threat of demolition (since carried out), and perhaps because of this 17 per cent of respondents directed their answers solely to the preservation of old buildings. But fewer respondents were unable to make up their minds about this issue, and the majority — over two-thirds — were in favour. Some, like Mr Sellars, had reservations: "I think conservation has a place in the scheme of things, but many conservationists are just rat-bags. They don't seem to understand that we've still got to have progress."

Approval of conservation was very general for all groups, with the older cohorts rating highest. Upper-status males were least likely to approve, probably because of emotional as well as financial investment in capitalistic enterprise such as mining and industrial development, involving exploitation of the land.

On the whole, exploration of political issues revealed a considerable variety of opinion. Any assumption of a biologically imposed rigidity could not be justified from the answers given.

Political effectiveness

As individuals, old people are over-represented in political leadership (Hudson and Binstock, 1976:380), and even octogenarians have been by no means rare on the world scene. The aged as a group, however, are commonly pictured as an oppressed and powerless minority, unable to bring any influence to bear on the decisions of government.

Arnold Rose, writing in 1962, was among the first to suggest that amid what he called "the sub-culture of the aging", some were beginning to see themselves not simply as a category, but as a group. In spite of their presumed conservative bias, they were supporting "radical" (in the American context) measures for the health care of the aged, and in Rose's opinion, "seem to be on their way to becoming a voting bloc" (1968:33). On the other hand Streib, in an article first printed in 1965, concludes from the evidence that the aged have little feeling of identification with their own age-group (1968:46).

More than a decade later, the same view of pressure-groups for the aged as non-existent or ineffectual is probably still the prevailing one both in the United States and in Australia. These views are soundly based on rejection of homogeneity as in any way characteristic of the aged; all existing research tends to underline the fact that "the aged" are even less of a homogeneous group than "the young". Nevertheless, Medicare is now well-established in the United States, and Maggie Kuhn's Gray Panthers, which began with six members in 1970, has spread internationally. With the Vietnam war as their first rallying point, the aim of the Gray Panters is to radicalize opinions on issues of general relevance, "old and young together"; but in some places the wider issues have been neglected for a direct appeal to old people's "hip pocket nerve". At least in West Germany and in Australia, the focus has been on raising pension levels — perhaps a necessary stage in the growth of group-consciousness among the aged.

As Duckett (1979) points out, pressure-groups do not necessarily attain their effectiveness through delivering block votes, though they may imply that they can do so, and induce politicians to believe them. More commonly, they may challenge a government's competence by publicizing unmet needs and thereby influence the opinions of a sympathetic public.

Ward points out that "The individual's experience of ageing is fundamentally affected by where he/she stands in relation to the property dividing line" (1979:49). Most Toowong respondents had an interest in property of some kind (a house, furniture, bank savings), and though a majority (53 per cent) reported the pension as their sole source of income, only 5 per cent saw themselves as hard-pressed financially. To this extent respondents were more characteristic of those 90 per cent of Australian old people whose problems are more likely to be perceived as physical or social than economic or political (Henderson, 1972).

As far as could be judged, respondents seldom looked to the political process as a possible means for solution of their problems. For Mrs King, for instance, right-wing activism had something of the flavour of a hobby. For Mrs Connors, a continued political involvement seemed to be mostly a matter of family loyalty. Mr Glenister's changing vote was apparently based on a predeliction for puzzles of a rather intellectual type, while Mr Drew's firm lower-status conservatism seemed based on a lifelong identification with the opponents of upheaval. For Mrs Donohue, as for Mrs Connors, political preference was a family matter, but for Mrs Hope a dislike of injustice had prompted her adoption of unconventional views. Perhaps Mrs Hurd, in changing her affiliation to accord with those she saw as "do-ers" rather than "talkers", was taking a political stance on what she saw as her own interests. And certainly Mr Sellars, uninterested in pensions but concerned with the proper invest-ment of superannuation funds, used his vote to advance those ends.

To the extent that these people are representative of people who are already very old, there seems little to support Wild's contention that they will "increasingly become aware of their common political, economic and social position and attempt to transfer this awareness into a broad-based social movement" (1977:28). He cites elections in New South Wales where the aged vote determined the results. But whether or not a "broad-based social movement" emerges, politicians cannot rely on any biologically determined rigidity as characteristic of ageing populations.

Much of the literature on politics in old age is concerned with the issue of increasing conservatism, on the assumption that this is an inevitable result of psycho-social processes which make the aged more and more resistant to change. Conservative politicians who take comfort in such a proposition, as indicating that an ageing population will support the status quo, should beware. Despite the very wide heterogeneity of their views and the reasons for them, nearly a quarter of Toowong respondents proved by the very cogent means of a change in voting habits that they were by no means set in their political ways.

To date, the most influential theories in social gerontology have concentrated on individual adjustment, resulting in a typically functionalist conservatism that reduces public issues to private problems, as Mills (1959) so neatly put it. Recently there have been signs of redirection. A course on ageing offered at an Australian university encourages a critical examination of the prevailing gerontological perspective, and suggests the value of conflict theory for a sociological appreciation of the place of old people in modern society (Dempsey, 1980). In the United States, an article by Marshall and Tindale puts a compelling case for a "radical gerontology" with recognition of "a variety of social processes which can be summed up as comprised of conflict, negotiation and compromise" (1978/79:167).

Ageism has weighted intergenerational conflict against the old in favour of the young, and debased the terms on which compromise is negotiated. As ageism is relegated to history, the authentic grounds of conflict will be specified more openly as it occurs, and the irrelevance of age itself as an issue will make problems more amenable to solution.

Chapter 12: Religion

I was never religious in the ordinary way but I lived to Christian principles, and I still do. And it's more than that. The experiences I had in Palestine. . . . I've been in Nazareth, I've bathed in Galilee, I picked pansies in the Garden of Gethsemane, I walked the trail from Bethany down to the Mount of Olives and to the Garden — These at a young age, they had a lasting effect on me. I'm not religious, but I'm Christian. I have my own religion.

Look, love, you know what I say? If we do anything wrong we're punished on earth, not when we die. The man I worked for, I was his housekeeper — nothing wrong, I used to cook and clean for him — Well, he used to be religious, but not when he got older, he said, I'm not so silly now! My husband died in 1950, he's up in the cemetery there with — We lost one of our boys. He was only 13 and 10 months. He was out and a car knocked him over and — He was a good boy. When the war came I used to say Eric's better where he is, because he was — shy, grown-up. He wasn't girly or anything, but he was thoughtful. That last Sunday he was alive — He used to always bring me a cup of tea and some toast on Sunday morning because I worked every morning, see, and sometimes I'd have to go back to clean — but I never left the children alone, their father was with them, you see. This time he said, you know, Mum, you shouldn't eat quick, because it gives you indigestion! I've never forgotten it. He was only 13, but he was a thoughtful boy. I've still got his toothbrush there, and a glass, I can't somehow bring myself to — When I die, that will be the end. I've told them now — I was going to have the ashes put over in the grave, you know, but it's like another funeral; so I said, sprinkle my ashes, girls, I'll be just as happy. I'm not religious now.

Studies of religion in old age have long been bedevilled by two conflicting hypotheses. The first — that religious faith increases in old age — is "part of the folklore of the psychology of religion" (Maves, 1960:723), and is probably based on a psycho-social model of ageing which assumes that people seek religious compensation for their disengagement from society and the approach of death. On the other hand, research on the religious behaviour of the aged has frequently concluded that there is a decline in religious observance with age. Mindel and Vaughn (1978) argue that two opposing definitions of religiosity are responsible for the conflict. Moberg made the same point earlier, concluding that "religion as a set of external extradomiciliary rituals apparently decreases in old age, while the internal responses linked with man's relationship to God apparently increase among religious people" (1968:508).

The extent to which Toowong respondents still engaged in objective "external rituals" connected with some religious organization can be gauged by considering their answers to questions about religious affiliation and church attendance. Their "internal responses", the subjective experience of religion, are indicated by their answers about the importance of religion, belief in life after death, and the meaning of life. In general, the answers they gave were much too subtle and complex to fit ageist stereotypes for either the objective or subjective dimension.

External observances

(a) Religious affiliation

Eighty-nine per cent of respondents were willing to identify themselves with a particular religion (though for five per cent it was only "Christian" or "Protestant"). Comparison with their reports of religious affiliation in childhood revealed some slight changes over the years, especially in the proportions claiming no religion at all. Only 2 per cent said they had had no religion in childhood; in old age this had increased to 11 per cent, a figure very similar to recent census findings for the population as a whole. This suggests that the very old have kept in step with an increasing tendency to reject identification with a particular religion, or with religion itself. Mr Ingham was one example: "I've got no time for religion any more. It's extremely divisive, for one thing — that's what causes most of the trouble between the Serbs and the Croats, for instance." He fingered the book about the partisans in Yugoslavia which he had been reading when the interviewer arrived. "Of course, Christ's teachings — they were very good, but people aren't good enough to keep up with them. If He came back to earth He'd be crucified again for sure. I've got no time for the churches — they're all out to gain what they can for themselves, they don't worry about the people in them. No." He shook his head slowly. "Religion's just a sugar coating, that's all."

But Mr Ingham and the other unbelievers were in a minority. The largest percentage of respondents (34 per cent) were Church of England, as in Brisbane as a whole. Those coded as belonging to "Protestant churches/sects" (27 per cent) including the congregations now combined in the Uniting Church (Methodist, Presbyterian, Congregationalist), plus Baptists, Brethren, Church of Christ, and Seventh Day Adventists. Roman Catholics (19 per cent) were under-represented compared with Brisbane as a whole, but the proportion of this faith has increased since the war with the influx of Italian and other European migrants; it now stands at 26 per cent. The category "Protestant/Christian" provided for those who refused to be more specific, and "Other" (3 per cent) included Russian Orthodox and Jewish respondents.

Unbelievers tended to be male (20 per cent) rather than female (7 per cent), but socio-economic and cohort differentials were negligible. There was a greater concentration of Church of England membership in the upper socio-economic stratum (48 per cent), and very few Roman Catholics (8 per cent), but all other denominations, except for Brethren, were fairly evenly divided in this respect. Brethren, originally known as Plymouth

Brethren, are doctrinally fundamentalist and have a lay leadership, meeting in Gospel Halls rather than a church. All respondents who claimed this affiliation had been born into their membership, and none belonged to the more extreme branch known as Exclusive Brethren. Among Toowong respondents, Brethren were usually lower or lower-middle status, and for all of them their membership had maintained its lifelong significance into extreme old age.

(b) Church attendance

The question of church attendance is complicated by two factors: religious affiliation and health status. In Australia, Roman Catholics are very much more likely to attend church every week than Protestants, but the extreme age of the Toowong respondents makes theirs a special case. In a Brisbane study Hewitt found a substantial age-related difference in attendance at mass in 1971, 54 per cent of those under 40 and 75 per cent over that age attending every week (1978:113). It seems likely that the old tend to maintain an earlier pattern of religious practice longer than the young, but in the Toowong study, only 26 per cent of the sample as a whole said that they still attended church every week, compared with 76 per cent who did so in their childhood. At the same time, those who "never" went to church had increased from 8 per cent in childhood to 43 per cent in old age. The figures are strikingly similar to those in an Australian study by Dowdy and Lupton (1978).

Structural analyses revealed that women were more regular churchgoers than men, a finding very widely supported in the literature. In the Toowong sample, churchgoing amongst women was fairly evenly divided between those who went every week (30 per cent), occasionally (34 per cent), and never (36 per cent); and amongst the latter, the reason usually given for non-attendance was ill-health. For instance, Mrs Barclay, whose solicitor husband had been dead for 30 years, was living alone and managing all her own housework and cooking; but at 82 her eyesight was poor and she was subject to falls, so she seldom left the house.

She was one of the few respondents who confessed to being "terribly lonely", in spite of having 4 children and no less than 13 great-grandchildren all living in Brisbane. Mrs Dopper, who in her eightieth year was living with her daughter, at first said she no longer went to church because angina made walking difficult for her, but then qualified her answer by saying, "now and again I might go, but I don't go much to church now"; so she was coded as one of those going occasionally.

Mrs Mitchell represents those who went to church every week. She was 87 and living with her son and daughter-in-law, and as a Catholic family they never missed going to mass. An unassuming person with a warm clear voice, she spoke of her childhood in England and her mother's death:

> So when I was nine we were put into the convent. The Sisters of Nazareth. They were very kind. Of course things were very much different from now. They were very strict with religion, and everywhere you went — Strict silence to be observed in this corridor! Strict silence to be observed in the dormitory! Strict silence to be observed in the refectory! I had all my schooling there, I was there till I was about 17. We had to do housework when we left. I got half a crown a week, got up at six in the morning and you worked all day until late at night. The nuns were very good to me when my father died. I was working for these people, and the night my father died — he was very ill and my auntie was staying with him, he couldn't be left. But she had to have some rest, and the people I worked for — When I went back next day my clothes were on the steps. We don't need you any more — taking time off — That's what they said. And they were practising Catholics! My father's people weren't Catholics, and when I told his sister that he had died and I hadn't any money to bury him, she said, "Oh no, your father had you brought up as Papists; you can't get anything from us!" So I had to borrow money from the nuns, and it took me two years to pay it off.

Of the men, only 17 per cent said they went to church every week. Mr Fulwood was one of these; he belonged to the Open Brethren and said that he and his wife never missed a Sunday. He was 87, very thin, and with a face much scarred by the removal of skin cancers. The interviewer said that he seemed a little nervous lest his much-younger wife find out he had done the interview and for some reason disapprove, but in other respects he was vigorous and very definite in his opinions — especially on the iniquity of strikes.

Well over half the men said they never went to church, and seldom bothered to excuse their non-attendance on the grounds of health, as the women tended to do. Mr Owen, for instance, was in a nursing home less because of his own health than because of his wife's, with whom he shared a room there. When asked about churchgoing he said simply: "No, I don't go to church. I'm not a keen follower of religion."

Slightly more than half upper-status respondents never went to church, compared to 36 per cent among the lower-status and with the middle stratum between the two. There seems to be a linear relationship between socio-economic status and the degree of secularization that has become evident in the population as a whole. Those respondents who were most likely to be opinion-leaders (i.e., upper-status males) reflected this historical trend most accurately.

Internal responses

(a) *Importance of religion*

Many Australians do not consider that regular churchgoing is necessary for leading a good Christian life, and this sentiment was frequently expressed by Toowong residents: "I haven't been to church for donkey's years", said 89-year-old Mr Townsend. Apart from a First world war injury that was still causing "an obstruction in the gullet", Mr Townsend's health was good, and the son-in-law he lived with would have taken him to church had he wanted to go. "But that's not what it's all about", he said. "Church isn't — I try to do unto others, sort of thing. Besides. . . ." He paused, then went on with a wry smile:

> I had a row with the church! When we were in France the Ninth Battalion had a raid on the enemy trenches, and we lost six men killed, and they were buried in the military cemetery one-and-a-half miles from the front line. Fire that missed the front line parapet

fell in the cemetery. The pioneers had to dig the graves and all that, but the chaplain — he wouldn't read the service over the grave! He went across the street and got behind a brick wall!

A disillusionment with chaplains, and with religion in general because of war, was mentioned in other interviews, and by women as well as by men. Some revealed the common conviction that religion was essential for the socialization of the young but peripheral to adult interests. Mr Aylwood was one: "When I came back from the war I had a lot of doubts about religion. There can't be a God when He'd allow things to go on like that. I didn't think it was right. Still. . . ." He paused, pulling thoughtfully at his ear.

Well, when the family came along, the wife — She said, they've got to believe in something. She wanted to just send the kids down and — But I thought that wouldn't be right either. I thought about it for quite a few weeks, and then I said, I'll take the children down to church. I took them down to Sunday school every Sunday, and then I got interested, and me being a carpenter and joiner, there was a terrible lot about the church they wanted to do and I got into that. Anyway, I went to church up until the boys got that way that they didn't want to go.

He seemed to take this as an inevitable development, and ended firmly: "I don't go to church now."

Others, like wiry little Mrs Bentley, explained their dereliction to changes within the church itself: "Right up till last year", she said with a broad Scottish burr, "I'd have said that religion was still important to me. We were Presbyterian." Her brown eyes twinkled wickedly behind her glasses. "But when the churches united — I wouldn't go!"

But on the whole women retained their loyalty to their religious faith. Seventy per cent of them said it was still important to them in their old age, leaving only thirty per cent who had wavered to the extent of denying its importance. Among men almost the opposite was the case. Forty per cent said religion was still important in their lives, and a sixty per cent majority averred that it was not.

(b) Belief in life after death

Belief in life after death is a central tenet of Christian dogma, but acceptance of it varies considerably with religious affiliation, at least in Australia. Hewitt found 72 per cent believers among Catholics, compared with 46 per cent for non-Catholics (1978:36). Inglis (1975) quotes Gallup Poll findings (1961) which disclosed that believers were a minority among men (41 per cent) and 52 per cent among women. For both sexes over the age of 70 the same poll found 50 per cent who were believers.

The Toowong survey revealed a high degree of uncertainty on this issue. Mrs Barclay, though she still said her prayers every night and said firmly that religion was still important to her, confessed that she could not make up her mind whether she believed in an after-life or not: "Sometimes I do, sometimes I don't — but I feel we have to be here for something."

Even 92-year-old Mrs O'Hagan, who said proudly that she was born a Catholic, had married a Catholic, would die a Catholic, and all her family were Catholics, paused when the question was put to her, then repeated the question softly: "Believe in life after death? You mean — heaven and — " Again she paused, looking into the interviewer's eyes as if searching for the reason for such a question. Then she said, with a return to her customary firmness: "No, actually I don't. I think when you die, you die."

Mrs Mitchell, another Catholic, wavered just a little: "Oh — that's a puzzling question! I often wonder, because — Well, nobody comes back to tell us, do they!" She smiled at the thought, then said: "But we're taught to believe, and — I think I do, really!"

Mr Ingham was the son of a Methodist minister, but in his old age his rejection of formal religion extended to a denial of immortality: "No, no, there can't be anything like that. We're all — like the trees. We'll just be buried and rot. No, that doesn't worry me. Why should it?"

Thirty-six per cent had no doubts about the matter at all — like Mrs Brooks, who said fervently, "Oh, I do, I do believe in it!" She went on to recount a near-death experience in which she had "died" during an operation. She had been met by her dead daughter in a world where "everything was beautiful and green", and seen "a magnificent glow" that became Jesus Christ.

Mrs Dopper had had no such experience but was "quite, quite sure" that she would meet her husband again — "though I mightn't know him!" Apparently Mrs Dopper was prepared to envisage heaven in less material terms than most respondents, for some of whom space exploration had aroused doubts in their minds about life after death. In this respect Toowong respondents revealed a reliance on concrete evidence characteristic of a scientific era. For nearly two-thirds of the sample there had been some wavering from the unquestioning acceptance of the literal truth of Christian dogma in which most of them had been brought up. Over the years most had revised their interpretation of early teachings to fit more comfortably into the secularized society they had helped to mould.

Eighty-eight-year-old Mrs Bentley had revised Presbyterian dogma rather drastically. She laughed when asked if she believed in an after-life: "Well, as to that", she said, "I fall out with everybody! They seem to think you meet your husband and — No, I don't think that!" She gave a little derisive snort. "I don't see how you can. You'd have everybody floating around in the air! No", she said, her Scottish accent thickening, "I think we are re-born. Re-born."

She was not the only one to express this particular unorthodoxy. Ninety-three-year-old Mr Leslie, who when asked for his religious denomination said with a laugh that he was a "Goddian", articulated his beliefs about immortality with his usual verve:

> I certainly do believe in life after death — I've been back lots of times! Reincarnation — yes. I do firmly. My belief is this, If I were to die now [he snapped his fingers] the life that is in me would immediately alight in an unborn child. I think a child is conceived as one dies. It's not a new life, it's the same one.

There was no difference between the sexes in the proportion propounding unorthodox beliefs in one form or another, but more females than males wavered into the "don't know" category on the issue of immortality, and males were almost twice as likely as females to state an uncompromising disbelief.

(c) Meaning of life

Respondents were asked to explain the meaning of life as they saw it, and not unexpectedly, more than half declined the invitation. Five per cent had never thought about it or just had no idea; twenty-three per cent had given it some thought but found it too difficult or "too deep for me"; and ten per cent were convinced there was indeed a meaning, but were unable to suggest what it might be.

Thirty-seven per cent tackled the question in terms of an ethical or religious purpose, and among them were the two ministers of religion in the survey. One was the oldest respondent of all. At 97, he was both mentally and physically active, and the interviewer commented on an air of deep tranquillity and contentment. Because he is well known and expressed some anxiety about the confidentiality of the interview, few details can be given here. In his remarks on the meaning of life he spoke of the love of God as "spiritual oxygen", and went on to say:

> It's all so mysterious, we are travelling an unknown path. I like to be in the hands of One who knows the road. I think we are meant to — correspond with the environment. With goodwill and friendliness. Those are your best companions. It's a working philosophy of life.

The bigotry she had suffered in her youth had not embittered Mrs Mitchell, but in her old age she pondered on the meaning of life and the presence in it of evil:

> I often give it thought, you have such a lot to think about when you're older. I think if you're born into this world, you should try and do good for someone or something, if you can. I never thought about it when I was younger, you were always thinking of something better, something brighter. But there are some dreadful things in the world. That's why I wonder if our Lord, now — We're taught to believe that He's here, but I think of these terrible things, when the Germans put all those Jews in the oven — why did God

allow it? That's what I do think of. If He's a just God? Why did those poor things — They didn't do anything — You just wonder. And some of those poor things when the atomic bomb was dropped — they're still suffering. Yes, I do think quite a lot about what life's all about — yes, I do. But you don't think of those things when you're young. [She smiled tolerantly]. You're always thinking, what will I do when my day off comes! I suppose we're more selfish when we're young.

For six per cent, life had no discernible meaning; they had consciously renounced all sense of any ultimate purpose along with their renunciation of religion. But among the atheists were some, like Mr Ingham, who had thought their way through to an answer that satisfied them: "I think it all gets back to Nature. I think everything is governed by Nature, and in the long run, if we just go along with that — We've got a sort of responsibility, because of our intellect, to — help instead of hinder, if you know what I mean."

This "naturism", if such it may be called, was evident even among some for whom religion had remained important, though they might have wavered in their belief in personal immortality. "I suppose the meaning of life is — matemanship", said Mrs Barclay, who was one such waverer.

Like — the trees grow and die, and life goes on, and each generation follows each generation. You don't really begin to think why we are here until your life is already lived. You live your life and you have your answer in what's already been done.

The ambiguities in the phrase "meaning of life" brought some responses that took the form of a definition of the meaning of the word:

Well — an electrical charge — an ordinary battery, it's got life in it, you put it to work, connect the two ends and it works. My idea is that our life is like an electrical charge in the battery, and when it's worn out it's like a battery that's fully discharged, it's — finished. That electric charge — goes into nothing.

The tendency to define the meaning of "life" semantically was confined entirely to males. More females than males replied in terms of some ethical or religious purpose, but there was very little difference between the proportions of males and females who were convinced that life held no meaning at all. Socio-economic and cohort membership had negligible influence.

The Toowong findings indicate patterns of religious thought and behaviour during the passage of 80 or more years. The patterns recollected as characteristic of their childhood had not been, and could not be, maintained in today's world. But though interference with tradition was sometimes resented, the transcripts offer no support for the hypothesis that psycho-social ageing reflects a biologically induced rigidity and imperviousness to change. Mr Ingham had become a 'government chemist'; perhaps his scientific training had led him to discard his early indoctrination and construct a personal philosophy that combined rationality with ethics. Mr Townsend had arrived at much the same position, though he had not had the same educational advantages — as the son of a struggling dairy-farmer there had been little time for school, and when eventually he had taken over the farm it had taken all his energies to make ends meet. Irrepressible Mr Leslie, once a watchmaker, had rejected his Baptist upbringing to work out for himself what made things "tick". Mr Fulwood, on the other hand, had retained the fundamentalist beliefs of his childhood, but not without expanding and enriching them.

The women were, on the whole, less ready to discard old beliefs outright, but no less ready to question and consider and develop hypotheses that integrated the old with the new. Mild-mannered Mrs Barclay, sharp-tongued Mrs Bentley, warm-hearted Mrs Mitchell — in their eighties, far from rigidifying, they were turning over in their minds all that had gone before and seeking to make sense of it in the light of their experience. That experience varied greatly. Mrs O'Hagan was the wife of a schoolteacher and had done some teaching herself. Mrs Brooks and Mrs Mitchell had both had an impoverished childhood, but Mrs Mitchell's husband (a bricklayer) had prospered, while Mrs Brook's had not. Mrs Dopper had married a railwayman and given her life, as had most women, to network-maintenance; in her eightieth year she took pride in the fact that in spite of severe angina she was "never idle" — she cooked and sewed

Most wives had given their lives to network-maintenance.

not only for her children and grandchildren but for "the stalls".

These people represent, in the diversity of their circumstances, their interests, and their devoutness or lack of it, the range of responses to what Mrs Tavey called "the universal questions". The ageist notion that the old automatically become more religious underrates to the point of absurdity the complexity of their responses. According to Peter Berger, religion is a "sacred canopy", the "ultimate shield against the terror of anomy" (1973:36). Respondents had probed that canopy with doubt and propped it up with faith — dismantling, repairing, reconstructing. With or without the protection of this fragile edifice, they looked out on a shrinking future, and came to terms as best they could with the meaning of life and death.

Chapter 13: Health

My health during childhood was good. . . . I had four children, and lost two — very bad births. Not like the beautiful attention — They didn't have the Women's Hospital. I went into a private nursing home where it was understaffed and underequipped. They died after birth. I don't want to talk about it. I tried to have more children, but I had a miscarriage, and they told me I wouldn't be able to have any more. There was no birth control. Well, there used to be some kind of tablets women inserted that irritated so they nearly went mad! You've no idea the processes — There was no — They used to say, Go and douche immediately, but who cares about douching then? And then of course there was the other process, withdrawal, which wasn't good for the man. So there was a lot of — unhappiness — and all the enjoyment of sexual contact was taken away. I had a hysterectomy after the miscarriage, so I had change of life then. I had a fibroid growth. I had terrible flushes. . . . I'm slightly diabetic now, but it's not of major concern, it can be controlled by a tiny little tablet. It's just recent.

I wasn't always healthy as a child. I was under the doctor quite a lot, they couldn't get the curse to come on me for one thing, and I don't know how old I was — 16 I think — before they got them to come properly. Then I was very anaemic, in fact I still am. I wanted to be a teacher but the doctor wouldn't let me because my brain was too active, he said. I used to walk the floor at night and Dad used to come and bring me back, and the doctor said it was all because I was studying so much. . . . I only had two children — the boy and the girl. That was as much as I could manage, I think — I had a very hard time with both of them. I couldn't carry the babies either, I couldn't lift them up or anything. My neighbour used to come and bath them. But I didn't have any trouble with change of life. . . . You ought to see the pills I take! Seven before breakfast and three at lunch and three at dinnertime. I've been on pills for years. . . .

During the lifetime of respondents there occurred what Gordon has called "the greatest explosion of health ever experienced by mankind" (1976:171). Mostly, as McKeown (1965) and others have argued, this "explosion of health" was due to non-medical innovations such as purer water supplies, more efficient drainage and waste disposal, and a rising standard of living. The result was greater control over infectious diseases and a decline in the rate of infant mortality, illustrated by the fact that during the closing years of the nineteenth century, when the majority of Toowong respondents were born, 112 infants died per 1000 born; the rate some 80 years later was 15 infant deaths to 1000 births.

Older children of the respondents' generation died from diphtheria, whooping-cough, broncho-pneumonia and occcasionally from typhoid or scarlet fever. In early adulthood tuberculosis was a comparatively common and usually fatal disease, and in 1919 contemporaries of the respondents died from the influenza epidemic that swept the world. Recovery from most illnesses was slow, and treatments frequently painful or inadequate. One respondent reported that when she had diphtheria her mother had rubbed the white spots on her throat with kerosene; several mentioned using cobwebs in lieu of stitches for a cut; and for pneumonia there was nothing to do but wait for the crisis and pray for its successful resolution. Cases of accidental drowning were eight to ten times more frequent than today (Gordon, 1976:163), and the rate for other accidents seems to have been comparable. Nevertheless, people managed to survive these hazards in greater numbers than ever before, and the Toowong respondents were among them.

At the turn of the century there was a surge of interest in "nutrition, child welfare, and personal cleanliness" (Gordon, 1976:167), a concern quite novel in terms of human history, especially in the range of people it affected. The stress on hygiene was instigated by the germ theory of disease, and the stress on nutrition by deficiency theories. Simplified versions of these theories were expressed in official public health measures, newspaper articles, and school-book exhortations, and eventually filtered down to the parents of respondents and to the respondents themselves. The great majority of respondents, whatever their level of education, had obviously internalized these values, and in many cases seemed to have consciously set about designing lifestyles in accordance with them. Almost all set store on being neat and clean, and believed in "moderation in all things" — typical middle-status values, though social strata were represented in the Toowong sample in proportions fairly typical of Australian society as a whole.

Health data included information on the longevity of parents; health and illness in childhood, mid-life, and old age; menstruation, menopause, and childbirth experiences; wartime injuries and illnesses; diet, exercise, smoking and drinking; hospitalization; medication, and attitudes to health professionals. In addition to these self-reports, interviewers filled out a cover-sheet listing their own estimates of respondents' mobility, eyesight, hearing, mental state, general health, and use of hearing, walking, or other aids. But the primary source of health data, as with other aspects of the survey, consisted of the answers and recollections of the respondents themselves.

Longevity of parents

On the grounds that health and longevity might to some extent be determined at birth by the traditional "choice" of long-lived parents, respondents were asked the age of their parents at death. It was obvious that respondents had indeed chosen their parents wisely, whether through the inheritance of favourable genes or the cultural inheritance of survival-enhancing lifestyles, or both.

Two respondents had had centenarian mothers, one of whom lived to be 108. Another's parents had *both* passed the century mark (102 for her mother, 101 for her father). She had been told that statistically this represented one chance in eleven million. Mothers were particularly long-lived, with slightly more than half surviving to their eighties or longer. In the 1954 census (by which time most respondents had experienced the death of their parents), the proportion of Australians surviving to be 80 or over was 0.9 per cent for males and 1.2 per cent for females. The Toowong respondents obviously came from unusually long-lived and presumably healthy stock.

Health in childhood and mid-life

Respondents were evenly divided in their recollections of health in childhood. Half said they had always been healthy and had no illnesses worth mentioning; the other 50 per cent talked of one or more incidents of varying seriousness. In the big families of the time it was not unusual to lose at least one sibling at birth or soon after, and virulent infections such as scarlet fever, diphtheria, and typhoid fever were survived by quite a number of respondents: "I remember when my father and brother was working on the trenches — that's bringing the water from Mt Crosby through to Brisbane", eighty-six-year-old Mrs Godfrey recalled.

> There was a lot of tents and there was a lot of new chums, as we called them, in tents, and the drinking water wasn't very good, it was droughty weather, and my brother got typhoid fever. He went into the General Hospital — it was only a little old place then. But I remember the ambulance came out to Moggill and they had a little stretcher with two wheels on and a little grey pony. I think there was two men, and they walked beside the pony and took my brother away at night-time into hospital. Two days after that I was taken ill, I got it too, and I was taken in. And my brother, when he got better, they wheeled him into my ward. That was the most serious sickness I ever had.

Parental concern for the health of their children was revealed by reports of such measures as a weekly dose of salts or castor oil for all the family, and perhaps more efficaciously, by deliberate exercise programmes, which were mentioned by several respondents. "My father was very keen on exercises", said Mrs Beed. "I used to have to skip 1000 before breakfast, and do dumb-bells, clubs and all those things."

More usually, exercise was obtained incidentally as a result of vigorous outdoor life-styles, at least for the boys, and also for the numerous girls who evaded parental edicts about suitable behaviour and became "tomboys". Diet was sometimes given deliberate attention, and on the whole seemed better than merely adequate. The family cow was a commonplace even in metropolitan areas, and people who did not buy vegetables from the Chinese market gardens often grew their own: "My mother was a great believer in giving us plenty of vegetables", said Miss Nicol.

> What you didn't like you had to eat just the same. We had plenty of milk — we had two cows — and we had our own fowls, so we had plenty of eggs, we were never short in that way. And we had rice puddings and all that kind of thing. We had plenty of suet puddings, they liked that good old English suet pudding. Mum would boil it and then she'd put slices of it under the roast, you know, in the gravy, and it went brown there, like dumpling. Those who didn't like it that way would have syrup on it. At times we had a lot of home-grown vegetables, and bananas, and passion-fruit. . . .

According to Gordon (1976), massive malnutrition and famine have been almost unknown in Australia, though sub-acute forms of scurvy may have been suffered in the outback, at least by those who did not supplement the prevailing diet of salt beef and damper with possums and wallabies and other wild life, as Mr Todd and his family had done. Scottish-born Mr Cunningham said that porridge was the staple food in their family night as well as morning, with bread and jam in the middle of the day. Several mentioned jam or "treacle" sandwiches for lunch, in which the filling soaked unappetizingly into the bread, but those who remembered eating bread and dripping usually did so with relish.

Health in mid-life appeared to be better for the men than for the women — a finding consistent with the literature, which reports a higher rate of illnesses among females occurring throughout life. Wilson (1970) suggests that "being a little ill quite often" might help protect women against the aggressive, risk-taking, weakness-denying confrontation with events characteristic of men. The possibility that male illness is under-reported is also raised by Mechanic (1968), but Twaddle and Hessler refer to a health examination conducted in 1961 and conclude that it is true that women suffer more illness than men: ". . . the only disease entity reported from the examination survey that shows higher rates among men is definite coronary heart disease" (1977:62).

The degree to which the female reproductive role contributes to higher morbidity rates is given little attention in the literature, although its effect on mortality is a matter of some controversy. In the opinion of feminist writers, the situation of twentieth-century women has been revolutionized by "the dramatic decline in their fertility, which gave them increased leisure, better health, and a longer expectation of life" (Encel, MacKenzie and Tebbutt, 1974:21). The male excess mortality which now exists in all modern industrialized societies, like the increase in life expectancy itself, is largely a twentieth-century phenomenon, and represents either a very sharp accentuation, or in some cases a reversal, of patterns existing less than a century ago (Wunsch, 1980).

The contribution of reduced fertility to the longer female life-expectancy is by no means universally accepted. A much-quoted study comparing male and female celibates (Madigan, 1957) demonstrated that the female advantage in life expectancy was independent of marital status, and a genetic explanation — specifically the fact that the male possesses only one x chromosome while the female has two — is usually proposed. But as Mechanic (1968) points out, this does not explain the dramatic increase in female life expectancy this century. He considers that the increasing significance of cardiovascular-renal diseases among males, and their greater vulnerability to accident, are most important for producing male excess mortality, but gives first mention to the fact that "the risk of child-bearing has very substantially decreased" (1968:241).

But this concentration on the risks of childbirth itself is shortsighted. Death in childbirth has always been a comparatively rare event in most societies. The spectacular increase in female life expectancy suggests some relationship with the equally spectacular decline in multiparity which occurred at the same time, rather than the lessening of risk in chilbirth itself. Multiparity is not a cause of death listed in mortality tables. Its physical and mental effects are cumulative, and may not manifest themselves in a specific illness, or death, for many years afterwards.

Both men and women in the Toowong survey were asked about childbirth; only 15 per cent of husbands remembered any trouble. Female respondents were more negative about the experience, with less than half remembering it as having presented no problems. This may be at least partly due to the fact that childbirth was socially defined as a dangerous and excruciatingly painful event; because "everybody knew" that this was a time when trouble could be expected, difficulties did in fact occur quite often. Also, physical fitness was probably reduced by the fact that pregnancy was considered disgusting, so that exercise consisted of a walk under cover of darkness, while the mother-to-be was exhorted to "eat enough for two".

However, only 9 per cent of Toowong respondents had 5 or more children, and Mrs Myles, as a mother of 12, was alone in the extent of her multi-parity. The fact that she was still alive at the age of 90 should not obscure the serious ill-health which she had had to cope with through most of her life. Interspersed with her six nervous breakdowns, she suffered from appendicitis and other crises:

> I suffered appendix for eight years. I had bad turns every six or eight weeks. Till one morning — I was washing, and I was found hanging over the tub and I couldn't move. I was sent to Dr Rivett, a lady doctor, and she says, Oh my God — hospital immediately! I said, I can't, I've got too many children and a little baby at home. So I went to the Valley and bought some flannelette and sewed all night, and I was in hospital the next morning. And when she made the incision it burst and splashed in her face. One of the nurses was crooked on me because I had long hair. But apart from that the nurses and doctors were really lovely. The doctor was marvellous — I owe my life to Dr Rivett. When I went home she used to come

and visit me every three or four weeks for about six months. The next operation I had was my gall bladder, and I suffered it for years before they took it out. Then I had a growth round the womb, and it clung to my bladder, and they had to strip all the roots off. And I owe my life to the matron in Turrawan Hospital. She pumped this black stuff out of my stomach. Then twelve years ago I had to be opened up from there to there [drawing a line from her breastbone to her groin]. It was for adhesions, they'd got wound round my bowel and closed it. I nearly went out to it on that one too. . . .

Whether these episodes bore any relationship to her 12 confinements is outside the province of medical science as it presently exists. There do seem to be grounds for concluding that her exceptional exposure to stress may have led to the nervous disorders that plagued her. The only others who reported "nervous breakdowns" were an introspective middle-status housewife, and career-woman Miss Levison:

I had a hysterectomy when I was 40. Very nasty. I was three weeks in hospital and there were problems with my family, because my mother was angry with me at the time for not letting my sister live with me. I had premature change of life — it lasted with me a long time. Probably it might have been my mental and nervous make-up and the worries on my mind. I wasn't happy in those days because of the worries I had, and responsibilities.

She paused, looking unseeingly out the window as though she was looking back through the years. "I think I might have been a little bit stiff", she confessed. "I had a nasty 10 or 12 years — I averaged about 3 months a year away from work, but they kept paying my salary. It was a nasty period, and" — she grimaced.

I had a nervous breakdown. Just after my mother died. I had this friend with me, who was gradually getting worse and worse, in her health. she — And I was unworthy enough to think — Well, I've been relieved of the responsibilities of my mother, and now I've got this cast on me! And the resentment, I think, caused the nervous state. No resentment against her, but resentment that life wasn't giving me a chance. I remember once, I felt so dreadful, I said to her, I wish somebody would relieve me of the responsibility of living.

The interviewer asked if she had had to go to hospital.

No, thank goodness! I couldn't get a doctor to help me at all. They said it's all in the mind, it's all in the mind — there's nothing more aggravating than to be told that! It *is* all in the mind, but surely they should be trained to help people to deal with it. Then I found a neurologist who was terribly kind to me. I was walking round like a zombie because I was full of drugs. As a matter of fact he himself — eventually he committed suicide with drugs!

"What about now?" said the interviewer. "Are you taking anything now?" "Oh yes, the local doctor put me onto a little tablet. I've been taking it for years. I can't stop it."

Miss Levison seems to have been expected to fulfill nurturant female roles despite her position in the workforce. Sex-role conflicts may lead to psychological and even physical health problems more often than is generally realized, and there is no reason to suppose that they are confined to those who do not marry. Though there is considerable evidence that marriage is positively associated with higher health status, closer analysis has revealed that it is males, not females, whom marriage best protects against illness and death. Gove suggests that this may be due to "the nature of the marital roles" (1975:275), but as Miss Levison's story illustrates, the role of an unmarried woman is by no means free of stress. As work-roles become less differentiated by sex, women may be increasingly subjected to the health risks at present associated chiefly with event-confrontation.

In general, mid-life histories provided many accounts of illness, sometimes of a life-threatening nature. Six women had had a breast removed because of cancer, and two men had also successfully conquered this disease; others had withstood tuberculosis, lung damage caused by poison gas, and bouts of rheumatic fever. In extreme old age, however, nearly two-thirds of respondents claimed to enjoy health that was either very good or "good for my age", and though some of these could be what Shanas and Maddox have designated as "health optimists", (1976:604), on the whole interviewers' estimates confirmed their judgment.

Health in old age

Ageist stereotypes suggest that old age is synonymous with disease. This is not the case, of course. It is true that length of life increases susceptibility to particular sorts of disease — though there are *no* diseases that are in actual fact "peculiar to old age". Episodes of acute illness tend to decrease with age, though when they do occur in old age they are more likely to be of longer duration or to be of a life-threatening severity. Old people, however, are far more likely to suffer from chronic arthritis, cardiovascular and other diseases, which increase in prevalence after middle age. Chronicity is the most characteristic feature of pathology in old age; Gordon estimates that in Australia it can be expected to affect about 50 per cent of those aged 65 and over, with about 25 per cent disability (1976:256). The proportion affected increases with age, as does the degree of incapacity.

Attempts to discriminate between disease and the process of ageing itself is methodologically exceedingly difficult. In an 11-year study begun by Birren et al. (1963) and completed by Granick and Patterson (1971), 47 healthy old men were minutely examined. Electro-encephalogram readings revealed a slowing of electrical activity within the brain and of reaction times for all muscles and sensory modalities, although both were within the normal range of young adults and were accentuated by psycho-social factors such as loss of spouse. The study was particularly successful in demonstrating the effect of even sub-clinical disease on cognitive performance, and of the interdependence of social, psychological and physical factors for producing symptoms commonly regarded as part of biological ageing.

(a) Self-assessments

The old get sick more often than young adults, but not more often than children do. As Dr Earle Hackett (1982) has pointed out, no more than five per cent of them are sick at any one time, including those who are in their final illness. The proportions are higher for people aged 80+, but Toowong respondents are probably representative of their age-group in that a majority (nearly two-thirds) reported their health as good, and a further 21 per cent rated it as "fair".

The Toowong respondents are not alone among the "old-old" in mostly rating their health as good, and those who said it was poor were in very much the same proportion as in the three-nation study by Shanas et al. In Toowong, 14 per cent said that their health was poor; for those of a similar age in the Shanas et al. survey, it varied between 14 per cent and 18 per cent according to nationality. In Toowong, though a majority of all groups reported their health as good, they were fewest among those aged 85 and over, and most numerous among those in the upper socio-economic stratum.

More males than females claimed to have good health. A cultural image of maleness as being strong and uncomplaining may have generated a degree of health optimism, but on the other hand octogenarian males have survived at least 12 years longer than the average for their sex (compared with 6 years for females). Their assessment may well have been based on a realistic comparison with men who had predeceased them.

Some respondents who reported poor health may have been experiencing the terminal drop which makes distance from death a more important dimension of ageing than distance from birth (Lieberman and Coplan, 1969). Others may have been victims of ageist norms which help to make failing health in old age a self-fulfilling prophecy.

Health status as perceived by respondents included self-reports of illnesses, which were of a range and multiplicity that defied tabulation. Arthritis, fractures, or other conditions involving bones or joints were the most frequently reported; unfortunately no effort was made to check on vertigo, which was probably the cause of fractures in a high proportion of cases. Mrs Eliot, who was 85 and living alone, is one example:

> The trouble is I fall a lot, I have trouble getting around and I fall down. I broke that wrist — and me thumb, too, that was the latest. The doctor comes once a week and the nurses come twice, and the Meals on Wheels ladies — I don't cook, you see. I'm not allowed to cook, since I broke me back —.

The interviewer gave a startled exclamation.

> Yes, me back. I fell right over and — The doctor wants me to go into a home, but not me, I can manage here. I'm not going unless I'm absolutely pushed to. I've only got one son alive now, and he's living in Sydney. But my granddaughter comes down from Ipswich, she comes and takes me for a drive. And I've got nice neighbours, the one that just come in, she's one in a million! Every day she pops in. . . .

Upper-status Mr Beech, on the other hand, was one of the 20 per cent who claimed to be entirely free of symptoms:

> I still play bowls three days a week. My health is very good. I've never had a serious illness in my life. No, no, I don't take any tablets or anything — don't need any!

Most respondents were taking a variety of tablets and other medication, but nonagenarians were more likely than any other group to be taking no medication at all. Several of them expressed distrust of modern drugs. "Oh — doctors — they can come if they want to", 91-year-old Mr Sale said cheerfully. "But the stuff they give me — I just shove it down the toilet!"

Health status, of course, affects residential situation, and though the relationship is by no means one-way, declining health is the usual reason given for seeking institutionalization. In the Toowong sample only half, and sometimes fewer, of the institutionalized replied to many of these questions. The bias introduced by such a high level of non-response probably over-represents the healthy; presumably those who were unable or unwilling to be interviewed would tend to be less in contact with the world than those who participated.

(b) Lifestyles

Palmore summarizes the findings of the Duke Longitudinal Study by saying:

> . . . the most important ways to increase longevity are: (1) to maintain a useful and satisfying role in society, (2) to maintain a positive view of life, (3) to maintain good physical functioning, and (4) to avoid smoking. . . . (1971:246).

Many Toowong respondents made strenuous efforts to maintain a useful and satisfying role in life, but in many instances were defeated by ageist attitudes. Regarding the other three points they may have had somewhat more success; many seemed conscious of the value of diet and exercise. Slightly more than half reported a preference for outdoor activities such as walking or gardening or, in a few cases, outdoor bowls; this was especially evident among males, members of the upper stratum, and respondents who were already in their nineties. In this respect they were decidedly more active than Shepherd's Canadian sample, which showed 92 per cent of those aged over 65 as taking no deliberate exercise and spending over 4 hours per day watching television — largely due, he considers, to cultural expectations that from their sixties on people should "slow down" and "take a well-earned rest" (1978:148).

Among the Toowong respondents who demonstrated some resistance to cultural expectations about the necessity for declining activity was Miss Nicol, aged 83: "My health is good", she said. "Very good! Except for — unfortunately about six weeks ago when I was doing some high kicks I must have broken a tendon down there in the groin, and it's still a bit sore. It's stopped me from doing all that I usually do. I still do a lot of walking, though."

In matters of diet, too, few Toowong respondents conformed to stereotypes about the elderly as existing on tea and biscuits. Although many — especially the women — preferred milk puddings to a meat course, they liked their "veggies", as some put it, and at least one piece of fruit per day was a frequently mentioned item. Mrs Beed said that she always included "a little bit of yellow, little bit of green" in her cooking every day.

Palmore's fourth point is the avoidance of smoking. Only a small minority (12 per cent) were smokers at the time of interview. Respondents were also asked about the drinking of alcohol, and though one respondent admitted that earlier in her life she had "been on the booze", most were abstemious. Thirty-four per cent said they drank "occasionally", which usually seemed to mean about two or three times a year, and over half never drank alcohol at all.

Lifelong health-related habits chosen by Toowong

respondents, then, tended to be conducive to the attainment of longevity, and at the same time, to good health. The cover-sheets filled in by interviewers confirmed these impressions.

(c) Interviewers' estimates

Except for the few who had had experience as nurses, inter-viewers had no medical training, and the estimates made of respondents' hearing, eyesight, mobility, and mental state were based only on simple observation and assessment of evidence acquired during contacts and interviews.

Hearing loss is a well-documented aspect of increasing age, though reports of its incidence are probably increased by the research methods commonly in use, which presuppose young-adult educational and motivational levels (Bennett and Ahammer, 1977). Botwinick (1978) found that the old were more cautious than the young in indicating that they had heard a low-volume sound. The incidence of presbycusis (high tone disability) was greater among men and appeared to be related to environmental factors such as noise pollution at work.

Mrs Beed was 84 and wore a hearing-aid. When she was asked if she would like to live to be 100 she sighed and shook her head.

It would be all right if you had your faculties. But if — Well, with me it's my hearing. With those trains, and this instrument — I wouldn't like to live and be deafer and deafer, I think that would be an awful thing. When you're deaf you live in a world of your own. Yesterday before you came, a friend came over and she sat in that chair and she said, "You know, you've got quiet, haven't you!" And I know that I have. One time I would be in everything. But now —.

Failing eyesight was usually accepted stoically as an unavoidable handicap of advanced age. Mrs Allsop, however, was inclined to blame the printers: "They make the letters too light these days", she said, frowning. "Even in these large-print books, they're — And price tags, they're disgraceful! Even my daughter has trouble reading them!"

Deficiencies in eyesight begin very early in childhood. There is a decline in the ability to focus on near objects from the age of five, and visual acuity typically reaches its peak in late adolescence and gradually diminishes thereafter. Only one or two respondents could read without the aid of glasses.

As with other disabilities, difficulties in moving about tended to be accepted with stocism. "I had a fall out of bed", said 93-year-old Mrs Olney.

> I can only move very slowly now, but less than 12 months ago I could walk any distance you like. Now I just creep around, just manage to get from that door to this one. My daughter takes me shopping, but — I get a bit bored with myself sometimes, but — oh [with a rather wistful little laugh]. I get over it! I didn't like it at the hospital — I had to go to the hospital for physio-therapy. It made me nervous, I've never been to a hospital before. And when I said to the physio-therapist, I said I mightn't come back, she said to me, "You'll do as you're told!" Just like that! You'll do as you're told!

And again she laughed, this time with a discernible note of indignation.

The great majority of respondents were clearly in full posses-sion of their mental faculties. More than half were coded as "bright, alert", demonstrating a lively intelligence, while 21 per cent were probably less gifted initially but had maintained what might be termed a "good average". These were combined for the category "good". A few had lapses of memory or wandered from the point to a degree which led interviewers to classify them as "a bit vague". Thirteen per cent were coded as "confused"; these included some who were described as such by relatives or institutional staff. Sometimes interviewers were given no opportunity to meet them personally, and could not ascertain whether the status of "mentally confused" was justified or not.

Mrs McCoy certainly seemed to be confused. She was 83 and in a nursing home, a good-looking woman with curly hair and large brown eyes which would not meet the interviewer's. She confused her husband with her father and gave contradic-tory accounts of the number of children she had. She was always reporting that her belongings were missing, but a search would find them under her mattress, or tied into the sleeves of a dressing gown, or hidden in a pillow case. At the time of the survey reality orientation and re-motivation therapies were not in practice in this nursing home, although they have since been introduced.

All four modalities were examined for relationships with socio-economic status, sex and age. On the whole socio-economic relationships were fairly weak (though in the expected direction — i.e., favouring higher status). A masculine advantage was found on all four counts. As younger cohorts scored better than older ones for each capacity, analysis by sex was controlled for age; but the masculine advantage held, and for eyesight and mental state, increased with increasing age.

About two per cent of the life-expectancy advantage of women over men can be accounted for as biologically conferred; the rest is probably due to higher male exposure to accident, stress, smoking, and excessive drinking (Powles, 1975). These patterns may be changing, but for the generation to which the Toowong respondents belonged, early socialization experiences, reinforced throughout life, encouraged among women a greater degree of conformity and fatalism that was evident among the men — especially high-status men. Few men defined themselves as powerless in the face of adverse circumstances. They had been brought up to confront events rather than submit to them. For example, when Mr Burkett suffered an attack of gallstones and was told that his doctor had a policy of not operating on people over 80, he said he "staged a sit-in strike", refusing to end the consultation until eventually his doctor agreed to operate. Even women like strong-minded Mrs Allsop would have been unlikely to attempt such a test of will.

Among the social advantages enjoyed by males who had succeeded in living to be very old was the fact that they usually did so with the companionship and support of a wife younger than themselves. One 97-year-old male was still in such a situation; the oldest female respondent (also 97) was in an institution.

Consider the case of Mrs Golden, who, at 87, had been widowed for many years. She had just moved *out* of a retirement village because she found she did not care for communal living, and had taken a unit in the same building as her daughter, who had her own circle of friends and quite different interests from her mother's. On the surface Mrs Golden seemed well-placed. Her material needs were amply catered for, and her daughter was available in case of need.

But Mrs Golden was a cultured and intelligent person who had slipped into reading the same books over and over again. She no longer found it worth the effort to go to the theatre alone, and she despised television. She suffered from a lack of mental stimulus to the point of sensory deprivation, and she certainly lacked what Palmore refers to as a useful and satisfying role in society. "I cumber the earth!" she said with a laugh. And with nothing, nobody, to call forth her considerable reserves of intellectual competence, is it any wonder that she was beginning to worry about a failing memory?

To remember something, we must first pay attention to it; and to pay attention to it, it must seem worth the effort of attention. What was there in Mrs Golden's situation to make her feel that any one repetitive little incident was worth paying attention to? What we don't use, we lose. If Mrs Golden did lose her memory, it would be because the society she lived in had made her feel that she cumbered the earth. The social definition of ageing as synonymous with senility precludes intellectual challenge of the most modest kind, and by withdrawing stimulus, guarantees at least some atrophy of mental powers.

Differential capacities between the sexes have been shown to have largely social causes; where they do exist, they tend to favour female rather than male survival. But society offers males more overt sources of challenge (to which more of them succumb), while those that do survive appear to have resisted the pressures towards decline somewhat better than the average of the women. In other words, at the end of life, lifelong socialization patterns culminate in an acceptance of passivity by the female. In old age passivity is required of both sexes, but may more often be resisted by the men, for whom it is a reversal rather than an extension of sex roles. In resisting these pressures, more men than women die, and more women live on into extreme old age deprived of much that makes life worth living.

Toowong respondents were members of a generation who were historically well-placed to survive into old age; but in outliving most of their contemporaries they demonstrated exceptional powers in this regard. Their extreme longevity may have been, in part, a biological endowment, but they themselves contributed to this result by health-promoting lifestyle preferences. By the time they reached old age, however, they tended to be trapped in circumstances that stripped them of a range of social contacts, mental stimulus, decision-making opportunities, and the chance of fulfilling useful roles.

Given their situation, it is remarkable that so few, of either sex, had declined towards the ageist stereotype of senile frailty.

Part 3   Finale

Chapter 14: On Being Very Old

Oh, I've had a lovely life! I often sit and — browse — about different things that happened. I used to get up at four o'clock every
morning to get my husband off to work, and I'd set the bread, and I
always had a baby sitting in the chair beside me. And then you'd
bun-bake twice a week. Then go down and milk two cows. I was
married when I was 20, my husband was an engine-driver in the
pits. He started when he was 15, he had a long time at the engines
— right up till he retired. We got five pounds a week, and we had
to pay rent out of that, and live on it. Well, we managed! We all
did. None of us had any — extras. Everyone was in the same boat.
No, we didn't grow anything — there was never any water, we
had to depend on the tanks. We always had to be very careful, we
didn't waste any water. I always had a lot of pot-plants, and every
little drop went on the pot-plants. We were all so happy! My life
has been so happy, ever since I was a little girl — I've been very
happy. We would sing out to one another, Come up and have a
cup of tea — I've just made some scones! Little things like that. . . .
Live to be 100? No! That's too long. I'd like to go while I'm full of
life, and can enjoy life. I'd like to live till I was 90, anyway — the
children are all giving me a party! They gave me a lovely party for
my 89th birthday. . . .

Robert Havighurst defines "successful ageing" as an ability to
extract "a maximum of satisfaction and happiness" from a
society that "maintains an appropriate balance among satisfac-
tions for the various groups which make it up — old, middle-

aged, and young, men and women, etc. . . ." (1961:8) The criteria of "an appropriate balance" are not explored, leaving the field to ageist assumptions that the old are biologically inferior to the young and therefore cannot expect to claim equivalent rewards. This puts the onus on the old person to adjust to their inferior status and accept it as inevitable.

By and large this is what most old people do. The rebels are few, and score low on any life satisfaction index. The "well-adjusted" who are highly satisfied are also a minority, though in the Toowong survey they were nearly three times the proportion of the "maladjusted". The great majority are simply resigned.

Toowong respondents were asked how they liked being their present age; whether they would like to be 20 again, or to live to be 100; whether they ever worried about dying; and for advice on how to reach a happy old age. Answers to the first question in particular provided data on their morale or "life satisfaction".

On life satisfaction

The range of answers to how they liked being their present age can be represented on a continuum from highly dissatisfied to highly satisfied. Eight per cent were clustered around the negative end, twenty-one per cent at the positive end, with the great majority (seventy-one per cent) demonstrating attitudes that were categorized as representing various degrees of resignation. Each of these three main clusters of attitudes will be dealt with separately, but their distinctiveness is an artifact of the coding, and the degree of overlap should be kept in mind.

(a) Highly dissatisfied

The 8 per cent who were coded as having definitely negative attitudes consisted of 14 people — 4 males and 10 females. Typically they were more likely to be younger than older, female than male, and slightly more likely to be middle rather than upper or lower status — in other words, in these and most other respects they differed in no discernible way from the rest of the sample. Despite the small numbers, however, some differences were apparent, especially when compared with the 36 persons whose attitudes were coded as definitely positive.

Both subjectively (i.e., judged by self-perceptions) and objectively (judged by interviewers' impressions), health ratings tended to be lower for those who disliked being their present age than for those in the middle or at the positive end of the continuum. This was especially the case for mobility, where five of those with negative attitudes (over a third) were rated as seriously handicapped in this respect, compared with three (eight per cent) of those with high morale. Eight of the fourteen used a hearing or walking aid, and six used both. A much larger majority were taking medications of various kinds compared with those at the positive end of the scale, where only slightly more than half did. Three still smoked, compared with only one among those with high morale. On the other hand, none had a daily drink, a habit enjoyed by 23 per cent of those with positive attitudes.

Attitudes that could be categorized as definitely negative were characteristic of such a small minority that conclusions must remain very tentative. Even in this small group, lifetime experiences could be classified as exhibiting opposite patterns, which were alike in only one respect: a lack of any marked attention to network-maintenance. Some of these respondents were intelligent, restless, independent people whose lives had been characterized by eventfulness. They seemed to have been accustomed to tackling problems and achieving a successful outcome, and they were not afraid of saying that they found their present situation intolerably burdensome: "Oh, I hate it!" cried Mrs Draper. "I just hate being 89! I hate it like poison!"

The widow of an architect, she was classified as upper status, and the home she shared with an unmarried daughter was a comfortable and tasteful one. She had short, soft hair framing a well-shaped face and was fashionably dressed and made up, but her voice trembled with feeling as she went on. "Old age is so uncomfortable! So miserable!"

The daughter of a civil engineer, she remembered the effects of the Special Retrenchment Act of 1893, when "everybody's salary was reduced, and his salary wasn't big enough for his commitments". Those commitments included the formal social life at the time:

> Ladies in those days — a lot of calling went on. Mother's "At Home" day was every second Thursday, people would come and just talk and — they were given afternoon tea, and if they called on the day the lady of the house was out they just left their cards, and sometimes if they didn't want to see the lady but just wanted to show her some respect they just left their cards and went — one of their own cards and two of their husband's.

She had come dux of the private school she attended:

> We sat for the Cambridge exams, Cambridge Junior and Senior, and I got distinction in the Senior, distinction in quite a few subjects. My father would have liked me to go to the university, but I'd have had to go Sydney, in those days there was no university here, and board there. It was quite out of the question, it wouldn't be fair to have spent all that money on me.

She had decided to train as a nurse. "I don't know why. I think I just wanted employment." "I'll go and get the medals you won", said her daughter. Mrs Draper had consistently topped her year, and soon became matron of a Red Cross nursing home. In 1915 she joined the British Army, and her three years of nursing service abroad seemed in many respects to have been the highlight of her life. She had had a happy marriage and won the devotion of her daughter, whom she described with a wry little laugh as "very bossy these days!" She added hurriedly, "But she's very good to me — she's very good to everyone. Even — my son — somehow the two of them never got on, but she was always — forgiving. He lives in Sydney now. They haven't any children. No, I'm not one of those who pine for grandchildren. . . ."

For Mrs Draper and for others like her, primary relationships tended to be few but intense, and bereavement apt to be a shattering experience. Ill-health was resented as imposing an unaccustomed weakness and dependence on others. Mrs

Draper, for instance, who suffered from diverticulitis and high blood pressure, seemed to be unable to reconcile herself to her condition.

Others were more passively inclined and seemed to have always expected their problems to be solved by someone else. These tended to have neglected network-maintenance, but less because they were absorbed in other activities than through inertia, or even through a rejection of network values. They had few social contacts left, and could justifiably be assessed as suffering from isolation as well as desolation.

Only one of the 14 — Mrs Draper — found any real solace in religion. On the whole, low morale appeared to be associated with social isolation, bereavement, and decline in activity and independent functioning related to ill-health.

(b) Highly satisfied

A total of 36 respondents displayed definitely positive attitudes about their experience of old age. Older respondents were slightly more likely to express positive feelings than those in their early 80s, but this, of course, does not mean that morale increases with age. Rather it suggests that cheerfulness may be characteristic of the minority who live to extreme old age. Sex made no difference at all, and those who were still married were only slightly more likely to express positive attitudes than those who had never been married, but the widowed were con- siderably less likely to do so — no doubt reflecting the depres- sion that follows bereavement and perhaps a lingering "cathectic impoverishment" (Peck, 1968:89) — i.e., a lack of close attachment.

All told, in old age the highly satisfied had a greater range of amusements, activities and contacts than revealed by the rest of the respondents. They had remained more interested in politics, and were much more inclined to hold firm opinions on nuclear power, Aboriginal land rights, and conservation. Their attitudes to Aboriginals and to the present generation were more often rated favourably, and they preferred outdoor activities to indoor far more than the rest. Two-thirds of them had travelled overseas at some time — the only group in which a majority had had this experience.

Religious denomination was of little account, and the group included three who had no religion at all, but their attitudes to religion were interesting. A majority seldom or never went to church, and they were less likely than the resigned to say that religion was still important to them; but a greater proportion than in either of the other groups expressed a firm belief in life after death — sometimes of an unorthodox kind. Though 4 of the 14 with negative attitudes stated that life had no meaning at all, none of the 36 at the positive end of the continuum came to this conclusion. Instead, they attempted an explanation in ethical terms. Fifty-eight per cent of them said they would like to be twenty again, and they were the only group in which even a bare majority (fifty-two per cent) were in favour of living to be a hundred. They were also slightly more likely than others to admit to sometimes worrying about dying. They were quite ready to proffer advice, of a wide-ranging type that often proved difficult to classify.

They perceived their health as better than most, and this was borne out by interviewers' estimates, particularly with regard to mobility, for which 92 per cent were rated good or fair. Few of them used aids other than glasses, and nearly half took no medication. Rather surprisingly, they were more inclined than others to criticize doctors and other medical personnel. Ninety-seven per cent no longer smoked and nearly as many had not done so for at least fifty years, but twenty-three per cent had a daily drink — much the highest of any group. Studies by Mishara et al. (1975) are among those that have shown beneficial effects for a moderate consumption of alcohol in old age.

They were also the least likely to use community services or to be institutionalized.

The answers given by these 36 life-affirmers cannot be explained by a blanket tendency to thoughtless good cheer. Their lifetime experiences were at least as eventful as those of other respondents; they recalled times of suffering during war, depression, bereavement, and illness, and they were more likely than most to take a stand on any issue than arose. But biologically they appear to have been endowed with good health and culturally with an interest in lifestyles likely to maintain it. Socio-economically they tended towards material circumstances that were moderately fortunate. Within these propitious preconditions they were well-equipped to respond creatively to lifestage crises. Their lifestyles in old age tended, on the whole, to be active and out-reaching, within a family or friendship network of long-established stability.

Mrs Ferrier was gardening when the interviewer arrived. She was a middle-status widow in her eightieth year, living alone in a small and well-kept house. Asked about how she liked being 80, she had no doubts at all:

> Oh, I enjoy it! I enjoy every moment of it! I think life is wonderful, don't you? Just to see the trees and the flowers and — Oh yes, I like being 80! I'm happy! I wouldn't have said that a few years ago, when my husband first died. I suppose in my life there's been good and bad, there were times that so much seemed to be happening — and not all of it good. But looking back I can't say I regret — any — I've had a good life, considering everything.

When the interviewer asked if she would like to be 20 again Mrs Ferrier shook her head, laughing.

"Oh no — not really. I'm happy as I am."

"How about living to 100? Would you like to live as long as that?"

"A hundred!" Again she laughed, then paused, considering it. Then, "No!" she said definitely. "No, I wouldn't. It's — too much. You're past your age-limit then."

(c) Resigned

Respondents with definitely positive and definitely negative attitudes were relatively simple to classify, but the majority displayed such a degree of overlap that attempts to locate them along the continuum with any exactitude were eventually discarded. The most that can be said is that the distribution was skewed towards the positive end; respondents displayed a determination to make the best of things, and appeared largely to have succeeded. Being such a large majority, they were far

"I think life is wonderful, don't you?"

more typical of old age generally than those at either extreme of the continuum, but they included a diversity of opinion and circumstance that is in itself typical of the aged.

It is possible that resignation increases with age, as the largest proportion (85 per cent) was found among nonagenarians — quite a sharp increase from the low of 64 per cent among the mid-eighties group and the 72 per cent in the early eighties. For sex and socio-economic status they conformed closely to the figures for the sample as a whole, except for a slight decrease among the upper stratum. Forty-three per cent lived in a family situation, 35 per cent alone, and 22 per cent were in an institution. Compared with those who enjoyed life, they were considerably less likely to live in a family situation, equally likely to live alone, and far more likely to be institutionalized.

In old age, their level of activities fell consistently between the two extremes presented by those with high and low morale. This may have been partly due to differences in health; eyesight, for example, was almost twice as likely to be poor as among those with high morale. Deafness was more than twice as common, and 22 per cent of them had mobility problems. Of the three groups, they were most likely to be rated by interviewers as "vague" or "confused". For other health variables, they tend to rate considerably lower than those with high satisfaction, although well above those with definitely negative attitudes.

Religious affiliations were similar to the sample as a whole, except for a slight over-representation of Roman Catholics. Religion was still important for nearly two-thirds of them, though 42 per cent seldom or never went to church. Half definitely believed in life after death, and a further quarter said they did not know. All but a small minority (six per cent) were convinced that life had a meaning, but they were the least likely of the three groups to try to put it into words. They were also least likely to give advice on how to reach a happy old age. They were evenly divided about the idea of being 20 again, but a majority (60 per cent) did not want to live to be 100. Eighty-seven per cent — more than in either of the other groups — said that they were not in the least worried about dying.

These, the resigned, constituted such a large proportion of
respondents that they must be taken as typical, in all their
diversity, of the sample as a whole. Mrs Morrison, for
instance, was typical in that her resignation was of a fairly
positive kind; also, she was a middle-status widow with no other
income besides her pension, and her health was good. She was
85, and lived with a widowed daughter. Atypically, she was
Catholic, and still went regularly to church.

"No. I'm not exactly lonely", she said in answer to the
interviewer's question. "Not too bad. I read and sleep — talk
to the birds and the cats. I've been able to get out more
through the kindness of friends and the Good Samaritan
group at the church and that. . . . I watch the news, that's
about all. I'll have the radio on occasionally, but I can't say
I'm that much interested in world events. What can we do
about them? You can say a few prayers for their guidance,
that's all I can do. Bored?" She considered a moment. "No,
not too bad. At times I might get a bit lonely and I play a
game of Scrabble with myself — right hand against left
hand. . . ."

Attitudes to the experience of being old can be regarded as
one of the end results of the lifelong construction of old age.
For most respondents this construction had proceeded according to one of two socially provided "blueprints". For males,
the mode of construction they were expected to undertake
was of an active, instrumental kind which favoured the confronting of life-events as problems to be solved by individual
effort. The stress of event-confrontation may have contributed to the shorter life-expectancy of their sex, but those
who survived into their 80s seemed, on the whole, to have
benefited physically and mentally from the stimulus of
stressful life-events. At the same time most of them were able
to rely on integration within a kin and friendship network
owed chiefly to a wife; but the loss of a spouse was a life-
event with which few were well-equipped to cope.

For females the behavioural "blueprint" was based on
network-maintenance, and most had successfully built up
long-lasting relationships, especially with kin, throughout the

course of their lives. An old age founded on relationships is especially vulnerable to destructive life-events like bereavement, but for the women, some degree of anticipatory socialization was evident in their acceptance of widowhood when it occurred in old age. On the other hand, a tendency towards event-avoidance may have contributed to a lower standard of physical health and mental alertness than was typical of surviving males.

The "blueprints", of course, consisted only of broad outlines of the behaviour expected of respondents, and they varied for socio-economic status as well as for sex. Higher status usually incorporated expectations of successful event-confrontation for both sexes (though especially for males), reducing anxiety and fearfulness and enlarging leisure opportunities as well as increasing the level of material comforts. All contributed to the degree of life-satisfaction experienced by respondents wherever ageist norms proved amenable to successful confrontation. On the other hand, *un*successful confrontation with events reduced the possibility of resignation and opened the door to despair.

On how to reach a happy old age

In asking for advice on how to reach a *happy* old age the question of "successful" ageing was inadvertently defined for respondents in terms of life satisfaction. Perhaps this was why 20 per cent declined to answer the question — it may well have been seen as inappropriate: "I wouldn't be so presumptuous", Mrs Monckton said. "In the first place, people don't take your advice and anyway — I'm still not sure I've got the answers to anything. I think people have to work things out for themselves."

There was plenty of evidence that for most respondents old age gained its significance only in relation to the whole life-span. For many this meant dismissing their circumstances in old age as of minor importance. They were abidingly conscious of a lifetime behind them in a way that gives the term "life satisfaction" a wider meaning. "I wouldn't know about advice", Mrs Denham said slowly. "I know I've had a good life myself, I suppose I've been — lucky. Just live your life, don't hurt anybody — if you do a wrong you get it back again. I don't say I've done good, but —."

Upper-status respondents were least reluctant to proffer advice, and nonagenarians were somewhat less inclined to do so than younger cohorts. Sex made no appreciable difference in this respect. The nature of the advice was often ethical, and the upper stratum was especially prone to speak in ethical terms. Moderation was also a popular form of advice, especially among the middle stratum, though the eight per cent who specifically mentioned "a clean life" (apparently meaning moderation in sexual matters) all happened to be lower status. Many spoke of the importance of good food and "looking after your health". The middle stratum predominated among those recommending activity: "I'd say, keep working if you can", advised Mr Finnigan, who at 86 was living alone. He was one of the very few men who had never married, and had shared a house with his sister until she predeceased him. "Or if you can't work, have plenty of — hobbies. Keep busy. Keep your mind occupied. That's the main thing."

Perhaps not surprisingly, those who emphasized content-ment and the importance of not worrying were usually from a lower-status background, like Mrs Burnie: "Peace and content-ment", she said. "That's my advice. And not to expect too much out of life. You can't have everything."

Many seemed to see happiness as a duty to themselves and to their fellows, and a cheerful stoicism as the most appropriate way of facing the difficulties of old age. Mrs Irons, who had recently been admitted to a nursing home, said that her husband's death had affected her very badly: "But I've got to accept it. So I'd say — don't go along with a long face. I'm against all that. I must do it in a very cheerful manner. Don't let people have to — sort of — put up with you."

On being young again

Respondents were asked if they would like to be 20 again, and Mr Narracott, for one, thought it was a ridiculous question: "Well, I couldn't be 20 again, could I! Whether I wanted to or not!"

Nevertheless, most respondents were sufficiently intrigued by the question to use it as an exercise in imagination. They were evenly divided on the issue. Among the 50 per cent in favour, some stipulated that they would like it only if they could go back in time, while nearly as many insisted on the opposite condition — that they could be 20 in today's world, without having to re-live their lives as they had already lived them. The 50 per cent who did not want to be 20 again included 8 per cent who thought 20 altogether too young and mentioned some other age — 40, 60, even 70.

There was a slight sex differential, with more women than men attracted by the idea of being young again. Respondents' age at the time of interview did not affect the issue at all, but upper-status respondents who favoured being 20 again were in a minority, compared with a slight majority in both the other strata.

The question sometimes led to reflections suggestive of a "life review", which Robert Butler regards as an almost universal process, and an important form of therapy aiding the "developmental work" unique to old age (1977/1978: 13–19).

The great majority (72 per cent) made it plain that on the whole they were satisfied with what they had made of their lives: "I consider I'd do the same thing as what I have today", Mr Arrowsmith said. "I have no regrets whatsoever. No regrets." He was one of those who felt that, on the whole, they had made the best of the opportunities life had presented to them, and perhaps had never expected very much in any case. They accepted the constraints of old age with a resignation closer to contentment than despair, and to the extent that they compared their present circumstances with former times, quite explicitly counted their blessings. This satisfaction *with their life as a whole* pushed up some to the definitely positive end of the continuum, sustaining them in spirit through the various indignities of extreme old age, and making chronological age to some degree irrelevant.

The rest did express regrets of one kind or another. Mrs Dean, who had just turned 80, seemed to be preoccupied with a conviction that she had not made the most of her life: "Yes, I do think I would like to be 20 again. I think I would live my life and be — different — because —" She paused, gathering her thoughts. "I could have done a lot more useful things and — been — more useful." She sighed. "I suppose it's a terrible thing to say, but I think when you're dead you're dead, so — Oh no, I'm not a bit worried about dying! Not a bit."

On death and dying

For the very old the future means death. If it is true that "One can no more look steadily at death than at the sun" (La Roche-foucald, quoted by Feifel, 1965:xi), then the aged must choose to contemplate only the past and the immediate concerns of a narrow present, or else find self-transcending modes of looking beyond death to a future in which they have no part. Chellam (1977/78) argues that self-engagement is the natural culmination of disengagement processes in old age, and is directly related to awareness of death. These ideas are consonant with Lieberman's findings of "deteriorative psychological changes" which make distance from death a more important dimension than chronological age. He suggests that these changes are not observed in non-terminal illness, and may explain some of the decremental phenomena usually attributed to ageing per se. The fear of death may contribute to these deteriorative changes, even when its imminence is not intellectually apprehended.

There are two opposing schools of thought about the degree to which this fear may dominate human life. Wahl (1965) points out that, following Freud, most psychiatric literature dismisses it as a derivative phenomenon, secondary to the fear of castration or separation anxiety. This glossing-over is still evident in contemporary literature: Kubler-Ross (1969) for instance, does not explicitly include fear in her five stages of dying (denial, anger, bargaining, depression, acceptance). On the other hand Ernest Becker sees fear of death, or "terror", as he prefers to call it, as "the mainspring of human activity — activity designed largely to avoid the fatality of death, to overcome it by denying in some way that it is the final destiny for man" (1973:ix).

In an Australian survey on attitudes to death, 14 per cent said that the most distasteful aspect of death was that the process of dying might be painful (Warren and Chopra, 1979:138). When Toowong respondents were asked whether they worried about dying, several mentioned the possibility of pain, and expressed a wish to die in their sleep.

Because such a large proportion (83 per cent) denied that they ever worried about dying, the question was re-coded, categorizing respondents as death-deniers, death-postponers, death-acceptors, and death-welcomers. Ten per cent were death-deniers, and said firmly that they preferred not to think about it. Another 24 per cent were death-postponers, like 89-year-old Mr Gussey:

> I can't say I really worry about dying, when it comes it comes. But I tell you what I want to see — Halley's comet! I think it's in about six or seven years. It comes every 75 years, and I saw the last one. I was up on a cattle station then, that's where I was working. About five o'clock in the morning I was out bringing the horses in, and I saw this, it was like a big electric light bulb giving a goldy coloured light — I never saw such a sight in my life. The nearest to it was a German bomb, they used to shoot up a tremendous fire and — shower right out [he spread out his arms] like that!

Nineteen respondents — thirteen women and six men — made it plain that they would welcome death. Mr Vickers, who at 83 was in a nursing home, was very definite about it: "The sooner I die the better!" he said, clutching at the swelling in his groin. "Getting around like this, it's — It's bloody awful!"

But death-welcomers were not necessarily depressed or dissatisfied with their present age. Ninety-three-year-old Mr Leslie was still active and in good health, but he said cheerfully that the thought of dying did not worry him at all. "In fact sometimes", he said with a quizzical little smile, "Oh, I wouldn't mind! I wouldn't mind going to bed tonight, knowing I wouldn't wake up in the morning. In fact that'd — that'd please me a lot!" He chuckled at the interviewer's expression of surprise. "I think that's how I'll go off, you know", he went on. "I don't think I'll have a sickness. I might have, you never know, but I don't think so."

Eighty-five-year-old Mr Donald had a less assertive personality, but expressed very similar sentiments: "No, I don't worry about dying now. Years ago I might have, but now — No, it doesn't worry me. Sometimes I sit here meditating over that, and I sort of — I look forward to dying, just to satisfy my curiosity about what happens after death!" He chuckled at the paradoxes this posed, then went on with increasing seriousness: "Death comes easy to old people, you know. You get tired with life, and passing on doesn't worry you. The only thing that worries me is the — My wife and family, they'd grieve over me. That's the only thing. Otherwise it wouldn't worry me in the slightest."

For those who have outlived their closest ties, like Mr Robson at the hostel, this was reason enough for welcoming death: "I've had a good go, but I don't want to live any longer. I've had me day and I've lost my partner so — I've had enough."

The majority of respondents (55 per cent) were classified as death-acceptors, pointing out in one way or another that this was their natural destiny. Three respondents, however, did not consider that the matter should be left entirely to nature, and Mrs Pound was one of them: "I want to go out like a light", she said.

> I'd hate to be a cabbage. I'd just as soon they bung something into me that'd do me in. That'd do me — I could take it. The trouble is, they wouldn't do it. They're not supposed to be allowed to do anything, but it's ridiculous — it's your life, you should be allowed to do what you like with it, if you don't want to live!

For a Catholic — even a non-practising one like Mrs Pound — these were certainly unconventional opinions. She was not contemplating euthanasia as any immediate prospect; she asserted that she did not at all mind being 82, and though she was coded as one of the more positively oriented of those who were "resigned", the word does not do justice to her bright personality and the extent of her activities and interests. She was a tiny person: "Jack used to say he had to put his finger on me when the light went out, I was that skinny!" She spoke of her long-dead husband, who had been a coal-carter, as though he was still present in her life: "I remarked to Jack one day, it seemed funny, everybody was complaining about this change of life, it didn't worry me, and he said, you don't stop still long enough for it to catch up with you!"

Analysis by socio-economic status revealed a strikingly higher proportion of death-welcomers among the lower stratum — 21 per cent compared with 6 per cent for the middle stratum and 8 per cent for the upper. More older than younger cohorts welcomed the thought of death, but there were no sex differentials for this variable.

These attitudes were examined for relationships with a belief in life after death. Denial of death was least evident among unbelievers, who were also most likely to say that they would welcome death. Vacillators, who could not make up their minds either way about their belief in immortality, were most likely to put the thought of death from them, but on the other hand showed the biggest majority accepting death with equanimity. Though the number coded as "unorthodox" was far too small to justify percentaging, they were unorthodox in this as in the content of their beliefs, in that none conformed to the modal tendency towards acceptance.

It seems that for Toowong respondents the subjective reality of extreme old age conformed to ageist norms of inevitable decline — but on the whole the rate of that decline was less steep than respondents themselves expected. Most of them were more satisfied than not with being old. With the rest of society most of them had accepted stereotypes depicting old age as biological pre-programming for death, but lifelong habits of activity and independence had to some extent reduced the negative effects of these ageist norms as self-fulfilling prophecies. At the same time, ageism systematically deprived them of opportunity and incentive for testing the validity of stereotypical old age, other than in idiosyncratic ways, and anaesthetized most respondents into more or less cheerful resignation.

A recipe

Contrasting the lifestyles and opinions of the highly satisfied with the highly dissatisfied, and taking into account the factors that make for resignation, a sort of recipe can be arrived at:

To make the most of growing old . . .

- Don't smoke.
- If you enjoy it, do have an alcoholic drink at the end of the day, preferably in company.
- Cut down on sugar, salt, and animal fats in your diet. End each meal with a piece of fresh fruit, and drink plenty of water.
- Five days out of seven, walk briskly for at least a kilometre, or take some other congenial form of regular outdoor exercise. In addition, and if your doctor agrees, jog or skip or run on the spot or dance aerobically or do other vigorous exercise to the point where your breath quickens noticeably. Physically, what you don't use, you lose.
- Accept that your sleep patterns change as you grow older and learn to relax or meditate if you find yourself lying awake. Remember that a glass of warm milk, or some form of sexual expression, is a much better sedative than sleeping pills.
- Regard any sort of medication as a temporary measure and a last resort. Make sure you understand what your doctor's giving you and why.
- Train your memory by deliberately learning something new each day and recalling it next morning. Mentally, what you don't use, you lose.
- Keep in touch with all your old friends and endeavour to make new ones.

- Maintain a close relationship with at least one much younger person.
- Try to prepare yourself emotionally, financially, and practically for inevitable bereavements.
- Learn to listen.
- Don't give up sex before you have to. Interpret the meaning of "sexual expression" as widely as you feel comfortable with. Sexually, what you don't use, you lose.
- Prepare yourself for the possibility of disabilities in hearing, eyesight, and mobility.
- Give a lot of thought to where you want to live. Taste and try before you buy. Try to avoid having to move in a time of crisis.
- Check your home for safety hazards and have them fixed. Install grab-rails and ramps before you need them.
- Find out about your social service entitlements and make intelligent use of them when necessary.
- Find yourself a hobby. Set yourself realistic goals for attainment within a set period.
- Keep up with the news.
- Learn to laugh at minor matters that might once have annoyed you.
- Reminiscing is good for you — but ask people to tell you if you repeat yourself. Tape-record your memories and listen to them yourself.
- Clarify your values and maintain links with organizations that support them, but guard against ramming your beliefs down anybody else's throat.
- Don't be a slave to routine. Do the things you never had time for before. Go places. Take risks.
- Contribute to your community.
- Fight ageism in all its forms.

Chapter 15: Towards an Age-integrated Future

Ageism, like racism and sexism, promotes segregation — in housing, health services, education, work, and most other social institutions. It results in a virulent apartheid that insulates the old from their fear of the young and the young from their fear of being old, and in doing so deprives both of mutually beneficial contacts.

The alternative is not assimilation — an empty pretence that no differences exist. These lead merely to pathetic attempts by those in the devalued status (whether blacks, women, or the old) to try to "pass" as indistinguishable from those who have been defined as their betters. Rather, the alternative is integration, which presupposes an acceptance of differences as enriching rather than a threat.

Nowadays blacks celebrate their blackness, but not by putting walls around their ghettos. Feminists, who no longer consider it deplorable that women are endowed with breasts, do not advocate incarceration in harems. But the segregation of the old from the young, fuelled by big business interests, is proceeding apace, and is promoted by gerontologists who recommend "(1) the reduction of contact and weakening of ties with younger people, and (2) the concentration of socially similar older persons within a local setting, preferably residential" (Rosow, 1974:156).

There is no reason to suppose that Toowong respondents

were any different from others in their age-group in the high value they placed on family contacts. "The family", said one of them, "is everything" — and he spoke for most. Reducing contact and weakening ties with the people they loved most (who were almost inevitably younger) was precisely their greatest dread. Nor was there any evidence that the young would welcome such a severance.

But this does not mean that they wanted to "live in each other's pockets", as several put it. Their preference was, in Rosenmayr's (1972) phrase, for intimacy at a distance — but not at such a distance as our present day cities impose.

Twenty-first century integrated housing

Housing in the 21st century can help to eliminate ageism along with several other problems by promoting the principle of integration rather than segregation. Modern cities segregate workplaces from leisure-places, schools from residences, fathers from mothers, old from young. Suburban housing may often be as many traffic-jammed kilometres away from a sports-ground as it is from Dad's office; its use as a dormitory and its distance from so many of the requirements of community life imposes segregation like a blight. Housing has yet to catch up with such realities of modern life as one-parent families, working mothers, and pre-school children with no one to mind them, let alone with an increase in elderly widows, some of whom might be available to do the minding if they did not have to do so all day every day. Small high-density housing in garden surroundings, providing *work* opportunities in a computerized on-site work-centre (surely the wave of the future), as well as leisure and shopping facilities in close proximity to a variety of residential options, would meet the needs of all age-groups without intrusion upon privacy.

Most old people, given a choice, would prefer "staying put" to moving anywhere, and this is at last becoming a recognized option with encouragement by local authorities, at least in Britain (Wheeler, 1982). In Australia the old are the least mobile section of the population (Kendig, 1981), but the possibility of having to move, especially on the death of a spouse, increases with increasing age.

The retirement village industry is cashing in on a realistic assessment of the difficulties posed by the maintenance of what was once the family home, and on a rather less realistic assumption that old age is a "slippery slope" requiring three-tier accommodation for increasing degrees of disability. In actuality, though it is culturally prescribed that at whatever age we die, the place to do so is in hospital, the other gradients of the slippery slope are unused in the great majority.of cases. And though retirement villages may offer an acceptable solution for the few who prefer that way of life, age-integrated housing projects (especially if they also integrated work and leisure opportunities) could provide all their advantages without the sterility of segregation.

There is no reason to suppose that only the old desire such features in their housing as low maintenance and built-in security, in pleasant garden surroundings with access to communal leisure facilities. Ramps and call-buttons and access to on-site "sitters" would be decidedly advantageous for mothers of young children, for instance; a rent-paying teenager might appreciate the ramps when wheeling home a load of groceries, the call-button when alarmed by a prowler in the night, and the chance to do some on-site baby-sitting for pay. But age-integrated housing does not require old and young to live cheek by jowl (except for those who choose to do so). Sections of the same "village" could offer different types of facilities, open to all residents but likely to appeal more to some groups than to others.

Such a village might be designed as a series of concentric circles, the centremost offering units designed for those (of any age) who preferred quiet and a full range of safety features. It might include a library, a spa, a small sick bay, a croquet lawn, a secluded garden/restaurant offering delivered meals on request, a craftsroom, and communal lounge. Gardens and walkways might separate it from the next housing circle, consisting of larger residences — townhouses — catering for two-generation families. Beyond that again there might be playgrounds, sportsfields, a larger swimming-pool; and finally, an outer circle encompassing the whole, offering one- or two-bedroom units, or inexpensive lock-up bedsitters with communal kitchens and bathrooms, in conjunction with shops, discotheques, coffee shops, at least one theatre, and a computerized work-centre with telex, word processor, electric typewriters, photocopiers, and other appropriate technology for hire. Laundromats and other communal facilities might be scattered throughout the complex, their number and size depending on the socio-economic standing of residents and their wish to pay for private installation and usage.

An integrated residential village of this type would provide for lifestyles favoured by Grandma in the quiet centremost circle, by Dad and/or Mum and their children in the middle, and teenagers trying their wings on the exterior. But there would be no rules requiring such a choice. Conceivably a shy teenager might choose to live in the quiet of the innermost circle, and a Grandma who preferred hustle and bustle might prefer a room on the outermost. And the sick bay and the services of the resident caretaker — as well as the laundromats, the theatre, the playing-fields, the gardens, the shops, the work-centre, and every other facility — would be available to all. Garage space and provision for public transport could be similarly flexible. The various facilities and their maintenance would provide work opportunities for all age-groups, as would the provision of baby-sitting and granny-sitting services.

Age-integrated housing of the sort suggested would provide for the largest possible element of *choice* in the degree of intermixing taking place between the generations. This would vary according to individual personality, circumstances, and mood. Sometimes Grandma might choose to use the laundromat next to the disco; sometimes the disco patrons might retreat to the quiet of the library. Individuals who chose to stay in one circle or another would not have had that choice forced upon them by their residential situation.

Age-integrated health services

There is a good case for arguing that there should be no such specialty as geriatrics, and that the institutions associated with the so-called diseases of old age should be divided up into smaller units specializing in the treatment of arthritis, strokes, hip fractures, incontinence, organic brain syndrome, angina, etc., at whatever age they occur (and none of them is peculiar to old age).

On the other hand, geriatricians can justify their calling on the undeniable ground that a special characteristic of pathology in old age is that several disease-patterns are often simultaneously present. Also, symptoms may be subtle and reaction to treatment paradoxical, when judged against young-adult standards for normality. If geriatricians can be expected to take more of a "whole person" approach, taking into account the many special social and psychological difficulties that face the old and the interplay between these and physiology, then geriatrics, like paediatrics and gynaecology, can be regarded as essential to a properly integrated system of non-discriminatory health care.

To date, however, ageism manifests itself in discriminating against the old in the quality of services provided for them, which are typically shoddy, inadequate, and of low prestige. Modern hospitals are geared towards cure rather than care, and dramatic interventionist strategies have a much greater appeal than the management of the chronicity that typically afflicts the old. People who fail to get better quickly retard the high turnover in bed-occupancy which is the goal of hospital administrators, and offer medical personnel little of the glamour associated with crisis-intervention techniques. Old people, of course, do suffer medical crises, and frequently die of them, but as Maddison points out, "the social value placed on the life of an elderly person is remarkably low in today's world" (1979:86).

Assimilationist medicine, which assumes that the young adult should be the norm for all procedures, has led to a very high degree of iatrogenic disease among the old. According to a distinguished British physician, "Perhaps the greatest danger to the physical and mental health of older people today lies in the number of drugs prescribed for them" (Anderson, 1977:173). He goes on to deplore the tendency of doctors to consider that an old person's illness must necessarily be of a fatal kind, whereas, "In fact, commonly the disease is treatable, especially if diagnosed early."

With the elimination of ageism, old age can be seen as a time when diseases are still treatable, disability still relievable, decline still reversible, and *development* — in the sense of improvement, adaptation, the learning of new skills, and growth towards wisdom — still eminently possible, provided the social climate makes it so.

And the social climate may change rapidly as new facts emerge regarding the biology of ageing. For example, Swedish research is discovering that the health of successive cohorts appears to be continually improving: people who turn 70 in 1982 are likely to be healthier, according to all kinds of exhaustive tests, than people who turned 70 in 1977. This offers support for Fries and Crapo's (1981) argument for a "rectangular curve" of human longevity. According to this model, the onset of maladies associated with old age are being increasingly delayed and compressed into a relatively short period at the far end of the lifespan, so that the old can not only expect to live longer, but to continue in good health until a final illness sometime in their tenth decade of life.

Sooner or later, living ends in death, and if it is later rather than sooner, death is preceded by old age. But the "facts" so often and so confidently associated with the one certainty of death must be qualified by conditionals such as "if", "but", "probably", "in some cases", "perhaps", "sometimes", and "usually". Usually (but not always) death occurs less than 100 years from birth. Usually (but not always) death is preceded by a period of physiological and mental vulnerability which is socially defined as symptomatic of decay. The extreme vulnerability of early infancy, on the other hand, is socially defined as developmental.

If we choose, we can define the ageing process also as potentially developmental, and the very act of so defining it will clear the way towards its fulfilment. Disease and disability are known to be amenable to social action, and a prerequisite for social action for the reduction of disease and disability in old age is a re-definition of what it means to be old.

As an example, take pregnancy and childbirth. These are biological experiences that have been socially re-defined within the lifetime of Toowong respondents. Shame, ignorance, danger, and pain were traditionally associated with parturition in Western industrial societies, and legitimated on religious as well as biological grounds. But the subjective reality of childbearing has been re-defined more positively, and social action has occurred at the same time. Expressed externally in such behaviour as relaxation exercises, pain and danger have been reduced, and shame and ignorance virtually eliminated. The new knowledge has received institutionalized support for an experience now commonly regarded as a highpoint for both parents.

A similar re-definition of old age as rewarding, rather than degrading, is both possible and overdue. With it will come non-ageist services that accord the aged as much right to good health and continuing development as any other human being.

Age-integrated education

Old people want to learn, and learn they can — given the opportunity. Opportunities are multiplying, as is testified by the success of further education classes and of mature-age university students. But the way is open for imaginative programmes more actively integrating age-groups in learning experiences beneficial to both.

As they stand, schools are monuments to ageism. Children and adolescents are defined as learners; adults as teachers; old people as incapable of either learning or teaching — they are hustled out of the system entirely at a pre-set retiring age. Yet children might well teach adults elementary computer skills, for instance; and old people could teach, among many other things, crochet and carpentry and local history. There seems to be no logical justification for separating learners from teachers simply on the grounds of age, or for decreeing that adult learners should be catered for only in age-segregated classrooms.

With the information explosion upon us, schools need to open up to the world and set aside their function as child-minding institutions to become a relevant part of that enlightening explosion. Anyone, from an out-of-work teenager to a lively nonagenarian, should have the right to acquire new knowledge or brush up on old at the nearest educational establishment suitable for the purpose — whether it be at primary, secondary, or tertiary level.

It is easy to envisage specific age-integrated courses designed to make the most of interaction between old and young. The most obvious is a course on human relationships, perhaps with conflict resolution as the key. Conflict occurs not only between generations, but between individuals, between groups, between nations, and the skills and insight gained from a successful course might well carry over into all these fields. Primary and secondary schools could offer eight-week courses open to the public, perhaps with special concessions to the elderly to attract their participation. In groups that changed their composition to suit the problem under discussion, they could practise the skills of conflict resolution with enough academic detachment to de-fuse possible antagonisms, but at the same time with sufficient personal involvement for the lessons learned to be incorporated into daily life.

But for the very old, like the Toowong respondents, the indoctrination of a lifetime as well as practical considerations of transport or disability might make it difficult for them to avail themselves of such an opportunity, even where it existed. For these — especially for those living alone — some positive discrimination is called for. People who are isolated in any way, whether through social circumstances or disability, lack opportunities to practise elementary skills of verbal recall in conversational give-and-take, and are therefore (whatever their age) likely to suffer some degree of aphasia and loss of intellectual alertness. For the old, these losses are exacerbated by self-fulfilling prophecies. Most have long accepted the notion that they are biologically rather than socially deprived of learning opportunities, and that some degree of senile malfunction is their irreversible fate. The extent to which senile malfunction is due to sensory deprivations imposed by living alone, in institutions, or within the so-called "safety" of deeply routinized habits, is at present unknown, but an educational programme for the aged must deal with the facts of the social environments typical of its clients if it is to have any hope of success. For the old as for the young, educational material must be relevant to the learner's life-situation or learning is unlikely to take place.

The same applies to what is remembered. Old people seldom do well at remembering a chance assortment of articles or words, because their life-experience has taught them not to bother about the meaningless. But their memory for everyday life situations may exceed that of younger people (Rabbitt, 1981). At the same time, most were brought up to believe that learning consists of the memorization of facts, and that memory-loss inevitably accompanies old age. They are apt to interpret lapses of memory (which are common in all age-groups, and are primarily due to inattention) as evidence of approaching senility. So an educational programme custom-built for the aged, aimed at integrating them with the mainstream of society, would be first and foremost a consciousness- and morale-raising programme. It would be designed to convince participants that *developmental* ageing is well within their powers and that the rewards are more than worth any effort involved. And it would concentrate on memory training. The material for memorization could aid developmental ageing by stimulating an interest in the requisites of physical and mental health, but wider interests, such as current events or the arts, could be added at will. In these days of telephones and conference hook-ups, video machines, and the newer communication technologies, there is no reason for old age or disability to isolate people in their homes from the world of learning.

Age-integration in a pensioner society

Many Toowong respondents saw the future as menacing, and

not without good reason. International leaders (some of them old enough to know better) seem to be trapped within an outdated view of the world as consisting of goodies and baddies with the solution a matter of shooting it out — Armageddon, as respondents saw it. Others among them interpreted the signs more hopefully. They thought there was more concern with justice, a wider vision, than they had been aware of in their youth. But all were very conscious that change was endemic and rushing upon us with alarming speed.

Among those changes is the fact that work is done increasingly by machines, with less and less available for the employment of human beings. In itself this seems to be no more a reason for gloom than the universal attainment of longevity. Only the fortunate few actually enjoy working. People have always preferred having slaves to do their dirty work, and their strenuous and monotonous work, too. Replacing human slaves and servants with machines seems to be a very substantial step in the direction of a just society — if we can solve the distribution problem.

In the immediate future it seems likely that work will still be eagerly sought after, and may become mostly a temporary affair awarded by short-term contracts. Specialized skills will be needed, of a kind scarcely predictable from year to year. Those who guess right will have equipped themselves educationally through intensive short-term training to tender for jobs that become available, and race, sex or age will probably be of minor importance compared to having the right skills at the right time.

But the majority will guess wrong, or be unable to find appropriate training, or will consider it all too much of an effort and accept the minimum-income pension available to all. When the workless become the majority, that minimum will provide adequately for most human needs, and it will no longer be known as the dole. There will be no technical difficulties in providing plenty of material goods for the workless majority, if we presume, as we surely can, that our machines are good enough. And the fact that the workless *are* the majority should ensure that they will not meekly suffer oppression by the ambitious few.

In this scenario the aged will not meekly suffer oppression either. They will be healthy, vigorous, well-educated, and there will be a lot of them. If they want work, they will pit their brains against anyone, and win contracts on their merits. If they want leisure, they will not all be content with bingo. Increasingly, they will choose their way of life and demand non-discriminatory treatment, seeing no reason for shame in the fact of being old.

These predictions are conjectural, as all predictions must be. What is *certain* about old age, now and in the future, is this and nothing more: to be old is to have lived a long time. There is nothing intrinsically disadvantageous in having lived a long time. On the contrary, *old is experienced*, just as black is beautiful. If self-fulfilling ageist stereotypes are to be ousted so that the full potentialities of old age may have a chance of realization, the old must learn to hold up their heads, just as blacks, and women, and other disadvantaged groups, are learning to do at last.

Bibliography

Aitkin, D.A. 1977. *Stability and change in Australian Politics*. Canberra: Australian National University Press.

Alexander, F. 1967. *Australia since federation*. Melbourne: Nelson.

Anderson, F. 1977. The role of the physician. In F.A. Exton-Smith & J. Grimley Evans (eds.), *Care of the elderly: meeting the challenge of dependency*. London: Academic Press, 169-74.

Andrews, F.M., and Withey, S.B. 1976. *Social indicators of well-being: Americans' perceptions of life quality*. New York: Plenum Press.

Aries, P. 1973. *Centuries of childhood: a social history of family life*. Harmondsworth: Penguin.

Bardwick, J.M., and Douvan, E. 1971. Ambivalence: the socialization of women. In *Woman in sexist society: studies in power and powerless*, eds. V. Gornick and B.K. Moran. New York: Basic Books.

Baumrind, D. 1973. Authoritarian vs. authoritative parental control. In *Socialization*, eds. S. Scarr-Salapatek and P. Salapatek, pp. 31–43. Columbus, Ohio: Merrill.

Beard, Bella B. 1967. *Social competence of centenarians*. Social Science Research Institute. Athens, Georgia: University of Georgia.

Becker, E. 1973. *The denial of death*. New York: Free Press.

Bennett, K.C., and Ahammer, I.M. 1977. Towards a social deficit model of ageing. *Australian Journal of Social Issues* 12 (1): 3–17.

Bennett, K. 1977. The social deficit model re-visited. Paper presented at the 13th Annual Conference, 1976. Australian Association of Gerontology, Adelaide.

Berelson, B.; Lazarsfeld, P.; and McPhee, W. 1954. *Voting*. Chicago: University of Chicago Press.

Berger, P.L. 1973. *The Social Reality of Religion*. Harmondsworth: Penguin Books.

———, and Luckmann, T. 1979. *The social construction of reality: a treatise in the sociology of knowledge*. Harmondsworth: Penguin Books.

Birren, J.E., Butler, R., Greenhouse, S., Sokoloff, L., and Yarrow, M., eds. 1963. *Human aging: a biological and behavioural study*. Publication No. (HSM) 71-9051. Washington, D.C.: U.S. Government Printing Office.

Bland, F.A. 1968. Unemployment relief. In *The depression of the thirties*, eds. L. Louis and I. Turner. Melbourne: Cassell.

Botwinick, J. 1978. *Aging and behavior: a comprehensive integration of research findings*. New York: Springer.

Brown, G.W. 1976. Social Causes of Disease. In *An introduction to medical sociology*, ed. D. Tuckett, pp. 291-333. London: Tavistock.

Brundtland, G.H., and Walloe, L. 1976. Menarcheal age in Norway in the 19th century: a re-evaluation of the historical sources. *Annals of Human Biology* 3 (4): 363–74.

Butler, R. 1969. Ageism: another form of bigotry. *Gerontologist* 9: 243.

Caldwell, B.M., and Richmond, J.B. 1967. The Impact of Theories of Child Development. In *Readings in human development*, eds. H. Bernard and W. Huckins, pp. 3–13. Boston: Allyn and Bacon.

Chellam, Grace 1977/78. Awareness of death and self-engagement in later life: the engagement continuum. *International Journal of Aging and Human Development* 8 (2): 111–27.

Cities Commission 1975. *Brisbane at the census, 1971: a social atlas*. Canberra: Summit Press.

Cohen, B., and Black, D. 1976. *Twentieth century Australia*. Perth, W.A.: Carroll.

Comfort, A. 1976. Age prejudice in America. *Social Policy* November/December, pp. 3–8.

———. 1977. *A good age*. Melbourne: Macmillan.

Costar, B.J. 1978. Brisbane or Prague?: the 1912 and 1948 strikes. In *Brisbane retrospect: eight aspects of Brisbane history*. Brisbane: Library Board of Queensland.

Cumming, E.; Henry, W.E.; and Parlagreco, M.L. 1961. The very old. In *Growing old: the process of disengagement*, eds. E. Cumming and W.E. Henry, pp. 201–9. New York: Basic Books.

Day, L. 1975. Family Size and fertility. In *Australian society: a sociological introduction*, eds. A.F. Davies and S. Encel, pp. 16–30. 2nd ed. Melbourne: Cheshire.

Dean, J.P., and Whyte, W.F. 1969. How do you know if your informant is telling the truth? In *Issues in participant observation: a text and reader*, eds. G.L. McCall and J.L. Simmons. Reading, Mass.: Addison-Wesley.

Dempsey, K. 1980. Teaching the young about the old: introducing undergraduates to the sociology of ageing. Paper presented at the 1st Regional Congress, International Association of Gerontology, Asia/Oceania Region, December, Melbourne.

Dowdy, E., and Lupton, G. 1978. *The survey of declining recruitment to the ministry: final report*. Prepared for the Australian Council of Churches.

Duckett, S.J. 1979. The development of social policy for the aged. In *Ageing in Australia*, eds. J.M. Donald, A.V. Everitt, and P.J. Wheeler, pp. 40–56. Sydney: Australian Association of Gerontology.

Dunstan, K. 1968. *Wowsers*. Melbourne: Cassell Australia.

Encel, S.; MacKenzie, N.; and Tebbutt, M. 1974. *Women and society: an Australian study*. Melbourne: Cheshire.

Exton-Smith, A.N., and Grimley-Evans, J., eds. 1977. *Care of the elderly: meeting the challenge of dependency*. London: Academic Press.

Feifel, H., ed. 1965. *The meaning of death*. New York: McGraw-Hill.

Fries, J., and Crapo, L. 1980. *Vitality and aging: implications of the rectangular curve*. San Francisco: W.H. Freeman.

Game, A., and Pringle, R. 1979. Sexuality and the suburban dream. *Australian and New Zealand Journal of Sociology* 15 (2): 4–15.

Gault, U., and Reeve, R.A. 1980. Forgetting in older people: probing the stereotype. Paper presented at the 1st Regional Congress, International Association of Gerontology, Asia/Oceania Region, December, Melbourne.

Gold, R.L. 1969. Roles in sociological field observation. In *Issues in participant observation: a text and reader*, eds. G.L. McCall and J.L. Simmons, pp. 30–38. Reading, Mass.: Addison-Wesley.

Goodman, R. 1968. *Secondary education in Queensland, 1860–1960*. Canberra: Australian National University Press.

Gordon, D. 1976. *Health, sickness, and society: theoretical concepts in social and preventive medicine*. Brisbane: University of Queensland Press.

Gove, W.R. 1975. Sex, marital status and mortality. In *Population studies: selected essays and research*, ed. K.C.W. Kammeyer, pp. 257–80. 2nd ed. Chicago: Rand McNally.

Granick, S., and Patterson, R., eds. 1971. *Human aging II: an eleven-year followup biomedical and behavioral study*. Publication No. (HSM) 71-9037. Washington, D.C.: U.S. Government Printing Office.

Gregory, Helen 1977. *A church for its times: the story of St. Thomas's Church, Toowong*. Brisbane.

Hackett, E. 1982. Ageing. Tape-recorded segment of radio broadcast The Body Programme. Australian Broadcasting Commission.

Hall, A.; Selby, J.; and Vanclay, F. 1982. Sexual Ageism. *Australian Journal on Ageing* 1 (3) (August): 29–34.

Harwood, E. 1977. What is normal healthy ageing? Introduction to group discussion. Presented to Australian Association of Gerontology, Adelaide.

———, and Naylor, G. 1980. Age resistance quotient: a new parameter in gerontological assessment. Proceedings of the First Regional Congress of the International Association of Gerontoloty, Asia/Oceania Region.

Havighurst, R. 1961. Successful aging. *Gerontologist* 1: 8–13.

Hazan, H. 1980. *The limbo people: a study of the constitution of the time universe among the aged*. London: Routledge and Kegan Paul.

Henderson, R.F. 1972. The dimensions of poverty in Australia. In *The public sector: selected readings*, ed. J. Dixon, pp. 123–37. Harmondsworth: Penguin.

Hendricks, J., and Hendricks, C. 1977. *Aging in mass society: myths and realities*. Cambridge, Mass.: Winthrop.

Hewitt, P. 1978. *Catholics divided: a sociological investigation*. Brisbane: Archdiocesan Research Group.

Hudson, R., and Binstock, R. 1976. Political systems and aging. In *Handbook of aging and the Social Science*, eds. R. Binstock and E. Shanas, pp. 369–400. New York: Van Nostrand Reinhold.

Hyman, H.H. 1954. *Interviewing in social research*. Chicago: University of Chicago Press.

Inglis, K.S. 1975. Religious behaviour. In *Australian society: a sociological introduction*, eds. A. Davies, and S. Encel, 2nd ed. Melbourne: Cheshire.

Isaacs, B.; Livingstone, M.; and Neville, Y. 1972. *Survival of the unfittest: a study of geriatric care in Glasgow*. London: Routledge and Kegan Paul.

Job, E. 1982. *The social construction of old age: a study of people aged 80 and over*. Unpublished thesis, University of Queensland.

———; Jones, J.; Johansen, C.; and Spenceley, E. 1980. Interviewing very old people. Paper presented at 1st Regional Congress,

International Association of Gerontology, December, Melbourne.

Kalish, R.A. 1979. The new ageism and the failure models: a polemic. *Gerontologist* 19 (4): 398–402.

Kendig, H., 1981. Housing and living arrangements of the aged. In *Towards an Older Australia*, ed. A. Howe, pp. 85-101. Brisbane, University of Queensland Press.

Kimmel, D.C. 1974. *Adulthood and aging: an interdisciplinary developmental view*. New York: Wiley.

Krupinski, J., and Stoller, A., eds. 1974. *The family in Australia: social, demographic and psychological aspects*. Sydney: Pergamon Press.

Kubler-Ross, E. 1969. *On death and dying*. New York: Macmillan.

Labouvie-Vief, G., and Blanchard-Fields, U.F. 1982. Cognitive ageing and psychological growth. *Ageing and Society* 2 (2) (July): 183–210.

Laslett, P. 1976. Societal development and aging. In *Handbook of aging and the Social Sciences*, eds. R.N. Binstock and E. Shanas, pp. 87–116. New York: Van Nostrand Reinhold.

Lawson, R. 1973. *Brisbane in the 1890s: a study of an Australian urban society*. Brisbane: University of Queensland Press.

Levin, J., and Levin, W. 1980. *Ageism: prejudice and discrimination against the elderly*. Belmont, Calif.: Wadworth.

Lieberman, M., and Coplan, A. 1969. Distance from death as a variable in the study of aging. *Developmental Psychology* 2 (1): 71–84.

Lofland, J. 1971. *Analyzing social settings: a guide to qualitative observation and analysis*. Belmont, Calif.: Wadsworth.

Lopata, H. 1972. Roles changes in widowhood: a world perspective. In *Aging and modernization*, eds. D.O. Cowgill and L.D. Holmes, pp. 275–303. New York: Appleton-Century-Crofts.

Lowenstein, W. 1978. *Weevils in the flour: an oral record of the 1930s depression in Australia*. Melbourne: Hyland House.

Lowenthal, M. and Haven, C. 1968. Interaction and adaptation: intimacy as a crucial variable. In *Middle age and aging: a reader in social psychology*, ed. B. Neugarten, pp. 390-400. Chicago: University of Chicago Press.

Maddison, D. 1979. Medical education and attitudes to ageing. In *Ageing in Australia*, eds. J. Donald, A. Everitt, and P. Wheeler, pp. 85–87. Sydney: Australian Association of Gerontology.

Madigan, F.C. 1957. Are sex mortality differentials biologically caused? *Millbank Memorial Fund Quarterly* 35: 202-23.

Marshall, V.W., and Tindale, J. 1978/79. Notes for a radical geron-
    tology. *Aging and Human Development* 9: 163–75.
Maves, P.B. 1960. Aging, religion and the Church. In *Handbook of social
    gerontology*, ed. C. Tibbits, pp. 698-749. Chicago: University
    of Chicago Press.
McKeown, T. 1965. *Medicine in modern society: planning based on evaluation
    of medical achievement.* London: Allen and Unwin.
McQueen, H. 1975. *A new Brittania: an argument concerning the social
    origins of Australian nationalism and radicalism.* Harmondsworth:
    Penguin.
————. 1978. *Social sketches of Australia, 1888–1975.* Harmondsworth:
    Penguin.
Mechanic, D. 1968. *Medical sociology: a selective view.* New York: The
    Free Press.
Milbrath, L. 1965. *Political participation: how and why people get involved
    in politics.* Chicago: Rand McNally.
Mills, C.W. 1954. *The sociological imagination.* New York: Oxford
    University Press.
Mindel, C.H., and Vaughn, C.E. 1978. A multi-dimensional approach
    to religiosity and disengagement. *Journal of Gerontology* 33 (1):
    103–8.
Mishara, B.; Kastenbaum, R.; Baker, F.; and Patterson, R. 1975.
    Alcohol effects in old age: an experimental investigation.
    Social Science and Medicine 9 (10): 535–47.
Moberg, D. 1968. Religiosity in old age. In *Middle age and aging: a reader
    in social psychology*, ed. B.L. Neugarten, pp. 497–508. Chicago:
    University of Chicago Press.
Moser, C.A. 1969. *Survey methods in social investigation.* London:
    Heinemann.
Myerhoff, B., and Simic, A., eds. 1978. *Life's career — aging: cultural
    variations on growing old.* Beverly Hills, Calif.: Sage Publications.
Myers, G. 1979. Recent trends in mortality among the aged and their
    implications. In *Ageing in Australia*, eds. J.M. Donald, A.V.
    Everitt, and P.J. Wheeler, pp. 21–27. Sydney: Australian
    Association of Gerontology.
Naylor, G. 1974. Theoretical and practical application of 'Educability'
    in the elderly. *Proceedings of the Auckland conference on ageing.*
Neugarten, B.L., ed. 1968. *Middle age and aging: a reader in social
    psychology.* Chicago: University of Chicago Press.
————. 1974. Age groups in American society and the rise of the
    young-old. *Annals of American Academy* September,
    pp. 187–98.

_____. Wood, V.; Kraines, R.; and Loomis, B. 1968. Women's attitudes towards the menopause. In *Middle age and aging: a reader in social psychology*, ed. B.L. Neugarten, pp. 195–200. Chicago: University of Chicago Press.

Palmore, E., and Jeffers, F.C. 1971. *Prediction of life-span: recent findings*. Lexington, Mass.: Heath Lexington Books.

_____. 1977. Facts on ageing: a short quiz. *The Gerontologist*, 17 (4): 315–20.

Parker, S. 1971. *The Future of work and leisure*. London: Paladin.

Parkes, C.M.; Benjamin, B.; and Fitzgerald, R. 1969. Broken heart: a statistical survey of increased mortality among widowers. *British Medical Journal* 1, pp. 740–43.

Parsons, T. 1954. The kinship system of the contemporary United States. In *Essays in sociological theory*, ed. T. Parsons, pp. 89–93. 2nd ed. New York: Free Press.

_____. 1959. Voting and the equilibrium of the American political system. In *American voting behavior*, eds. É. Burdick and A. Brodbeck, pp. 80–120. New York: Free Press.

Peck, R.C. 1968. Psychological developments in the second half of life. In *Middle age and aging: a reader in social psychology*, ed. B.L. Neugarten, pp. 88-920. Chicago: University of Chicago Press.

Powles, J. 1975. Why do women live longer than men? *Growing Older* 6 (2): 2–5.

Rabbitt, P. Memory for everyday life situations. Paper presented at *XIIth International Congress of Gerontology*, Hamburg, 1981.

Rankin, D.H. 1939. *The history of the development of education in Victoria, 1836–1936*. Melbourne: Arrow.

Raphael, B. 1979. Life and love in the decades of loss. In *Ageing in Australia*, eds. J.M. Donald, A.V. Everitt, and P.J. Wheeler, pp. 83–84. Sydney: Australian Association of Gerontology.

Richardson, A.H., and Freeman, H.E., 1964. Behaviour, attitudes, and disengagement among the very old. Unpublished thesis, Brandeis University.

Rosaldo, M.Z. 1974. Women, culture and society: a theoretical overview. In *Woman, culture and society*, eds. M.Z. Rosaldo and L. Lamphere, pp. 17–42. Stanford, Calif.: Stanford University Press.

Rose, A. 1968. The subculture of the aging: a topic for sociological research. In *Middle Age and ageing: a reader in social psychology*, ed. B.L. Neugarten, pp. 29–34. Chicago: University of Chicago Press.

Rosenmayr, L. 1972. *The Elderly in Austrian Society*. In *Aging and modernization*, eds. D.O. Cowgill and L.D. Holmes, pp. 183-96. New York: Appleton-Century-Crofts.

Rosow, I. 1977/78. Institutional position of the aged. In *Readings in aging and death: contemporary perspectives*, ed. S.H. Zarit, pp. 79–83. New York: Harper and Row.

Royal Reader. 1901. London: Thos. Nelson and Sons.

Russell, C. 1981. *The aging experience*. Sydney: George Allen & Unwin.

Ruzicka, L.T., and Caldwell, J.C. 1977. *The end of demographic transition in Australia*. Australian Family Formation Project Monograph no. 5. Canberra: Australian National University.

Shanas, E., and Maddox, G. 1976. Aging, health and the organization of health resources. In *Handbook of aging and the Social Sciences*, eds. R.N. Binstock and E. Shanas, pp. 592–618. New York: Van Nostrand Reinhold.

———; Townsend, P.; Wedderburn, D.; Friis, H.; Milhoj, P.; and Stehouwer, J., eds. 1968. *Old people in three industrial societies*. London: Routledge and Kegan Paul.

Shann, E. 1948. *An economic history of Australia*. Cambridge: Cambridge University Press.

Shephard, R.J. 1978. *Physical activity and ageing*. London: Croom Helm.

Shigiya, R. 1978. *Report of interdisciplinary research on Japanese centenarians*. Tokyo: Japan Institute for Gerontological Research and Development.

Shock, N. 1973. Physiology of aging. In *Aging: its challenge to the individual and to society*, ed. W. Bier, pp. 47–60. New York: Fordham University Press.

Streib, G. 1968. Are the aged a minority group? In *Middle age and aging: a reader in social psychology*, ed. B.L. Neugarten, Chicago: University of Chicago Press.

Sussman, M.B. 1959. The isolated nuclear family: fact or fiction. *Social Problems* 6, pp. 333–40.

Tew, M. 1951. *Work and the welfare state*. Melbourne: Melbourne University Press.

Townsend, P. 1963. *The family life of old people: an inquiry in East London*. Harmondsworth: Penguin.

———. 1968b. The Structure of the family. In *Old people in three industrial societies*, eds. E. Shanas, P. Townsend, D. Wedderburn, H. Friis, P. Milhoj, and J. Stehouwer, pp. 132–76. London: Routledge and Kegan Paul.

Tuckett, D. ed. 1976. *An introduction to medical sociology*. London: Tavistock.

Twaddle, A.C., and Hessler, R.M. 1977. *A sociology of health*. St. Louis: C.V. Mosby.

Wahl, C.W. 1965. The fear of death. In *The meaning of death*, ed. H. Feifel, pp. 16–29. New York: McGraw-Hill.

Ward, J. 1979. Class and the aged. In *Ageing in Australia*, eds. J.M. Donald, A.V. Everitt, and P.J. Wheeler, pp. 49–52. Sydney: Australian Association of Gerontology.

Warren, W.G., and Chopra, P.N. 1979. An Australian survey of attitudes to death. *Australian Journal of Social Issues* 14 (2): 134–42.

Wharton, G. 1981. *Sexuality and aging*. Metuchen, N.J.: Scarecrow Press.

Wheeler, R. 1982. Staying put: a new development in policy? *Ageing and Society* 2 (3) (November) 299–330.

Whitehead, T. 1978. Ageing and the mind. In *The social challenge of ageing*, ed. D. Hobman, pp. 197–221. London: Croom Helm.

Wild, R.A. 1977. Social stratification and old age. *Australian Journal of Social Issues* 12 (1): 19–32.

Wilson, R.N. 1975. *The sociology of health: an introduction*. New York: Random House.

Wood, P. 1971. *Site and pre-war growth: Brisbane and its river*. Brisbane: 43rd ANZAAS Congress, 24–28 May, pp. 9–13.

Wunsch, G. 1980. Sex differentials and cause of death in some European countries. In *Demographic patterns in developed societies*, ed. R.W. Hiorns. London: Taylor and Francis.

Wyeth, E.R. 1953. *Education in Queensland: a history of education in Queensland and in the Moreton Bay District of New South Wales*. Melbourne: Australian Council for Educational Research.

Index

Aborigines: franchise for, 140; land
  rights for, 145, 148-49, 193
activity: importance of, 49, 85, 166,
  185, 200; indoor/outdoor, 88, 97,
  180, 193; lack of, 99, 133, 184; and
  life satisfaction, 193, 197;
  solitary/gregarious, 88, 93, 96, 97,
  99, 205, 206-7
advice, 190, 194, 197, 199-201, 206-7
age-cohort differentials: in
  advice-giving, 200; in age of
  menarche, 103; as analytic principle,
  21; in attitudes to being young
  again, 201; in attitudes to death and
  dying, 205; in attitudes to equality
  in marriage, 120; in education, 61,
  63; in health, 178, 179, 183; in life
  satisfaction, 190, 193, 197; in
  number of children, 128; in number
  of siblings, 44; in political and
  religious attitudes, 151, 157, 166; in
  residential situation, 137, 197; in
  work and leisure, 93, 180
ageing, 5, 7, 8, 59-60, 177, 215;
  biological model of, 3, 5, 7, 57, 68,
  190; conflict model of, 154; course
  on, 153; developmental, 70, 201,
  216; disengagement theory of, 5,
  202; social deficit theory of, 8;
  symbolic interactionist model of, 8
age-integration, 208-18; in education,
  214-15; in health services, 212-14;

  in housing, 209-11; in work, 216-17
ageism, 3-9, 22, 39, 40, 55, 190, 207,
  208, 209, 218; and activity, 99, 180;
  and decision-making, 138; and
  education, 68-70, 214, 215; and
  event-confrontation, 54; and
  gerontology, 5, 57; and health, 177,
  178, 185, 212; and life-satisfaction,
  199, 205; new ageism, 6-7, 8, 138;
  and politics, 154; and religion, 156,
  167; sexual ageism, 110-12; and
  work, 86
age-segregation, 208, 209, 210
age-stratification, 47-49, 82, 98
alcoholic drinks, 180, 191, 194, 206
Aitkin, D.A., 140, 141, 142
Alexander, F., 74
Anderson, F., 213
Andrews, F.M., and Withey, S.B., 115
Aries, P., 47
Australian Labor Party, 140, 143-44,
  146
authority: biological model of, 65;
  in childhood, 47, 50; fear of, 54,
  141; in marriage, 50, 119-21

Bardwick, J.M., and Douvan, E., 50
Baumrind, D.; 50
Beard, Bella B., 8
Becker, E., 203
being young again, 201-2
belief in life after death, 39, 155,

162-64, 194, 202; as reincarnation, 163; sex differentials in, 164

Bennett, K.C., and Ahammer, I.M., 8, 181

bereavement, 39, 70, 123-24, 193; compensation for, 135; death of adult children, 133-34; and life satisfaction, 192, 194, 199; loss of spouse, 124, 125, 177, 193, 198; and network-maintenance, 114

Berelson, B., Lazarsfeld, P., and McPhee, W., 145

Berger, P.L., 167

Berger, P.L., and Luckmann, T., 7

biology, 3, 5-6, 7, 8, 61, 185, 214; and inferiority of females, 3, 65; inferiority of old people, 3, 99, 190; and education, 57, 215; and death, 205; as determinant of social behaviour, 59, 61

Birren, J.E., 177

birth control, 19, 36, 101, 105-7, 168; celibacy as means of, 107; socio-economic status and, 107

Bland, F.A., 81

Boer War, 28, 29

boredom, 7, 37, 53, 98, 198

Botwinick, J., 7, 19, 181

Brown, G.W., 123

Brundtland, G.H., and Walloe, L., 101, 103

Butler, R., 6, 201

Caldwell, B.M., and Richmond, J.B., 47

celibacy, 173

centenarians, 8, 170, 171

Chellam, G., 202

childhood, 33-34, 40, 43-55; education in, 56-66; health in, 102-3, 168-70, 171-72; leisure activities in, 88-91; political socialization in, 140; religion in, 158, 159, 161, 166; work in, 58, 73, 74, 75

childlessness, 123, 128, 133

childbirth, 19, 49, 101, 214; attitudes to, 104; dangers of, 173-74; experiences of, 35, 126, 168, 170

church, 54, 85, 160, 161

church attendance, 20, 34, 38, 136, 158-60; and life satisfaction, 194, 198

Cities Commission, 24

Cohen, B., and Black, D., 73

Comfort, A., 83

community services, 11, 12, 86, 122, 194

conflict resolution, 215

confusion, 4, 14, 108, 182, 197. See also mental state; senility

conservation, 145, 150-51, 193

contraception. See birth control

Costar, B.J., 146

Cumming, E., and Henry, W.E., 5

dances, 37, 87, 91-93, 113

Day, L., 128

Dean, J.P., and Whyte, W.F., 17

death and dying, 39, 167, 190, 194, 197; attitudes to, 85, 134, 144, 202-5; death of children, 134, 155, 168; death of parents, 33

demography, 3, 6, 10, 12, 31

Dempsey, K., 131, 154

dependence, 10, 50, 51, 192

Depression, economic, 29, 30, 31; in 1890s, 27, 74; in 1930s, 36, 67, 71, 79-82, 194

depression, emotional, 7, 124, 193

development, 5-6, 66, 213, 214; developmental ageing, 70, 201, 216

diet, 43, 44, 172, 180, 200, 206

disability, 5, 39, 97, 182; and education, 214, 215, 216; preparation for, 207

disengagement theory, 5, 156

divorce and separation, 52, 117

doctors, 49, 78, 107-8, 168, 194, 206

Dowdy, E., and Lupton, G., 158

Duckett, S.J., 152

Dunstan, K., 92, 93

Encel, S., Mackenzie, N., and Tebbutt, M., 75, 173

equality: in marriage, 50, 119, 120, 125

education, 56-70, 192, 208; age-cohort differentials in, 61, 63; and age at leaving school, 48, 58, 61, 63; age-integrated, 214-16; and attitudes to menopause, 105; compulsory, 58, 62; in the country, 56, 63, 64; further education, 66-68; in old age, 67-70, 214-16; self-education, 63,

64; sex differentials in, 63; socio-economic differentials in, 32, 63, 68
ethnicity of sample, 31
ethnocentrism, 59, 60, 65
euthanasia, 4, 204
event-confrontation, 53-54, 79, 96, 124, 129, 135; and health, 173, 176, 199; as lifelong pattern, 130; and life-satisfaction, 191; and sex roles, 52, 54, 82, 85, 86, 198; and socio-economic status, 53-54
exercise: in childhood, 43, 49, 56, 172; in old age, 49, 70, 87, 179, 180, 206; during pregnancy, 174
extra-marital sex, 108, 109
eyesight, 170, 181-82, 197

family: contacts/relationships, 109, 131-34, 138, 195; enterprises, 75; importance of, 128, 129, 209; and myth of desertion by, 137-38; and politics, 153, 198; size of, 44, 45, 128; theories of, 137
Feifel, H., 202
feminism, 78, 106, 208
financial situation, 20, 29, 32, 83-85, 152; in childhood, 46; of women, 85, 189
First World War, 28-29, 36, 46, 78, 97, 114, 192
flexibility, 97, 105, 145, 151, 153, 166; myths about lack of, 7, 69
friends, 53, 124, 206; and life-satisfaction, 195
Fries, J., and Crapo, L., 213

Gallup, G., and Hill, E., 8
Game, A., and Pringle, R., 44
Gault, U., and Reeve, R.A., 7
geriatrics, 69, 212
gerontology, 5, 6, 82, 153-54, 208
Gold, R.L., 18
Goodman, R., 60
Gordon, D., 169, 172, 177
Gove, W.R., 176
grandchildren, 132-33
Gray Panthers, 152
Granick, S., and Patterson, R., 177
Gregory, H., 25

happiness, 65, 131, 189; of marriage, 16, 115-19

Hackett, E., 177
Haire, Norman, 106
Hall, A., Selby, J., and Vanclay, F., 111
Hanlon, F., 148
"Harvester judgment", 74, 75
Harwood, E., 57, 58, 69
Havighurst, R., 189
Hazan, H., 8
health, 12, 14, 83, 96, 168-85, 213; age-cohort differentials in, 178, 183; in childhood, 168, 169, 171-72; historical developments in 169-70; and life-satisfaction, 193, 198; in mid-life, 172-76; sex differentials in, 172-73; socio-economic differentials in, 178
hearing, 181; age-cohort differentials in, 183; and life-satisfaction, 181, 191
Henderson, R.F., 152
Hendricks, J., and Hendricks, C.D., 82
Hewitt, P., 158, 162
historical context: of Aboriginal land rights, 148; of age at menarche, 101, 103; of attitudes to child-rearing, 47; of attitudes to health, 169-70; of education, 58-60; of marital fertility, 44, 128; of marriage, 114, 119; of the period, 25-30; of political situation, 140, 143-44; of work opportunities, 73, 74, 75, 78
hobbies, 95, 97, 98, 200, 207
home duties, 74, 119, 121
home ownership, 32, 37, 84, 85
hospitals, hospitalization, 11, 49, 170, 171
hostels, 11, 17
housing: age-integrated, 209-11
Hudson, R., and Binstock, R., 151
Hyman, H.H., 18

independence, 4, 78, 205
infant mortality, 169, 171
Inglis, K.S., 162
illness, 171, 177-78, 193, 194, 213
institutionalization, 18, 31, 194, 197; and boredom, 99; dread of, 136; and family contacts, 133; and health, 179; and loneliness, 134; and marital status, 125; reasons for, 53

institutions, 7, 11, 86, 137;
interviewing in, 14, 17-18
interviewing, 12-21
"intimacy at a distance", 129, 131, 209
Isaacs, B., Livingstone, M., and
Neville, Y., 4
isolation, 193, 215, 216
Job, E., 13
Job, E., Johansen, C., Jones, J.,
and Spenceley, E., 21

Kalish, R.A., 6, 8, 138
Kendig, H., 210
Kimmel, D.C., 5
kin, kinship, 137, 198. See also family
Krupinski, J., and Stoller, A., 114
Kubler-Ross, E., 203
Kuhn, Maggie, 152

Labouvie-Vief, G., and Blanchard-
Fields, U.F., 7, 112
Laslett, P., 137
Lawson, R., 25, 140
leisure activities, 87-99; in childhood,
52, 87-91, 172; gregarious, 93,
96-97; indoor, 97; intensification of,
98; in mid-life, 93-96; modification
of, 97-98; in old age, 96-99, 180,
193, 218; outdoor, 88, 180, 193;
solitary, 93; in youth, 91-93
Lieberman, M., and Coplan, A., 178,
202
life expectancy, 31, 85, 173, 174, 183,
184, 198
life review, 201-2, 207
life-satisfaction, 189, 190-99, 201, 205
lifestyles, 3, 32, 101, 134, 170, 195
living arrangements. See Residence
Lofland, J., 12, 21
loneliness, 4, 7, 10, 37, 53, 118, 134,
159
longevity of parents, 33, 170-71
Lopata, H., 83
Lowenstein, W., 73, 80
Lowenthal, M., and Haven, C., 124

McKeown, T., 169
McQueen, H., 26, 74, 77, 79, 91
Maddison, D., 212
Madigan, F.C., 173
marriage, 113-25; authority patterns

in, 119-21; length of, 118; love as
proper basis for, 115, 117;
happiness of, 16, 35, 109, 115-19,
192
marital status, 12, 31, 53, 112, 114,
123-25, 199; divorce and separation,
117; and health, 176; and
institutionalization, 125
Marshall, V.W., and Tindale, J., 154
Maves, P.B., 156
Meals on Wheels, 11, 136, 178
meaning of life, 20, 164-67, 194, 197
Mechanic, D., 173
medication, 170, 179, 191, 194, 206,
213
memory, 7, 69, 121, 144, 182, 184,
206, 216
menarche, age at, 19, 36, 101; age-
cohort differentials in, 103;
forewarning of, 100, 103-4
menopause, 19, 101, 104-5, 170
menstruation, 77, 100, 101-5; bans on
bathing during, 103; pain during,
104, 113, 170
mental state, 10, 14, 170, 181, 182,
184; confusion, senility, 4, 14, 108,
182, 197
Milbrath, L., 142
Mills, C.W., 153
Mindel, C.H., and Vaughn, C.E., 156
Mishara, B., Kastenbaum, R., Baker,
F., and Patterson, R., 194
Moberg, D., 156
mobility, 170, 207; and life-
satisfaction, 191, 194
moderation, 59, 65, 82, 170, 200
Moser, C.A., 19
Myerhoff, B., and Simic, A., 8
Myers, G., 10

Naylor, G., 57, 69
neighbours, 24
Network-maintenance, 52-54, 86, 114;
and institutionalization, 53; and
leisure activities, 96; and life
satisfaction, 191, 193; and
parenthood, 129, 130, 132; and
politics, 142; and religion, 166; and
sex roles, 79, 82, 123, 136, 198
Neugarten, B., 8, 104-5
nonagenarians, 5, 31, 110, 130

Norton, J., 92
nuclear power, 38, 145, 149-50, 193
nursing services, 11, 17, 122
nursing-homes, 11; and boredom, 99;
   dread of, 137

occupation: as index of socio-
   economic status, 32, 72; variety of,
   73, 74
octogenarians, 8-9, 11, 30, 151
old-old, 8, 178

Palmore, E., 7, 179, 180, 184
parenthood, 126-38
Parker, S., 88
Parkes, C.M., Benjamin, B., and
   Fitzgerald, R., 124
Parlagreco, M.L., 5
Parsons, Talcott, 137, 145
Peck, R.C., 193
pensions, 11, 82, 83, 85, 216
place of birth, 32, 33
politics, 139-54; interest and
   participation in, 38, 141-43; 193;
   party affiliation, 143; political
   effectiveness, 151-54; political
   issues, 145-51
poverty, 43, 44, 45, 46
power, powerlessness: and age-
   stratification, 47; and the
   Depression, 81; and old people, 10,
   132, 151; and sex roles, 49; and
   socio-economic status, 183
Powles, J., 183
pre-marital sex, 100, 107, 108

Rabbitt, P., 216
racism, 3, 6, 208
Rankin, D.H., 58
Raphael, B., 3
rapport, 18-19, 20
reaction times, 7, 19, 177
reading: in childhood, 34, 45, 68;
   in old age, 68, 87, 95, 184
reality orientations, 183
religion, 144, 155-67, 214; and
   belief in life after death, 162-64; in
   childhood, 47, 157; and church
   attendance, 158-60; importance of,
   160-61; and life satisfaction, 59,
   194, 197; and meaning of life,

164-67; and mystical experiences,
   85, 155; 157; in old age, 85, 155;
   157; religious affiliation, 32, 156-58;
   and survival of fittest, 59
re-motivation, 183
residence, 4, 11, 12, 31, 131, 137,
   179, 209-22; age-cohort differentials
   in, 197; alone, 14, 17, 31, 125, 134,
   137, 138, 216; with children, 137;
   in family situation, 31, 125, 134,
   197; in institutions, 11, 31, 86, 98,
   99, 125, 136, 179, 194, 197;
   preference for living alone, 129,
   137; sex differentials in, 31, 114;
   with siblings, 31, 135; with spouse,
   112, 114
resignation, 195-99, 201, 206
retirement, 24, 36, 72, 82-83, 87, 122
retirement village, 184, 210
Richardson, A.H., and Freeman, H.E.,
   8
Rosaldo, M.Z., and Lamphere, L., 50
Rose, A., 151
Rosenmayr, L., 129, 209
Rosow, I., 69, 208
Royal Reader, 60
Russell, C., 8
Ruzicka, L.T., and Caldwell, J.C.,
   58, 106

Sanger, Margaret, 106
Second World War, 29, 31, 36, 78,
   79, 110
secularization, 160, 163
self-fulfilling prophecies, 3, 40, 69;
   and activity, 205; and childbirth,
   174; and education, 57; and health,
   178, 214, 215; and menopause, 105;
   and mental state, 184
senility, 4, 14, 182, 184, 185, 216.
   See also confusion
Senior citizens' centres, 11, 37, 97,
   134, 145
sex differentials: as analytic principle,
   21; in attitudes to sexuality, 112; in
   childlessness, 128, 136; in
   educational levels, 63; in effects of
   economic Depression, 81; in
   financial situation, 85, 189; in
   health, 173-74; 176, 183, 184; in life
   expectancy, 31, 85; in life

satisfaction, 193, 200; in power and powerlessness, 49; in marital status, 31, 128; in religiosity, 157, 158, 161, 163-64, 165, 166; in residential situation, 31, 114; in role expectations, 51-54, 74-79, 86, 119-22, 125; in sample numbers, 31
sexism, 3, 6, 54, 208
sex ratios, 31
sex roles, 49-52; as biologically based, 125; in childhood, 43, 49, 51-52, 56, 63; conflict in, 176; in household tasks, 121-22, 125; in leisure, 88, 90; for married women, 79, 119-22; for men, 74, 97; in politics, 142
sexual ageism, 110-12
sexuality, 100-112, 206, 207; birth control, 19, 36, 101, 105-7, 168; childbirth, 19, 35, 101, 104, 126, 168, 173-74, 214; menopause, 19, 36, 101, 104-5; menstruation, 77, 100, 101-5; pre-marital and extra-marital sex, 108, 109; sexual ageism, 110-12
Shanas, E., 5, 83, 125, 178
Shanas, E., and Maddox, G., 176
Shann, E., 74
Shigiya, R., 8
Shock, N., 7
siblings: and age stratification, 47, 49; contacts with, 53, 135; living with, 31, 135; number of, 44
singlehood, 31, 53, 123-25, 128
sleep, 14, 206
smoking, 170, 206; and life satisfaction, 191, 194; and longevity, 179
Social-Darwinism, 59-60
social deficit model, 8, 70
socio-economic differentials: as analytic principle, 21; in advice-giving, 200; in age at menarche, 102; in areas of Toowong, 24, 25; in attitudes to death and dying, 205; in educational levels, 63, 68; in event-confrontation, 53-54, 199; in financial situation, 32; in health, 78, 183; in husband-dominance, 119; in leisure activities, 52, 96; in membership of voluntary

organizations, 96; in number of siblings, 44, 47; in politics, 142, 143-44, 149, 151; in religion, 157, 160; in styles of upbringing, 47-48, 52; in work opportunities, 73, 78, 83
socio-economic status, 6, 12, 24, 32, 33, 191; and age at menarche, 101, 102; biological model of, 59; and health, 178; and leisure, 96; and politics, 142, 144, 149
sociology, 8, 15
Stopes, Marie, 106
solitary/gregarious leisure patterns, 88, 93-97
Streib, G., 151
strikes, 35, 74, 145-48, 160
structural compensation, 135-36
successful ageing, 189, 199
Sussman, M., 137
symbolic interactionism, 8

tape-recorder, 15-16
terminal drop, 178
Tew, M., 74
Townsend, P., 132, 134
trade unions, 74, 146, 149
Twaddle, A.C., and Hessler, R.M., 173

usefulness, 179, 180, 184, 185

Vietnam War, 29, 30, 150, 152
voluntary associations, 96, 97, 207
voluntary work, 85, 86

Wahl, C.W., 202
war, 27, 28, 161; and religion, 160-61. See also Boer War; First World War; Second World War; Vietnam War
Ward, J., 152
Warren, W.C., and Chopra, P.W., 203
Wharton, G., 110
Wheeler, R., 209
Whitehead, T., 69
widowhood, 83, 112, 123-25, 199
Wild, R.A., 153
Wilson, R.W., 173
women: assumed inferiority of, 3, 65; and authority, 49, 54, 119-21; and domestic skills, 52, 74, 130; and

financial vulnerability, 85; and
health, 173-76; as interviewers, 13,
19; life expectancy of, 31, 85; and
multiparity, 173-75; and politics,
141-43; and religion, 157, 158, 161,
163-64, 165, 166; and strikes, 148;
suffrage for, 140; surplus of, 114;
and work after marriage, 79; and
work before marriage, 74, 75, 78;
and work ethic, 59, 61, 85, 86, 166;
in workforce, 29, 75, 78; work roles
of, 75-79
Wood, P., 23
work, 71-86; after marriage, 79;
autonomy at, 72, 83; before
marriage, 74, 78; centres, 209; in
childhood, 73, 74, 75; ethic, 59, 61,
77, 85, 86, 166; and leisure, 88; in
old age, 82-86; retirement from, 72,
82-83; satisfaction, 72; seasonal, 73;
and sex roles, 74, 75-79; voluntary,
29, 85
work-centres, 209
work ethic, 59, 61, 85, 86, 166
work satisfaction, 72
wowserism, 92-93
Wunsch, G., 173
Wyeth, E.R., 58